DAVE THOMPSON

DEPECHE MODE

SOME GREAT REWARD

St. Martin's Press ⋯⋯⋯⋯⋯⋯⋯⋯ New York

Author's Note: It should be noted that for dramatic purposes I have occasionally taken the liberty of constructing scenes and dialogue, based on previously published statements by or about band members.

DEPECHE MODE. Copyright © 1994 by Dave Thompson. All rights reserved. Printed in the United States of America. No part of this book may be used or reproduced in any manner whatsoever without written permission except in the case of brief quotations embodied in critical articles or reviews. For information, address St. Martin's Press, 175 Fifth Avenue, New York, N.Y. 10010.

Design by Junie Lee

Library of Congress Cataloging-in-Publication Data

Thompson, Dave.
    Depeche Mode : some great reward / Dave Thompson.
        p. cm.
    Discographies: p. 243
    ISBN 0-312-11262-9
    1. Depeche Mode (Musical group)   2. Rock musicians—England—Biography.   I. Title.
ML421.D46T6   1994
782.42166'092'2—dc20
[B]   94-21469
                                  CIP
                                   MN

First Edition: December 1994

10 9 8 7 6 5 4 3 2 1

To Plushkin

CONTENTS

<Acknowledgments>

DEPECHE MODE IS an enigma.

There can be few bands who have appeared so visible yet remained so obscure, who have talked so much about their lives and work but ultimately said so little. From the moment Depeche Mode appeared on the music scene fourteen years ago, they have remained guarded, giving away as little as possible. Deliberately, they have obscured their backgrounds and their family lives; purposefully, they speak only of their music—and sometimes, even that is couched in mystery.

Like the artists who most inspired them, Kraftwerk and Can, David Bowie and Bryan Ferry, Depeche Mode has manipulated their image in a way that completely belies the aura of naiveté and innocence that has grown up around them, until even when events appeared to be spiraling beyond their control, the band's hands remained on the wheel.

More than any other facet of Depeche Mode's long, remarkable career, it was that which fascinated me the most—the Hows and Whys of a career which, according to every dictate of rock 'n' roll tradition, should never have lasted as long, or attained the heights of success, that it has. As this book came together, what started as a simple band biography began to change shape.

It remains Depeche Mode's story, of course, and only one of several which could have been written. Their music, and the manifold interpretations that have grown up around it, deserves a book unto itself; so do the private lives of the musicians who have made that music; and so does the story of the sheer weight of technology with which they created it. As Depeche Mode move into the second half of their second decade, those books, I'm sure, will come.

But as fascinating as they will undoubtedly be, it is still Depeche Mode's very survival which remains the most gripping tale: their evolution from a barely competent youth-club band to the fresh-faced crop of electronic fops who rode the synth-pop bandwagon to success; their cautious regrouping following a split which would have crippled almost any other band; the marshaling of their remaining assets, and the gradual consolidation of both their vision and their sense of purpose; and finally, their emergence among the most important and influential bands of the postpunk era. At any point along the way, they could have easily fallen apart, and on a couple of occasions they came very close to doing so.

But the energies which drive Depeche Mode would not permit surrender, and the group marched on—a marvel to its friends, a mystery to its critics, a phenomenon in a world which had forgotten what such things even were. Those words remain the key to Depeche Mode today—marvel, mystery, and phenomenon—and though they cannot be fully explained, they

<x>

ACKNOWLEDGMENTS

can be detailed and defined. That is what I set out to accomplish here, and, of course, I could not have done it alone.

I would, then, like to thank everybody who helped see this book through to completion: Tony Secunda, who put the deal together; Jo-Ann Greene, whose own memory for faces, dates, and names has rarely proved so invaluable; Rob Cherry, Joe Banks, and Jason Pettigrew—my editors at *Alternative Press* magazine—for pointing me in directions I might otherwise have missed completely; Grant Alden, whose enthusiasm for this project has been so inspiring; as well as Gaye Black, Marion Breeze, Liz Coldwell, Barb East, Matt Green, K-Mart (not the store!), Geoff Monmouth, Amy Mueller, Oedipus, Orifice, Julian Paul, Brian Perera, Lisa Ridley, Brian Robin, Tim Smith, Snarleyyow the Cat Fiend, Tim Stegall, Jeff Tamarkin at *Goldmine,* Sue Wack, and all at St. Martin's Press. Cheers also to everybody who, for reasons of their own, spoke only under condition of anonymity. Their own recollections, and the factual wrongs they righted, made all the difference!

I would also like to acknowledge the many books and magazines that I consulted during my research, singling out a handful as being of especial value: "Depeche Guevara," by Betty Page (*Sounds,* June 27, 1981); "Learning the Highway Mode," by Paul Colbert (*Melody Maker,* November 14, 1981); "Red Rockers over the Emerald Isle," by X. Moore (*New Musical Express,* September 17, 1983); "Basildon Bond," by Micky Senate (*Melody Maker,* March 10, 1984); "Coming Up Smiling," by Sheryl Garratt (*The Face,* No. 58); "Bacchanalia in Black," by Gavin Martin (*New Musical Express,* September 25, 1993); and "Revenge of the Euroweenies," by Stephen Daly (*Rolling Stone,* November 25, 1993).

Elsewhere, issues of *Alternative Press, American Music Press, Billboard, Detour, The Face, Goldmine, Ice, Interview, Island Ear, Keyboard World,* the *Los Angeles Times, Melody Maker, Musician, New Musical Express, New Times, People, Pulse, Record Collector, Record Mirror, Rolling Stone,*

Select, Smash Hits, Spin, the *Village Voice,* and *ZigZag* all proved invaluable.

    I would also like to acknowledge—and recommend—the following books: *When the Music's Over,* by Robin Denselow (Faber & Faber, 1989); *Recombinant Do Re Mi,* by Billy Bergman and Richard Horn (Quarto, 1985); *Like Punk Never Happened,* by Dave Rimmer (Faber & Faber, 1985); *The Best of Smash Hits,* compiled by Neil Tennant (EMAP, 1984); *Backward Masking Unmasked,* by Jacob Aranza (Huntington House, 1983). All were useful as I conducted my background research. I also extend my thanks to Dave Thomas, author of the first-ever biography of Depeche Mode, back in 1986 (Omnibus Books).

    Finally, the biggest bouquet goes to my wife, Jo-Ann, just for being here (and for proofing, typing, fixing punctuation—the list goes on and on . . .).

<xii>

ACKNOWLEDGMENTS

DEPECHE MODE

Chapter < 1 >

Which One of Those Drugs Do You Want?

SEATTLE, NOVEMBER 1993: Six months of near-solid touring affects different people in different ways. Some—most—simply look burned out, their skin a sallow cloud which needs that little bit more makeup every time they step out in front of another television camera, their eyes darting in search of shades when the public gets too close.

For Dave Gahan, the opposite appears true. Three years of living left him looking like death. Six months of the road's living death, however, have rejuvenated him beyond recognition.

Eighteen months ago, a friend spotted him in Madrid. He looked "scary, painfully thin . . . almost blue."

Now even the scratches and bruises on the insides of the singer's skinny arms, innocently acquired, have faded. His skin glows with ruddy vigor; his voice is stronger, even when he comes offstage, and it no longer threatens to croak into mid-set silence.

At the beginning of Depeche Mode's European tour, in early summer in Budapest, Dave admitted in print that he had suffered certain "problems"; that he meant to "sort them out." "[But] everyone knows a rock 'n' roll tour isn't really the place to start sorting things out," *NME* journalist Gavin Martin shot back.

As Depeche Mode busy themselves around the massive Seattle Arena, however, killing time while their road crew kills gremlins in their gear, Dave Gahan not only appears to have "sorted them out"—he might have exorcised them completely.

He didn't achieve the transformation alone, of course. "When you've been in a band for thirteen years," he imparts, four "weird energies" work together. So far as he's concerned, Depeche Mode's latest album, *Songs of Faith and Devotion,* was the focus of those energies. "Every single song on the album were the best things Martin could have done for me. As a friend to a friend, he helped me heal a lot of my personal problems, and he wasn't even trying."

Beside him, Martin Gore smiles behind his latest made-up mask. Maybe he wasn't trying, the smile agrees. Or maybe he was. He has never been one for discussing his songs too deeply. But Dave is a friend, and if there's one thing that has kept Depeche Mode together all these years, it is friendship—recognizing it, and working for it.

People had been saying things about Dave for a couple of years now, ever since he ran out on his wife and five-year-old son and moved to L.A., had a daughter by Depeche Mode's former PR officer, and spent his time living out of a suitcase, living out the Rock God dream.

The vast computer network through which Depeche Mode's fan base keeps in touch with one another hummed with the latest street rumors. These rumors were powerful, and when Depeche Mode did return to action, in 1993, the journalists who caught up with the band in Hungary only added to the confusion.

THE TRUE CONFESSIONS OF DAVE GAHAN, screamed British rock weekly *Melody Maker*. PENANCE EXTRA, countered archrival *New Musical Express*. Even when the fuss died down, and Dave had survived unscathed through two-thirds of the band's latest American tour, *Rolling Stone* could not resist hauling him over the coals of retribution once more. Dave, however, was not playing ball.

"Religion, drugs—which one of those fucking drugs do you want to talk about?" he queried innocently. "They're all so closely knit: good, evil, drugs, alcohol, honesty, guilt . . ." Only when his eyes flickered away did it even seem possible that he knew, after all, what his interrogator really meant.

To a pop psychologist, Dave's was a textbook case. Sadly, pop psychologists only turn up after the event, waiting till things are either too weird . . . or too late. "No one can understand what it's like to be a young man and you get all that money, all that fame," a "camp insider" mourned to *NME*. No one, that is, except those to whom it's already happened.

Depeche Mode were never party animals in the accepted sense of the phrase—have never numbered amongst that elite coterie of musicians who spend their careers living out one long lost weekend.

Even today, people turn a blind eye to their indiscretions. When the band members confessed their own proclivities, when Dave spoke openly of an alcohol problem that had scarcely even been hinted at in the past, but which came close to destroying him anyway, outsiders simply shrugged, and Depeche Mode didn't push the point.

"Going out is enjoyable," Martin once laughed. "Drinking is enjoyable, and collapsing is enjoyable." Still, in 1985 the band vigorously denied the report in Germany's *Bravo* magazine that after every performance Dave was carried to his dressing room and kept supplied with constant fluids.

In Quebec in September 1993, Dave and his long-time friend and road manager, Daryl Levy, were arrested for scuffling with a hotel employee. They were released without being charged because the witnesses could not agree on what they saw. And that's always been Depeche Mode's story—people cannot agree on what they see or hear.

Depeche Mode has long remained reluctant to join the superstar circuit. It was never Depeche Mode who were caught on candid camera—drunk, disorderly, and drained outside London's liveliest nightclubs—not they whose evening escapades became their breakfast-time embarrassments. That, then, was when the first alarm bells began ringing among Depeche Mode's contemporaries—when Dave and his new girlfriend, Teresa, started showing up at their parties.

<4> Seven years previous, Dave jokingly described Martin Gore as "going through the same sort of things as I went through in my teens." Martin had just broken up with his childhood sweetheart and fled abroad with a new lady friend. Now he lived in Berlin and wore dresses in public, but the rest of the group simply laughed indulgently. "He's just trying to get attention."

In 1992 it was Dave's turn to relive other people's youths, to try and get attention, to make one last, desperate grab for the wild life that his own early engagement and young marriage had deprived him of. Outsiders, willingly admitting that their imaginations played as great a part in the equation as the evidence of their own eyes, described the process.

"It was like watching someone build a Frankenstein pop star. He grew Al Jourgensen's old beard, got Anthony Kiedis's old tattoos . . . and developed Kurt Cobain's old habit." Rock 'n' roll in the Nineties has yet to produce an unholier trinity!

What these outsiders didn't know—the thing that nobody outside Depeche Mode's closest circles could have known—was that by the time the Frankenstein became public, and the writers lined up to quiz the creature, the worst was already over.

The scratches and bruises on Dave's arms came from one night in Mannheim, poised on the edge of a seething German audience—tottering, falling, and being torn to shreds by his fans before he landed. The tattoos simply augmented a tapestry he had started half a lifetime before, and as for the goatee—once again, Depeche Mode has grown up.

Not that that had ever really been in question, not over the last few years, anyway. Musically, Depeche Mode has set a pace that few other artists could ever match, pioneering technologies that rock 'n' roll is still struggling to fully assimilate.

It was Depeche Mode who opened the doors through which an endless stream of modern industrial bands now revolve, taking the harsh extremes of a lunatic art-noise experiment and making palatable music for the masses. It was Depeche Mode, too, who demonstrated the potential and the possibilities of the technology now on display. Without them, the sampler might still be the preserve of academics and the lunatic fringe, as untapped by the powers of pop commerce as the synthesizer was in the years before Brian Eno dragged it bleeping and burping into the soul of Roxy Music.

When Ministry's Al Jourgensen growled his apologies for his band's lightweight debut album, he accused his old record company of trying to turn him into the American Depeche Mode. But when he reinvented himself as the embryonic King of Aggro, he recruited two of the people who had sharpened Depeche Mode's own edges, producer Adrian Sherwood and engineer Gareth Jones.

The acclaimed Razormaid and Disconet remix companies all but cut their commercial teeth producing a string of Depeche Mode club remixes. Derrick May, the mastermind behind the Detroit "house" scene's enormously influential Rhythim Is Rhythim, admitted that he borrowed much from Depeche Mode's approach to sampling.

And when Kraftwerk—the German electronics pioneers whose example inspired the nascent Depeche Mode—updated their own greatest hits for 1991's *The Mix* album, more than one reviewer reported that the masters had finally become the servants.

"Depeche Mode hang heavier over Kraftwerk than the Germans ever did over them," wrote one. "They even share a remix master in Francois Kervorkian, and it must please Depeche no end to know that They Did It First!"

Depeche Mode has done a lot of things first, and a lot of things better than anyone else. But what is even more remarkable is that they have done it from within the glare of a limelight whose brilliance they could never have imagined.

It is very popular for journalists to either open or close their studies of Depeche Mode with an attempt to analyze the band's extraordinary success, to ponder aloud the attraction of a group whose idea of a final encore is a song which announces for its very first line, "Death is all around." You can't really blame them, either. Lyrically, Depeche Mode owes little to anything that has passed as pop in the past.

While Depeche Mode was fighting the likes of Blue Rondo à la Turk and Modern Romance for the crumbs of U.K. chart success, Martin Gore was listening to Neil Young and Leonard Cohen. While his rivals were writing "John Wayne Is Big Leggy" and "Karma Chameleon," Martin was penning "Everything Counts" and "The Landscape Is Changing." And while those others sang of love, Martin spoke about life—real life, ordinary life, the kind of life that ends with death. Under those kind of conditions, of course, it's "all around."

Yet when *Rolling Stone* magazine titled its November 1993 story "Revenge of the Euroweenies," that, too, fit the group like a glove. In 1995 Depeche Mode will be fifteen years old, but they have retained their original all-synthesizer lineup for so long that the wheels of fashion have turned full circle around them. In 1980, when the group started out, everybody was doing it, and the foursome was simply one more name in the electronic queue, lining up for another glossy photo shoot and filling out questionnaires whose most challenging question was "Favorite color?"

However, whereas their contemporaries were eventually to founder, unable to adapt their own visions to the constantly shifting patterns of the 1980s, Depeche Mode held firm—a sore thumb throbbing within a mid-decade climate that was gracefully rediscovering drums and guitars. At times Depeche Mode appeared so hopelessly anachronistic that it is a wonder they did not simply turn to dust; at other times, so far ahead of themselves that you could not even measure their progress in light-years.

By the early 1990s, however, electronic music was once again bursting to the commercial fore, and Depeche Mode were elder statesmen, respected as much for their longevity as for their music—for the way they'd both retained their vision and grown with it, single-mindedly developing themes that were laid down as early as their second and third albums, but which have remained a vital part of their music all the same.

<7>

Certainly the group has reacted to the demands of its audience. If, back in 1984, the thunderous "Master and Servant" and "Blasphemous Rumors" had been unanimously rejected, the Depeche Mode of today would be a very different group—might, in fact, no longer even exist, so central to the band's very being have those tracks become.

In other hands, however, the impact of those songs would have been so intense that there might have been no thought of ever even attempting to emulate, let alone enlarge upon them. For Depeche Mode, however, neither song is even a regular fixture within their live show anymore, so far along has the band progressed. At times, even they don't seem to appreciate precisely how far they are pushing forward.

But it is not only through their music and the popularity of that music that Depeche Mode is unlike any other band. In other groups, different members adopt different duties, and so it is with Depeche Mode. But how many others could deliberately, and delightedly, carry a member who by his own admission has little interest in pop music anymore, who plays only the most minimal part in the creative process, and who is as much at home hunched over an accounts ledger as he is standing over a synthesizer onstage—more so, in fact?

Elsewhere Andy would be excess baggage, an unnecessary fourth face on the record sleeves, a fourth bed on the hotel bill, a fourth wheel on a tricycle. And he is often a cause of strife—his own colleagues admit that. "Fletch has had a fight with everyone but me," Dave once admitted. "He's never actually tried to hit me. But just lately, I think he's potentially been thinking about it."

But Fletch is also the anchor that has held Depeche Mode firm through almost a decade and a half of turbulence. When Vince Clarke quit in 1980, running out before his bandmates could even walk on their own, it was Fletch who marshaled the other members' strengths, and gave them the will to go on.

When the band's critical stock began to dip to laughable, laughing, lows at home, it was Fletch who engineered their ascent to superstardom elsewhere. And when personal problems began straining the very fabric from which Depeche Mode was cut, it was Fletch around whom the band members gathered for support.

"He's part of what we started," insists Dave, "and he'll be part of what we'll finish." Nobody can accurately date the point where the heavyset, bespectacled Fletch ceased to involve himself in the band's music—Dave simply reckons, "Forever." But "he still has an opinion," Dave insists. "He has a function."

Without Martin Gore—flamboyant, flighty, and fey—there would be no songs; without Alan Wilder, the first synthesized rocker in pop, there would be no music; without Dave, who jokes that if he wasn't in a band, he'd probably be in jail—and has the juvenile record to prove it—there would be no voice.

But without Fletch, there would be no money, and money is what Depeche Mode's 1993 World Tour is all about, greasing the wheels of the largest, most ambitious outing the group has ever undertaken. In that respect alone, Depeche Mode is just like every other band.

And out on the road, they are just as insulated from the outside world in the cosseted, closeted heart of a machine whose every cog is so tightly choreographed that if a pin drops unexpectedly, there's somebody waiting to pick it back up.

Depeche Mode long ago came to terms with the knowledge that three men standing around playing synthesizers while the fourth cavorts in front of them offers a far from riveting spectacle. In the past, however, their live show labored to divert its audience's attentions away from the band. This time around, the group is reclaiming the spotlight. ⟨♫⟩

The stage is draped with giant black curtains, and as the lights dim and the music swells, there is no band, just a giant silhouette that cavorts behind the shades. The shape does not resolve itself until the first song, "Higher Love," is over, and if Dave Gahan looks tiny at first, it is only in relation to the rest of the set. Perched on a giant raised dais ten feet above him, "as ominous as a surgical theater, more kinetic than a video arcade," as the *Seattle Times* later put it, Martin, Fletch, and Alan stand nearly motionless at their synthesizers.

Gahan has grown increasingly confident since Depeche Mode's last American tour, three years ago. He looks, if not like Satan, at least like a Very Important Demon. During "Walking in My Shoes," while the screens behind him flicker with the sad, strutting bird-woman who appears in the same song's video, he appears positively infernal.

His dancing, once described as the missing link between Michael Jackson and Howard the Duck, has expanded to incorporate the agility of a soccer goalkeeper and the crudity of a vaudevillian stripper. "It's great fun!" he says with a smirk.

"You get to grab your dick in front of twenty thousand people and they all scream!" Every night he leans back and massages his crotch; every night an auditorium erupts.

Suddenly, however, he is no longer alone at the front of the stage. Eleven songs into the set, Martin Gore and Alan Wilder appear there too, descending from the podium, attendant imps to the Rock God from Hell. Sidling behind a drum kit that has miraculously appeared alongside him, Alan picks up the beat.

To his right, resplendently sporting glittering bondage trousers, Gore holds a white Les Paul guitar, striking a new pose with every fresh chord. The mock crucifixion is his favorite right now; no sooner do his hands touch the strings than his arms are outstretched beside him, and his closed eyes face the floor. The symbolism is not lost on the audience.

"Anyone still judging Depeche on their last stop through town was in for a shock," warned Jo-Ann Greene in the Northwest biweekly music paper, *The Rocket*. "The former synth darlings are now a rock force to be reckoned with." Martin's "fiery guitar . . . totally belied Mode's electronic image," and "when Alan Wilder took a seat behind the drum kit for 'I Feel You,' an already overheated audience erupted. It's virtually impossible to believe that this is the same flock of funny haircuts beloved by popsters in the early Eighties."

Impossible, and improbable. The rock 'n' roll portion of the show lasted for less than one-third of the set, but its image lingers long after the rest of the show is forgotten— through the electric grind of "I Feel You" opening the *Songs of Faith and Devotion—Live* album; through the stark, angular portraits that come to surreal life during the accompanying *Devotion* home video; and through the photographers who clicked feverishly away every night, each aware of just how precious every shot was.

Earlier in the year, when Depeche Mode made themselves available for magazine interviews, it was under the stringent condition that any accompanying photographs would be culled exclusively from the band's own preselected library.

Several magazines, no more willing to allow a band to choose its own pictures than to let them write their own articles, refused. Others—*Rolling Stone,* for instance—held off on their stories until the tour was under way and their own photographers would be permitted access.

Even so, official photo passes are issued for just three mid-set songs—those when Depeche Mode turns into a traditional rock 'n' roll group, a brilliantly conceived manipulation of both memory and image. The first time Depeche Mode visited the United States, journalists asked why they didn't use guitars. As the 1993 tour wound its way around, people were asking why they didn't use synthesizers any longer.

Their moment facing the spotlight over, the photographers are ushered outside again. There are no other cameras allowed inside the auditorium, and the exiles glare jealously at those that did get in—smuggled past the metal detectors and pat-downs that welcomed the audience to the show—whose brief, brilliant flashes now strike a blinding contrast to the warm glow of the cigarette lighters being held aloft by everybody else: a sea of flickering fire oozing the disreputable reverence of a bygone era. You expect somebody to call out for "Free Bird" any moment and sure enough, somebody does.

<|>

From the stage, Martin seems to acknowledge the request, filing it away in the library of lunacies he carries around in his head. He knows, just as the audience knows, that with Depeche Mode anything is possible. A month and a half ago, at New Jersey's Meadowlands Stadium, Martin performed a heart-stopping "Knocking on Heaven's Door," adding his voice to legion others, from Eric Clapton to Axl Rose, who have given voice to Bob Dylan's most plaintive lament.

On other occasions Depeche Mode has revisited "Route 66," 1987's frighteningly authentic reconstruction of another of Rock's Greatest Clichés. And squirming through the collectors' underground, fans furtively exchange tapes of Martin's bizarrely synthesized rendition of English glam master Gary Glitter's stomping "I Love You Love Me Love."

Indeed, anything is possible, for Depeche Mode has already achieved the impossible. Even a thumbnail sketch of their career to date leaves the band members scratching their heads. "How we survived certain periods," laughs Alan, "I'll never know."

Yet while Depeche Mode's fortunes waxed and waned around the world, overall their fame spread—not through the patronage of radio or video, nor through the time-honored slog of perpetual touring, but via that most underestimated of promotional networks, simple word of mouth.

Prior to "Personal Jesus," in 1990, MTV—arguably the most powerful promotion any band can have—had never once placed a Depeche Mode video in heavy rotation. Yet the group was already capable of selling out Pasadena's seventy thousand-capacity Rose Bowl. Depeche Mode had not scored an American hit single since 1985, but still their records dominated the club scene. And though they had remained gratuitously unfashionable since their inception, Depeche Mode not only became a byword for skillful electronic music—an influence on so much of what has followed—they are also acknowledged for pioneering rock 'n' roll's headlong tumble into other areas of computer technology.

In September 1993 Depeche Mode became the first band ever to go "on-line," staging an interactive Q & A session with three hundred fans. Afterward, their only regret was that they weren't able to hook up with more—when the event was first planned, some fifty thousand people had been intended to participate!

"We've always been out on our own," Dave once laughed. "We've always been unique in what we've done." And he recounted a story to anybody who was listening. It was, in many ways, insignificant; certainly it was flippant. But it summed up Depeche Mode better than virtually any other.

<12>

Some months earlier, Dave and Martin were sitting in the studio together, playing through some of their old records, in search of a certain sound. Then Martin turned down the volume and looked at Dave, his expression poised midway between delighted surprise and absolute shock. It was, remembered Dave, "as if he'd suddenly rediscovered Depeche Mode."

"You know what?" Martin was laughing now, while behind him "Blasphemous Rumours" recounted its peculiar message. "Depeche Mode are just *so fucking weird!*"

<|ɜ>

Chapter 2

You Didn't Even Need to Know How to Hold a Guitar

DANIEL MILLER DOES not look like the sort of man who moves mountains or changes worlds. Unfashionably wiry, even when that look flashed fashionably across the hip world; casual, but never appearing wholly comfortable; discouraging even the familiarity of "Dan" or "Danny"—even at the forefront of the revolution he had always dreamed of leading, Daniel Miller looked somehow anachronistic.

It was no coincidence that his first-ever record was released under the pseudonym the Normal, because Daniel Miller was the epitome of Normalcy, and respectable normalcy, too. It was only when you took a step away and combined everything you knew about him—which wouldn't turn out to be much—with everything you *didn't* know (which would eventually fill a couple of encyclopedias), that suddenly you caught a glimpse not only of what drove Daniel Miller, but of what drove everybody who came into his orbit. For Miller is one of nature's motivators. Softly spoken, he nevertheless conveys excitement with a gesture, outrage with a flicker, and innovation with an inflection.

Throughout the early 1970s, Miller was just one of several thousand would-be guitarists plugging his spare time in a succession of high-school pop groups. He was not, he insists, a particularly good musician—rather than bend his fingers out of joint trying to figure out complicated chords, he preferred simply to whack his guitar with pieces of metal or wood, just to see what happened.

Years later, his technique would be called "avant-garde," and be held up as an object lesson in musical experimentation by hordes of similarly disaffected young axemen. But throughout the pre-punk age of Jimmy Page and Ritchie Blackmore, when a guitarist's worth was measured by the number of notes he could play per minute, Miller was simply an irritant.

After leaving high school, Miller attended art school in Guildford, a small city lurking on the fringes of London's suburban skirt. There he turned his attention to filmmaking, and when he won a National Film Festival award with a twenty-minute comedy called *Don't Sit Too Close,* Miller's eyes turned curiously toward a career in celluloid.

The flirtation didn't last. By the middle of the decade, Miller was on the outside again, working as a disc jockey at an alpine Swiss tourist resort, blasting a nonstop diet of disco-pop at the vacationing would-be mountaineers.

Abba was big back then and in their wake came a host of little Abbas, all filling the dance halls with their inoffensive harmonies and pretty little songs. "Mamma Mia" would melt to "Mississippi," "Fernando" would fade into "Free," "Dancing Queen" to "December '63." From his booth above the dance floor, Miller kept his smile Superglued into place as he placed the latest Boney M. on the deck and watched "Daddy Cool" drag even the reluctant wallflowers onto the floor. And if someone requested "Yes Sir, I Can Boogie," Miller would nod in accordance—"Yes ma'am, I bet you can"—and that, too, would fill the chill night air.

But if Miller outwardly enjoyed what he did every night, inwardly he was seething. Trips back to Britain had shown him a whole new world erupting off the streets—the world of the Sex Pistols, the Damned, the Clash, and the Adverts—the great Punk Rock Explosion that would take the safe, staid world of alpine holiday resorts and turn it upside down, inside out, and every which way it could, ramming complacency and safety back down the throats of the buffoons who bopped their nights away on holiday.

Miller brought the punk records back with him, but he rarely got the chance to play them. Even at his most vengeful, he could see no way to segue Baccara into the Boys, not without provoking a self-righteous hail of plastic cocktail umbrellas. So it was all the more surprising when salvation did finally come, galloping across the dance floors like a deranged metallic cabaret, from the disco scene itself.

<17>

Donna Summer was a not-going-too-far American disco diva when she hooked up with German producer Giorgio Moroder in 1975, and might have remained such, had her desire for success not so far outweighed her need of acceptance. Stints in European productions of *Hair, Godspell,* and *Porgy and Bess* had already earmarked the twenty-six-year-old former LaDonna Adrian Gaines as a media star in her adopted German home; under Moroder's tutelage she was now to take one step beyond.

Moroder himself had haunted the edges of the Anglo-American pop consciousness since 1972, when, performing under his Christian name alone, he made the American Top Fifty with "Son of My Father"—a synthesized pop song which had already topped the British chart for Chicory Tip. Two years on, he was jamming with the Rolling Stones at his own Musicland Studios, as the band prepared for their groundbreaking *Black and Blue* album.

You Didn't Even Need to Know How to Hold a Guitar . . . .

But it was "Love to Love You Baby"—twenty minutes of moaning and groaning set to a soft-porn Motorik backbeat—that established both Moroder and Summer as names (or noises) to watch, and as he spun the record each night at the disco (the full-length album-side long version, not the emasculated premature ejaculation that made it out as a single), Miller could sense his audience's bewilderment. It was disco music, but it was more than disco music—you could dance to it, but there were other possibilities there, too.

Now, two years later, Miller realized what those possibilities were. If popular music had a future, one which could outlive the cleansing firestorm of punk, it lay in a direction that no one had yet embraced, one that hung as far from the basics of rock 'n' roll as you could get.

He looked to Moroder for guidance, and the producer did not disappoint. The holiday season of '77, writ large in the annals of rock history as the snot-drenched Summer of Punk, was not dominated by the Pistols—they had shot their bolt already, and after the napalmed frenzy of "God Save the Queen," the only way was down. It was dominated by the sense-destroying pounding of "I Feel Love," Donna Summer's second Moroder-made masterpiece and the first truly computer-generated dance hit ever recorded.

A number-one hit throughout Europe, a Top Tenner even across unadventurous America, "I Feel Love" had nothing to do with punk rock, but everything to do with punk. It disrupted the status quo, disturbed the shallow veneer of pop respectability which the industry, already fleeing for its life from the safety-pinned armies of Rotten, had erected to cover its tracks.

For them, still cocooned within the jerry-built mundanity of their corporate dance-pop universe, "I Feel Love" was the enemy within, a fire which flooded over the lip of the frying pan of punk. The record not only disdained conventional pop instrumentation, it ignored conventional pop structures as well.

<18>

The world was coming to an end . . . and who knew what would come to replace it?

Of course, the warning signs had begun flashing long before. "Son of My Father" and, the previous year, Hot Butter's infuriating "Popcorn" both made as much sense on the dance floor as they did anywhere else, while 1974 saw Kraftwerk score a surprise worldwide hit with "Autobahn"—like "Love to Love You Baby," a three-minute distillation of a longer album cut that nevertheless left no one under any misapprehensions about its true intentions. Even the popular misinterpretation of the record's lyric (it really *did* sound as though Ralf Hütter and Florian Schneider were singing, "Fun fun fun on the autobahn," conjuring up visions of grinning Teutonic Beach Boys) could not camouflage the alien nature of "Autobahn." In Britain, the record was popularly known as "Dr. Who" music, out of deference to Ron Grainer's pioneering electronic soundtracks to the long-running science-fiction television series.

<1 9>

Nineteen seventy-six brought fame to another German electronic band, Can, when they landed a Christmas U.K. hit with the chilling mantra "I Want More."

Then, in January 1977, David Bowie unleashed *Low,* a long-playing slab of emotionless misanthropy that his record company of the time, RCA, deemed so uncommercial that one label executive volunteered personally to buy Bowie a house in Philadelphia, "so he can write some more of that black music" instead. *Low,* and its attendant single, "Sound and Vision," went on to number among Bowie's greatest hits ever. Bowie even introduced his new sound to Iggy Pop's *The Idiot* album, and if there was something dichotomous, even blasphemous, about the original Street-Fighting Cheetah packing his punch behind a panel of buttons, Pop himself embraced the technology with abandon.

Even after so much turmoil, however, "I Feel Love" was different. Those other electronic hits—Bowie, Can, and

Kraftwerk included—sold as much on the strength of their novelty as their noise. They slashed musical boundaries, but they did not truly breach them. "I Feel Love," on the other hand, was unstoppable. It blared as loudly from the punk mecca the Vortex as it did from Studio 54; punks dug it, poseurs dug it, queens and Quakers flocked to its beat.

And while few could—or even would—take the time to diagnose their delight, those people who understood the tides of pop were left in no doubt whatsoever. Punk was simply the paint stripper, peeling last year's decor from the walls. "I Feel Love" was the first lick of genuine freshness rock 'n' roll had seen in years. Daniel Miller quit his deejay job almost immediately.

If rock 'n' roll was sired by the electrification of the guitar, its own electronic offspring was fathered by the synthesization of the keyboard.

In the simplest terms, the synthesizer is an electronic device that creates and shapes sound patterns. First developed during the 1920s, the modern instrument was refined by the American engineer Robert Moog, after whom one of the world's most enduring instruments was named. It was he who first attached a keyboard to a synth and in 1967, the Moog synthesizer made its rock 'n' roll debut: a few moments of twittering on the Monkees' "Star Collector."

Four years on, the portable Mini-Moog had found its way into the first touring rock shows, little more than a decade after Columbia Studios was forced to empty out an entire room simply to install a state-of-the-art synthesizer!

And though the instrument was still nominally the preserve of the gargantuan techno-maestros of Emerson, Lake and Palmer, Yes, and Pink Floyd, it was still viewed with downright suspicion by any musician birthed in the tenets of three chords and a prayer; it nevertheless embarked upon some surprising inroads into pop.

While pop-rockers Queen made a virtue of the fact

<20>

that their early albums were entirely synth-free, advertising that fact on the back of each of their first four albums, other bands—talents as disparate as Hawkwind, Roxy Music, and the Who—were indelibly etched with the versatility of the synth.

But it was Kraftwerk who truly embraced the potential of pure electronics. Indeed, it is often remarked that if all rock 'n' roll roads lead back to Chuck Berry, their electronic counterparts lead back to Kraftwerk. If that is the case, *Autobahn* is the Germans' "Johnny B. Goode," an album which reached so far beyond its creators' own brief that it literally redetermined the course of electronic music.

Kraftwerk's most fulfilled vision yet—*Trans-Europe Express*—was greeted with disbelief. By the simple expedient of rerouting the spectral "Autobahn" down a railroad track, Kraftwerk pulled humankind with it, dragging it toward a world where life itself was utterly dispensable, subservient to the power of the machine.

Trans-Europe Express relied absolutely upon electronic instrumentation, paring melody and rhythm to their lowest common denominator—an icy delivery against which Ralf Hütter's and Florian Schneider's deadpan vocals even sounded tuneful. In a year during which emotions already burned fierce in rock 'n' roll, Kraftwerk's brittle machinations confirmed punk's harshest rallying cry. There was no future—or if there was, it would be very different from the past. Kraftwerk's next album, 1978's *Man Machine,* not only made the U.K. Top Ten, it also spawned a number-one single, the eerie "The Model."

By the end of the 1970s, Kraftwerk's lead had been snatched up by a whole new generation of musicians, armed in turn with a new generation of synths. Suddenly, the instruments were not only portable, they were also inexpensive—so much so that even unsigned, untried bands were now dragging their own banks of computers around with them.

For observer-participants like Daniel Miller, there was an excitement in the air which cut to the very heart of Britain's own musical traditions. Twenty years earlier, during the first flourish of homegrown rock 'n' roll, young would-be musicians had improvised instruments from washboards and tea chests, an explosion of homemade sound which the media was quick to dub "skiffle."

They were following a similar agenda today, only the washboards had gone electronic, and the tea chests came from Radio Shack. Once again, musical ability had nothing to do with it. "A synth meant you didn't even need to know how to hold a guitar in order to express yourself," Daniel Miller pronounced, and from all around, a new breed of mutant rock 'n' rollers raised their unencumbered fists in approval.

Oftentimes, of course, this liberation from the tyranny of three chords and a backbeat made little difference—a bad band was a bad band no matter how high-tech their aspirations. But in the all-pervading firestorm of punk, it wasn't what you played that counted, it was the way that you played it.

By the end of 1977, groups like Ultravox, the Human League, and, across the Atlantic, Suicide had each taken their first tentative steps toward defining what would eventually become a new musical discipline. Behind the scenes, others—Gary Numan and his Tubeway Army, Rikki and the Last Days of Earth—were quietly twisting their own, preset musical destinies in a similar direction. And still others—Cabaret Voltaire, Wire, and Throbbing Gristle (whose own Industrial label eventually gave its very name to a new musical genre)— were preparing to burst fully-formed from the nameless obscurity to which pre-punk visionaries had hitherto been doomed to linger.

But punk did more than liberate music, it also liberated the means by which music could be distributed, and that was the direction in which Daniel Miller's attentions now turned. Previously, record labels were just that—brand names that functioned from behind a cloak of corporate anonymity, doling out the public's daily dose of rock 'n' roll only after it had

<22>

passed through the fiery auditions of "paying your dues" and "getting a deal."

Those labels that sprang up in spite of the system didn't believe in "paying dues"; frequently didn't even offer "deals." They seldom survived long, either—in Britain at least. Even the best-known of all U.K. independent labels, Andrew Loog Oldham's now-legendary Sixties dream, Immediate, eventually crumbled beneath the wheels of establishment pressure, and that despite boasting its own ready-made catalog of guaranteed chart-toppers.

More recently, Seventies upstarts like Stiff and Chiswick had rapidly discovered that their own dreams of uncompromised independence were best achieved by climbing into bed with one or another of the major labels. But while both were to gain higher public profiles, their newfound bondage demeaned them.

When Immediate finally closed its doors in 1969, the industry simply relinked its arms and it was business as usual. This time, however, the passing of Stiff's and Chiswick's initial free-spiritedness left a void—one that others were very quick to fill. Just months inside 1978, *ZigZag* magazine published the first in an eventual series of independent-label catalogs, noting eighty-four companies that had at least one privately produced single release to their name.

It was with his eyes firmly upon these two unexpected developments of the punk experience—the opening up, on the one hand, of pop's musical frontiers; on the other, of its commercial avenues—that Daniel Miller took his own first step into the waters of free enterprise.

That spring of 1978, Miller recorded what he perceived as a limited-edition single of two of his own most minimalistic electronic compositions: "Warm Leatherette," its concept lifted from J. G. Ballard's novel of wrecked auto-eroticism, *Crash,* and "TV O.D."—the ultimate anthem of couch-potato-hood. "It damn well exploded from the turntable,"

<23>

enthused *ZigZag*'s Chris Westwood, "and there was me, sitting all dumbfounded and shell-shocked . . . wondering how in the name of Ezra Pound any single 'droid could cook up a nitro-pancake like that all on his lonesome." He later revealed that two or three "eminent" record companies had already rejected the record. *That,* Westwood continued, proved how great it was!

Instead, "Warm Leatherette" was released on Miller's own Mute label, operating out of his northwest London apartment. But Miller was not completely alone in his endeavors. Impressed by his vision, the Rough Trade record store helped finance the record's manufacture, then promptly sold virtually every copy through its own burgeoning independent distribution network.

Miller adopted the name "the Normal" because he was. Hand-drawn graphics that accompanied his earliest publicity mailings were distinguished by their absolute lack of distinction; journalist Chris Westwood, attempting to conduct a Normal interview by mail for *ZigZag*, described Miller's characters as "generally devoid of personality, representing ordinary (i.e., 'normal') people in ordinary ('normal') situations."

Two "Normal-visuals" accompanied the resultant article, in the magazine's October 1978 issue: "The Normal Answering Fan Mail" and "The Normal Live at Madison Square Garden." The two pictures are virtually identical; in both, the Normal himself is viewed from the air, seated at a desk. The only difference is that there's an audience at Madison Square Garden. "Who are the audience?" asks Miller's handscrawled caption. "Who is the Normal? Your guess is as good as mine, mate!"

Sixteen years on, over forty thousand copies of "Warm Leatherette" have been sold. It has spun off a couple of visionary cover versions, one by Grace Jones, who titled her fourth album after her rendition of the song, and one by the industrial band Blok 57. Disc jockey Tony V. of WTBS in Boston named his weekly radio program after "TV O.D."

Miller remained unmoved by his success. Confessing that "I can never take anything I do totally seriously," he made tentative plans for a second Normal single, "First Frame," but abandoned it while it was still incomplete. "Much of the stuff he's laid on tape will probably never be heard," Westwood accurately prophesied; there would be just one further Normal release, a live EP recorded at West Rutland Pavilion in March 1979 with fellow electronics buff Robert Rental.

Nevertheless, emboldened by the success of his Normal activities, and convinced that there really was a market for a label specializing in experimental, non-pop pop records, Miller began expanding Mute's catalog.

The first act he approached was arch-experimentalist Boyd Rice, a San Francisco performer whose back catalog included one single with four holes punched in it, for "multi-axial rotation," another which cataloged every "cry" Lesley Gore ever sang, and an album that was playable at any speed the listener liked. Rice still records for Mute today.

Next to join the roster was the eccentrically inconsistent Fad Gadget, a.k.a. cartoonist Edwin Pouncey's flatmate Frank Tovey. His "Back to Nature" single became Mute's second release, with the Düsseldorf-based electro-punk bank DAF (Deutsche-Amerikanische Freundschaft) providing the fast-growing fledgling with its first album release, *Diekleinen und Diebosen.*

Already a known quantity, with a growing cult audience both at home and abroad, DAF was a key recruitment, establishing Mute as a "genuine" record label, as opposed to a handful of madmen messing around—a trough into which many of the era's most illuminative independents had already slipped. But it was Miller's own next enterprise that finally set the seal on Mute as a wellspring of both creative *and* commercial innovation.

The Silicon Teens was not, in essence, a particularly novel idea. For years, successive new musical fashions had de-

<25>

lighted in taking the hits of earlier eras and transforming them according to the dictates (and corresponding clichés) of the latest wave.

The Beatles and the Stones performed British Beat renditions of Carl Perkins and Muddy Waters; the next generation took psychedelic trips around interminable reassessments of Bo Diddley. The barely two-year-old story of punk, too, was strewn with the bloodied corpses of mutilated history. But from Sid Vicious hamstringing "My Way" onward, the question still remained: Where did novelty end and creativity begin?

This question certainly vexed Daniel Miller as he began piecing together what would become the Silicon Teens' album. Taking established rock 'n' roll classics and performing them as synthesizer speedball novelties, he was aware that he was treading on delicate ground. Could such a project be carried off without falling headlong into parody?

<26>

Once again, precedent loomed menacingly. During the first flurry of synthesizer mania, during the early 1970s, otherwise respected electronic musicians had laid both their integrity and their intelligence on the line by recording what amounted to stereo-demonstration albums with their po-faced recreations of sundry classical pieces.

They weren't all completely redundant, of course. Walter Carlos and Japan's Tomita both carved considerable niches for themselves within the slowly expanding electronics universe, with their takes on the work of Mozart and Debussy.

But it is one thing to restructure the classics, quite another to make a similar assault on rock 'n' roll, especially when your target audience is still in the throes of painstakingly painful deprogramming. Even among Miller's "target" audience—their senses and sensibilities already battered by the full-frontal assault of Rice, Tovey and Co.—songs like Chuck Berry's "Memphis Tennessee," Chris Montez's "Let's Dance," Heinz's "Just Like Eddie," and John Fred's "Judy in Disguise" retained a certain nostalgic value. And as he put the finishing touches to each successive synth mutation, Miller was aware that a lot more than simple time and money rode on the backs of the Silicon Teens. The real stake was his own credibility.

He needn't have worried. *Music for Parties,* the Silicon Teens' album, proved to be just that; the tunes of choice at every self-respecting New Wave party of 1979. And while the Teens themselves fell short of the charts (in Britain, unlike in the United States, the charts are the barometer by which even the most eclectic releases are measured), their influence did not.

Within months of *Music for Parties'* appearance in the spring of 1979, the Flying Lizards were scoring with a distinctly Teens-flavored deconstruction of the old Motown chestbeater "Money."

Almost simultaneously, glam veterans Sparks—gone and all but forgotten for the previous four years—resurfaced in tandem with Giorgio Moroder and rebuilt their career around a computerized throb. And in October 1979 Trevor <27> Horn and Geoff Downes teamed up as the Buggles, took a leaf from Daniel Miller's book, then recorded a song around a J. G. Ballard novel *(The Sound Sweep),* and chalked up one of the year's biggest hits—"Video Killed the Radio Star" ushered in the Eighties before the Seventies were even over.

Despite its science-fiction inspirations, "Video Killed the Radio Star" was essentially nothing less than unashamed nostalgia, a lament for the Golden Age of Radio and its death at the hands of the Hollywood talkies.

But the Buggles dressed like gay spacemen, and when they appeared on television, they brought their spaceship with them, plugging into a battery of computers whose most basic functions were otherworldly, alien. The Buggles made number one in Britain and abroad, and the electronics explosion that Daniel Miller had perceived two years before when he experienced "I Feel Love" was finally under way.

The catalyst around which these once-disparate threads all raged was Gary Numan (né Webb). Throughout 1977 and 1978, his Tubeway Army was just another ragtag punk band, high on adrenaline but low—so horribly, painfully low—on original ideas. A couple of singles did nothing; regular gigs at primal punk showcases the Vortex and the recently re-opened Roxy offered nothing to suggest that the band that closed its shows with a chaotic "White Light White Heat" was anything special whatsoever.

In vocalist Gary Webb, however, Tubeway Army had an advantage that even they did not fully comprehend. A committed Bowie fan, Webb openly confessed that he played punk because that was what the market demanded. He fed off contrivance, he insisted, and if what he regurgitated was equally contrived, then so be it.

But he also trumpeted the virtues of Ultravox, a go-nowhere electro-punk band fronted by the mechanoidal John Foxx, whose third album—produced in Germany by Connie Plank—had recently been released to widespread scorn. Talking to *Smash Hits* magazine in early 1979, Webb simply smiled to himself as his interrogator, Ian Cranna, described Ultravox as a "little rock band [with] unhealthy leanings towards glam posing and pretending to be weird. Eventually they ended up so pretentious and stilted that . . . it's small wonder they never caught on." Another two years would elapse before Ultravox erupted as one of the biggest bands of the age—two years during which they first had to displace Gary Webb himself.

Resurfacing with a new surname—Numan = New Man, a wicked pun which belied its owner's claim that he had picked it from a telephone directory—Webb redesigned Tubeway Army from the ground up. The accoutrements of regular rock 'n' roll were thrown aside; in their place, banks of winking synths were piled above the stage. Numan's own, once-frenetic stage persona was the next to go; in its stead, he became a barely moving manikin, clad in a space-age boiler suit and demanding to know, "Are Friends Electric?"

It was still very contrived, but that summer of 1979, Numan struck a chord in pop's body politik that had lain unmo-lested for years. Punk rock, and its related fallout, had accom-

<28>

plished much in the past two years, but what it hadn't done—
what it couldn't, by the very nature of its own psychotic hyper-
bole, ever do—was to create anything to rival the star machines
of earlier eras.

One could admire Johnny Rotten, Joe Strummer,
Paul Weller; one could even idolize them. But one could never
fall star-struck at their feet, and while that is probably a good
thing, it left a void as well, one that Numan was fast to fill.
Atonal, asexual, curiously inhuman—Numan fulfilled functions
that pop, in its haste to clasp the street credibility of punk to its
bosom, had given up for lost. And although sharp-eyed pundits
could date everything about Numan from his costuming to his
very demeanor to one single scene in the 1960s Peter Cooke–
Dudley Moore movie *Bedazzled,* the average pop-picker is not a
train-spotter.

For an incandescently glorious few months, Gary
Numan was untouchable, the biggest British pop star of his generation. And then he vanished. Within a year, his luster was
fading; within two, the magic had gone. But without Numan's
music, the floodgates would never have opened; without his eye
for imagery, the 1980s might have been a very drab place. Just
as the Buggles prophesied, video was indeed to kill the radio
star.

Image has always constituted an essential ingredient
in the marketing of rock 'n' roll—essential, but often ill-defined.
Throughout the 1970s, the number of artists who sprang fully
formed into the public consciousness on the strength of a ready-
made "look" was infinitesimal when compared to those whose
impact was initially derived from how *other* people saw them.

Marc Bolan, at the forefront of the early-Seventies
glam movement, was one such exception; Johnny Rotten, the
Crown Prince of Punk, was another; Gary Numan a third. Arguably, all who followed in their wake—glam rockers, punk rockers, synth-poppers—simply refined for their own use those
elements of these "originals" that most appealed to them.

Video shattered this truth completely. The concept

<29>

of shooting short films to accompany new records, of course, was hardly unique—the Beatles did it in the 1960s, and what was "The Monkees" but one long, glorious promotional film? But the idea of shooting them to accompany *every* record was new, and it was this notion of built-in continuity that made the difference.

Adam and his gaily painted Ants, rocketing out of punk-era mediocrity with a nonstop barrage of pounding pop pantomimes; Men Without Hats, morris-dancing through a French-Canadian approximation of a medieval English countryside; Men at Work, making a similar impression on the Australian outback; and Duran Duran, who took the travelogue directive to its most absurd lengths yet, shooting videos in locations that cost more than the records they were ostensibly promoting—these were the early pioneers, establishing through the medium of video, *and video alone,* the image they believed would carry them to the stars.

<30>

In America, of course, the advent of MTV—the cable-television station commenced broadcast on August 1, 1981—dictated that video would soon become *the* primary medium by which a new band should be marketed, simply by slipping into a ready-made niche somewhere between the self-imposed tyranny of popular AOR (album-oriented rock) radio, and the increasingly blinkered self-martyrdom of the college stations.

But it was very ironic that it was British bands who most readily filled that niche. The country only had three television channels—the two government-financed BBC stations, and the commercially financed Independent Television Network (ITV)—none of which made more than a token attempt to cover rock 'n' roll, and all of which viewed video with distrust.

Johnnie Stewart, creator of the long-running "Top of the Pops," explained, "On TV you must never try to be too clever, or you lose the thrill of what you are meant to be doing. A band physically performing is much better than all the video trickery that there'll ever be."

Video did bring a new dimension to these shows, but its impact was always going to be muted. The bands that exploded in a flurry of color, creativity, and cost (EMI spent over $200,000 flying Duran Duran to Sri Lanka to shoot three videos) on MTV were going to cut no ice whatsoever back home, not unless they had a look to match their lavish settings—and could re-create it on a TV-studio stage.

The New Romantic movement that dominated British rock throughout the early 1980s exploded, if not directly, at least as a direct result of this need. The fact that, in its earliest flowering, a berth on "Top of the Pops" was nothing more than a pipe dream for even the brightest of the nascent movement's exponents simply lent further authenticity to the art form.

For an art form it was, with its heart—not to mention the palette of rich colors and textures from which it would be painted—a Soho club called Billy's.

<3|>

Set just off Dean Street in London's West End, just around the corner from the famed Marquee Club, Billy's opened during the spring of 1978. At first it only really functioned on Fridays; the rest of the week it served as a conventional watering hole for conventional night owls. Fridays were when the freaks descended; the freaks, and anybody else who couldn't sleep.

For some, Billy's was simply one more stop in a lifelong whirl around the capital's gay clubs. But Bangs, Louise's, the Global Village, and Chaguarma's were all gone now, had been for eighteen months or more—ever since Chaguarma's became the Roxy, and filled up with punks.

Billy's, then, was fresh, and for a while it was also secret, with nothing more than the whispered word of mouth to draw all that was young, chic, and beautiful from the shadowy alleys of London's art community. Even when it outgrew its Friday-night berth and two of the regulars—Rusty Egan and Dave Claridge—announced that they would be taking over the club on Tuesdays as well, Billy's remained exclusive. Arguably, however, everything that was to happen over the next two years grew from that one decision.

The kids who hung out at Billy's in 1978 were those who fifteen years earlier would have frequented the Mod clubs in west London's Goldhawk Road: a predominantly working-class, teenaged crowd that spent its money on clothes and its time getting dressed—anything to detract from the gray monotony of the streets it grew up in.

Most were unemployed, some were unemployable—the dropout debris of a dying socialist government's inability to even stall the growth of Britain's dole queues. To an older generation, raised on work and work for all, kids like these were little more than parasites. At Billy's, though, they were peacocks—and peacocks are born to strut.

Squatters and soul boys, transvestites and tough nuts, students, punks, and student punks lined up at the door, all hoping that their chosen attire—for none were admitted uncostumed—would pass the scrutiny of the Welsh doorman, Steve Strange. Once they were inside, Egan would cast a second studied eye over the entrants. Nobody was on display at Billy's, but one false note could dampen the entire evening.

Once inside, they danced to Kraftwerk and the Velvet Underground, Roxy Music and T. Rex, Gary Numan and David Bowie; indeed, Tuesday nights *were* Bowie nights, Heroes Nights, with every Thin White Clone in the city turning up to eye the competition and dance to the house band, Ziggy Heroes.

One night Bowie himself dropped by the club, liked what he saw and immortalized it on vinyl, with 1979's "Boys Keep Swinging." The video that accompanied that single was itself shot at Billy's; the following year doorman Steve Strange was among the coterie of nightclub grotesqueries invited to accompany Bowie in his epochal "Ashes to Ashes" video. This whole period, recalls singer Midge Ure, "was rather like dying, and then waking up in Heaven."

Cliques formed and disbanded with restless energy.

<32>

One of those that stayed the course comprised a group of north London soul boys, busy forging the distinct identity that would eventually emerge as Spandau Ballet—one of the most successful young British bands of the decade.

In another corner, the painted transvestite outrage of "Boy George" O'Dowd and Peter "Marilyn" Robinson would be locked in scratch-your-eyes-out rivalry, competing with the roar of the crowd to get in one last, lasting put-down. Their barbs would turn up the following month in the movement's own magazines: the ultra-cultish *The Face* (which commenced publication in May 1980) and its down-market pop cousin, *Smash Hits*.

Life was fast and fickle. As word spread of Billy's, and the general public began joining the lines at the door, the party moved on to Blitz, a wine bar in trendy Covent Garden, just around the corner from Chaguarma's old site.

Splintering further, the scene played out a brief flirtation with the Cabaret Futura, a mock Berlinesque nightclub run by one of the new movement's own unacknowledged godfathers, ex–Doctors of Madness vocalist Richard Strange.

The importance of these two venues can be gauged from the haste with which their names were borrowed to christen the first wave of emerging new bands. The Blitz Kids, led by Spandau Ballet, played at Blitz; the Futurists—championed by Richard Strange (no relation, incidentally, to Steve!) and punk poet Richard Jobson—played the Cabaret. And all were New Romantics.

No one knows for sure who first coined the term, or how it rose above the many others that flew through the pages of the press. When *Smash Hits* interviewed Spandau Ballet in November 1980, writer Steve Taylor was complaining that "nobody's found a handle to describe this lot"; even the increasingly cliquey *Face*, that same month, was still calling them "the Cult with No Name." By the time the mainstream media *did* catch up with what was going on, the "New Dandies," the "Now Crowd," the faintly ominous "them," the distinctly derogatory "Post-Punk Blank Poseurs"—call them whatever a desperate journalist might—had already left the building.

Spandau Ballet—the first and always the most proficient of the Blitz Kids to make the leap from posing to playing—welded their own vision of Bowie to a loose white-funk backing, and by Christmas 1980, their debut single, "To Cut a Long Story Short" was selling twenty-three thousand records a day. Steve Strange's Visage, formed with Midge Ure and Rusty Egan (who had previously played together in Glen Matlock's Rich Kids), were in the Top Ten with "Fade to Grey." From the music papers to the tabloid press, news of the new cult spread fast. By the end of the year, New Romanticism was all but de rigueur on the rock 'n' pop circuit.

To those insiders left looking out, it was punk all over again. Now, as then, a clannish movement, Masonic in its ritual, innocent in its play, had been commercialized, sanitized, and finally, bitterly, exorcised, absorbed into the body politik of pop. But flashing through the pages of *The Face* and its ilk, New Romanticism flourished in a vacuum of its own creation.

The principles were simple, to emulate and to parody. A clothes sense which fell from a clothes horse. A musical sense learned in days of doodling rather than years of painful practice. And a willingness to play the game backward. Bands like Spandau Ballet, Visage, and Duran Duran (who emerged from a similar, Blitz-like scene in the midlands city of Birmingham, and whose own frilly-shirt-festooned debut, "Planet Earth," charted just months after Spandau's did) spiraled effortlessly from the fashion spreads to the top of the charts. In the past, it was usually the other way around entirely.

It was within this climate of fashionable foppery that the electronic bands—pioneered by the Normal and the Silicon Teens, but now resolving into the less esoteric sounds of Liverpool's Orchestral Maneuvers in the Dark and Sheffield's Human League—found the most willing reception. Soon they were dressing up as well.

Like the Blitz-based bands, groups like these drew

<34>

their energies from the icy example set by Kraftwerk and a handful of other, similar bands. If punk had looked to America for inspiration, sucking its strength from guitar-based rowdies like the Stooges and the New York Dolls, then Depeche Mode, OMD, the Human League, Soft Cell, and all faced in the opposite direction altogether—toward Europe. "With their flailing fringes, makeup, androgynous looks, and tinkling synthesizers," as journalist Pascal Bussy remarked, they sent thirty years of rock 'n' roll symbiosis spiraling into oblivion.

Even their backgrounds were, to put it mildly, "unconventional." None had spent half their careers slogging up the highway en route to another ill-paying club gig; none had grown up on a diet of truck-stop grease and coffee; none had "paid their dues."

The first generation of professional musicians to have spent the Sixties in a stroller instead of a van was also the first to question rock 'n' roll's tried-and-true formulae. It came <35> as no surprise, then, that in the time-honored tradition of birds of a feather, the bands that broke out of Britain's cities in the first months of the new decade should now flock together.

But links that appeared umbilical were largely superficial. Bands have always played follow-the-leader, seizing the preoccupations of the moment in a bid to hitch a ride to the top, and many of the new groups who made their "Top of the Pops" debut in the dandy shirts and funny haircuts that were so fashionable throughout the embryonic 1980s dropped the look the first chance they got.

Among the electronic bands who were so skillfully surfing the New Romantic movement, that alacrity was only accentuated by the individual musicians' own awareness of what they were doing. Musical rebellion was already flowing effortlessly from their fingers. What difference did it make if they painted those fingers first? The revolution was not going to be televised. It was going to be sold on video.

Throughout the musical traumas of 1980, Daniel Miller's Mute label continued to grow. He did his best to disassociate himself from what was going on outside, even though he knew that he was probably partially to blame. Many of the emergent bands cited the Normal as a formative influence; many more were clearly indebted to the Silicon Teens, and Miller's own reputation was such that several bands approached him in hopes of a deal.

They were quickly frightened off, either by Miller himself (his brusque reaction to one group of hopefuls—a resounding roar of "Yeeuch!"—is legendary even today) or by Mute's own peculiar working practices.

Miller offered neither contracts nor advances. Any expenses incurred in the making and marketing of a record would be shared equally by band and label, and though Miller pledged that the profits would be divided likewise, few would-be suitors stayed long enough to hear that. They would be off in search of a "real" record label, with real money to throw in their direction. Those haircuts didn't grow on trees!

Miller didn't regret those bands' passing. Mute was now a dozen singles old, and as established on the underground dance scene as any fledgling could hope to be. To Miller himself, Mute's championing of the eccentric and esoteric was as worthy as any chart hit—more so, because any idiot could release a hit single. It took a special kind of madness to put out four Fad Gadget records in the space of a year!

And besides, Mute was no longer a voice in the experimental wilderness. There was another label in town.

Throughout the summer of 1980, a disc jockey from the east London overflow of Dagenham announced that he intended to start up his own record company, a shop window for the ever-increasing number of homemade electronic tapes that were falling into his hands.

Stevo had worked the New Romantic circuit with visionary vigor. A regular at Billy's, Blitz, and the Chelsea Drugstore in King's Road, Stevo championed electronic music with a vengeance, broadening its horizons simply by broadening his own.

<48>

Clubs on the very fringes of London—Croc's in Rayleigh (named for the live crocodile that lived in a pool there), Scamp's in Southend—now held regular Futurist nights, expanding the formula that made the original cabaret so successful, and combining that with the verve of the old Heroes Nights. To many of the people in his audience, Stevo—the man who made such evenings possible—was more than a simple club deejay. He was the founding father of the new electro-pop scene. And now his children were coming home to roost.

Musical parenthood was not a mantel that Stevo adopted lightly, however. New bands were springing up everywhere, and as he packed up his equipment every evening, Stevo would find another cache of homemade demos piled upon his turntables. A lot of the bands, of course, were rubbish, but some showed genuine promise. A few even demanded documentation, a stab at making some history of their own. But they all trusted him to make the right decisions for them.

<37>

Stevo's intended compilation was just such a decision. It would bring together the very cream of the bands he had encountered over the last few months, a shop window for new talent. Confidently, he predicted that every band on the record would have a deal within the year.

In later years, when Stevo's own deliberately misspelt Some Bizzare label was off and running, this confidence was most evident in his insistence on arranging separate distribution deals for every band on the label. Just as every group had different talents, so, Stevo believed, did every major record company. His job was to bring them together. At this earlier but no less critical juncture, he was simply adamant that any act that granted him the rights to their precious demo tapes would never have cause to regret it.

He was not to know that within the very first crop of bands he intended consigning to vinyl, one was already kicking against the image that the Some Bizzare label conferred upon them, one that cringed with embarrassment whenever its name was brought up in connection with Stevo's beloved Futurist movement.

It was not Stevo's fault that he had fallen for the same visual hooks as everybody else who came into the orbit of this headstrong band, just as it wasn't really the group's fault that they, in their naiveté, had adopted both a look and a name that simply screamed "New Romanticism" at everyone who encountered it.

But both learned an invaluable lesson as they tried to come to terms with their mistakes. With Depeche Mode—then as now—nothing would ever be quite what it appeared.

<30>

Chapter 3

You Know That
Sound That Goes
"WAAAUUUUGH"?

IF THERE EVER was such a thing, Depeche Mode was the perfect pop group. Young and good-looking, they dressed as well as they behaved. Their largely self-composed repertoire comprised nothing but short, sharp lessons in contagion, with lyrics that sounded great but meant very little. Few of the people encountering them had any difficulty in imagining that here, and nowhere else, were the real Teenage Idols for whom the country had been searching for so long.

Depeche Mode had other ideas, however. They were cripplingly naive, they admitted that. But they also knew what they wanted, and while they were more than happy to be wined and dined by the entrepreneurial bigwigs who beat a path to their Basildon door, it was because they were thirsty and hungry, not because they were ready to be sculpted into something they weren't.

The fact that Depeche Mode slipped both sartorially and stylistically into the Futurist bag, they admitted, was through necessity rather than need. For a synthesized four-piece, there was no other scene they could join.

Actually, the band members sheepishly confessed, the synthesizers were a recent addition to their arsenal—had been suggested to them by what they were hearing at the clubs and discos they attended at night, by the music they themselves most enjoyed listening to. Indeed, as the summer of 1980 ebbed into history, Depeche Mode itself was still a brand-new concept, hatched when three teenage friends realized that they weren't getting anywhere with "conventional" musical instruments, but wanted to continue making music regardless.

<40> At the outset, the group's ringleader was Vince Clarke. He had started singing in his early teens, in the church choir and, for a short time, as one-half of an unstable gospel duo. It was, in fact, through the auspices of the local branch of the church-based Boys Brigade organization that he first ran into Andrew Fletcher, the second member of this quizzically-named new band.

The two hit it off immediately—they had so much in common! Their birthdays were just five days apart: Vince was born in Woodford, Essex, on July 3, 1960; Fletch in the Midlands city of Nottingham on July 8—like Vince, he was still a child when his parents packed up their belongings and moved to Basildon.

Both boys were devoted to the Boys Brigade, with its Scouts-like litany of healthy sports and activities, and so while their school friends hurtled regularly to London to clubs and concerts, Fletch later laughed, "I went to church seven nights a week. So did Vince. Vince was a real Bible basher!" Religion remained one of the handful of activities available in the "new town" of Basildon that didn't involve breaking the law.

New towns are a peculiarly English, and peculiarly 1960s, innovation. The postwar years had seen London boom, as a center of population and industry alike, and do so at a rate that far outpaced the building industry. Overcrowding was rife, with entire neighborhoods abandoned to slum housing. Even the well-intentioned erection of enormous, American-style concrete tower blocks—new homes for family piled upon family—could not lessen the strain.

They did, in fact, often exacerbate it, as it became apparent that the only families being moved into these projects were those who, through either educational or economical deprivation, were considered "problems"—stereotypically worn-out mothers with a brood of unruly children, a drunken husband in jail, and a larcenous son bent upon joining him there.

New towns were conceived, then, as a means of less- <41> ening the strains of inner-city life. If the "problem" families could be relocated to "nice" homes in leafy suburbs, maybe they would respond in kind. It was a frighteningly condescending point of view, but one that, history continues to prove, remains symptomatic of Western bureaucratic thinking. A ghetto is a ghetto is a ghetto, and all the grassy lawns in the world will not change that. But try telling that to someone who grew up with grassy lawns.

Encircling north and east London in a ring of tightly manicured concrete and steel, new towns were presented to the public as an alternative way of life—all the luxuries of the suburbs, all the conveniences of the city. No more than thirty or forty miles of lovingly maintained railway track separated them from London. Neighborhood shopping centers, with all the amenities one could dream of, catered to the family's every need.

Basildon, Stevenage, Harlow, Milton Keynes . . . these were not simple *towns,* they were communities. The only problem was, there was no *sense* of community, just a couple hundred thousand people from heavily contrasting backgrounds, crammed unwelcomingly in alongside one another.

Businessmen—relocated by avaricious companies, keen to take advantage of the low property prices—rubbed shoulders with hard-bitten laborers forced to migrate from their traditional homes by that selfsame relocation drive. These people had nothing in common, and wouldn't have wanted to if they could. The "them and us" structure of the English class system, forever seething beneath the surface even in the ancient cities, was pushed up and out in the tight "neighborly" confines of the new towns. But whereas once, those pressures had the safety valve of tradition to relieve them, in the cultural bottleneck of Techno City, everyone and everything was strange.

It was worst for the children. Adults could exhaust themselves commuting to work, or the shops. For the kids, though, free time yawned like a wasteland. In the cities, familiarity bucked the boredom and bred a strange contentment. The bomb sites, the youth clubs, the dance halls—each was steeped in local lore; you knew where you were, and you knew who you were with.

Within these strange new developments, however, youth counted for little. It was as though the architects who belched their pipe dreams into cold stone reality had forgotten that people came in all shapes and sizes, and that the small ones needed amusement too. And so, two very different subcultures began to emerge; no different, in many ways, from those that flourish in any community, but somehow twisted and exaggerated by the preplanned anonymity of their young lives. The "good" kids, like Vince Clarke and Andy Fletcher, threw themselves into "nice" activities: the church, the Scouts, the Army Cadets. The "bad" ones just ran riot.

Vince and Fletch—singing, marching, and preaching to their fellows—had very little time for the "bad" kids, seldom even allowed their paths to cross with them. When a rash of car thefts shook the neighborhood one summer, it was not the Clarkes and Fletchers who would be awakened by the

<42>

policeman's knock on the door. When petty arson reached epidemic proportions, the trail of scorched and twisted rubbish skips never led to their garden gates.

And when the pop-music bug finally sank its teeth into the pair, around 1977, it was not the snarling, spitting horror of punk rock that they set themselves to emulate, but the gentler sounds that their parents might have liked—the Beatles and the Eagles. Giving up the oboe lessons that he'd been taking for a couple of years now, Vince bought a guitar, Fletch picked up a bass, and with a revolving-door's-worth of fellow musicians, No Romance in China took its first tentative steps around the rehearsal room in late 1977.

The group's vocabulary was limited. Vince had written a few simple songs, but he encouraged his bandmates to bring along their favorite records as well: "I Like It," by Gerry and the Pacemakers; "The Price of Love," by the Everly Brothers; Phil Spector's "Then She Kissed Me"—oldies (but goldies!) like that. <43>

Even when No Romance in China started sensing a need to maintain at least a stylistic link with the current state of musical affairs, it was the Cure upon whom they modeled themselves—a Beatle-esque pop group whose future, darker side was still hidden beneath the twangy inflections of their candy-coat hooklines.

No Romance in China was to survive through the last three years of the Seventies. But even the extra rehearsal time freed up after its founder members left the Boys Brigade in 1978 did not change the band's outlook. Neither Vince nor Fletch saw No Romance in China as anything more than a way to kill an evening or two a week. The highlight of the band's career was to retain their sometimes-weekly appearances at the Van Gogh youth club—as featureless a hole as anything else in Basildon, but a welcoming one.

Show nights and free nights were spent hanging out with the other young musicians who haunted the club: Norman and the Worms, an acoustic duo whose repertoire included a show-stopping rendition of the theme from the Sixties children's TV series "Skippy the Bush Kangaroo"; and the Vicars, a comparatively better-accomplished R&B band from nearby Canvey Island, whose powerful female singer went under the unlikely name of Alf. A few years before, she'd been taking oboe lessons alongside Vince, and often credited those classes for the strength of her voice. "I always had big lungs from playing a wind instrument."

The Van Gogh—so named, it was joked, because "you only ever kept one ear to the bands that played there"— was popular with kids from both sides of the behavioral track. Fights broke out regularly, cultish rivalries ran high, and petty crime was a fact of life. The bands that played there learned very early, and sometimes painfully, never to close their eyes while they played and sang, nor to turn their backs on their audience. If they did, the chances were good that something would vanish.

Their vigilance only increased that evening in the fall of 1979 when one of Norman and the Worms turned up with a cheap Moog Prodigy synthesizer.

Partners in adversity, No Romance in China and Norman and the Worms had already developed a common bond. The two groups often shared an evening's billing, taking it in turns to headline the show. The arrival of Martin Gore's synth, however, was to send their friendship rocketing away in a new direction altogether.

Born on July 23, 1961, Martin was a year younger than Vince and Fletch. Like so many others at the Van Gogh, Martin was a relative newcomer to Basildon. He grew up in Dagenham, the London suburb that existed solely to house a massive Ford car plant. His parents, like most Dagenhamites, worked at Ford, and although they, too, had made the trek to Basildon in search of the great new life which the town's recruitment posters promised, all it really meant was that they had farther to go to get to work every morning.

<44>

As a child, Martin remembers, he was something of a school bully, right up until the day he was caught battering one of his schoolmates over the head with a brick. His father gave him "a good hiding," he recollects, "and that was the beginning of my being thoughtful."

Now, by his own determination, he was "very passive and harmless," an excellent scholar whose propensity for languages saw him enroll in a student-exchange program. He made several visits to Germany, swapping holiday homes with a like-minded pupil from the northern province of Schleswig-Holstein, and when Martin made up his mind to escape from Basildon the first chance he got, Germany was always the most likely place he would run to. If he had any wildness left inside him at all, that vague sense of wanderlust was it.

Martin left St. Nicholas' Comprehensive School in 1977 and took a job in a local bank—a dutiful teller whose polite charm rapidly marked him out for a lengthy career in the industry. He considered that as well; banking was not the most exciting job in the world, he knew, but it was safe, and the pay wasn't bad.

<45>

He just needed to get a few things out of his system first. Martin's employers knew about Norman and the Worms; encouraged it in the same way they might encourage a keen stamp collector, and admired the way the youngster salted away his earnings so that he could purchase new equipment. They were as proud as parents when he came in one morning and announced he'd bought the synthesizer he'd been talking about for what seemed like months. Now all he had to do was learn how to play it.

By today's standards, the monophonic Moog Prodigy ranks among the most primitive of all modern synthesizers, although it was a considerable step up from the machines with which the first generation of synth operatives were saddled. The first mass-market synthesizer to boast the ability to create new sounds, rather than simply re-create preset ones, the Prodigy's only major drawback was the number of knobs and switches one needed to come to grips with. There were so many of them that unless one was very familiar with the instrument, it was difficult to know which one to turn first.

"I'd had my synth for about a month before I realized you could change the sound," Martin would confess. "You know that sound that goes 'WAAAUUUUGH'? I was stuck on that one for ages."

"WAAAUUUUGH" or not, the arrival of a synthesizer into the hitherto guitar-dominated Basildon scene was an event of seismic proportions, particularly once it became apparent that it was completely incompatible with Norman and the Worms' existing sound. And with Vince sensing that No Romance in China, too, was on a fast road to nowhere, it was inevitable that he and Martin would quickly join forces.

The "new technology," as it was called, fascinated Vince. Hours spent doodling with Martin's Moog demonstrated so many of the home truths that Vince had heard about synthesizers—that they were easy to play, easy to transport, and when you got bored with making music, you could simply experiment with sound . . . and that became music as well.

Martin and Vince's first group was a duo called French Look, although the pair did little more than kick around their rehearsal space—Vince's bedroom—and study synthesizer catalogs while Vince's newly acquired drum machine clicked impatiently in the corner. Only after Fletch started attending these unproductive sessions did the germ of another band begin to take shape. Deferring to the still-untapped potential of Martin's Moog, they called it Composition of Sound.

"I don't think you'd really call either of them 'groups,'" remembers one of the trio's old schoolmates. "It was more like a hard core of friends—Vince, Martin, and Andy—who'd get together to dick around with their instruments, and a loose outer circle that would egg them on. People make a lot more of this period than it really deserves. . . . I don't think French Look ever even played a show, and Composition

<46>

of Sound couldn't have done more than three. And they were all disasters!"

The first of these shows took place not in the familiar bowels of the Van Gogh, but a dozen miles away in Southend, at the regionally famous Scamps nightclub, where Stevo was now hosting regular electronic nights. Fletch is generally credited with having found the gig, calling around every venue in the area until he found one that had an opening for a completely untried new group. And as the drum machine–powered three-piece—Martin on synth, Fletch on bass, Vince on guitar and vocals—prepared for action, it truly appeared as though the Big Time was beckoning. They had even heard of the band they were opening for—had read their name in the music papers. That in itself was a killer achievement!

In the event, it was to remain Film Noir's greatest-ever achievement that they once headlined over the embryonic Depeche Mode—and blew them away. <47>

Nerves and tempers alike were frayed as Composition of Sound ran tentatively through their set. Their repertoire, despite Vince's growing confidence as a songwriter, was still peppered with cover versions, rounded off with the instrumental "Mouldy Old Dough"—a thumping keyboard piece that, close to a decade before, had given the bizarrely named Lieutenant Pigeon a completely unexpected British best-seller.

That band's trademark was an old lady playing piano while a wooden pigeon nodded alongside her. Cruelly, witnesses to Composition of Sound's debut show—and beyond the handful of friends who traveled to Southend with them, there were few—reckon the pigeon was a formative influence on this new band. "They were certainly very wooden."

The show was a disaster from the beginning, but it got worse. From where Vince stood, center stage, Composition of Sound sounded plodding, amateurish, horrible. Martin's synthesizer was kicking out a tuneless barrage of burps and squeaks, the rigid syncopation of the drum machine was running rings around Fletch's stumbling bass, Vince's own guitar sounded out of tune, and his vocals were barely audible. The crowd was small but restless. Nothing was working right.

Suddenly, he exploded—not dramatically, because that was never his style. But quietly, almost unnoticed, he walked to the side of the stage and launched a savage kick at the plug board—promptly plunging band and stage alike into silent darkness. From the back of the club, the biggest cheer of the evening compounded his rage.

Composition of Sound's inauspicious debut was followed by an equally inauspicious encore. Just weeks after the Scamps show, the trio agreed to play a friend's party. "And it wasn't even a minor success," Fletch later reminisced. "The crowd didn't react [again], so Vince lost his temper [again]."

<48>

An already fraught situation was worsened by the audience, most of whom had never seen a synthesizer before. The entire performance was plagued by what Vince remembers as "fourteen-year-old kids" wandering onto the makeshift stage and twiddling with the knobs, demanding to know what "this one" did.

Himself still uncertain what the correct answer was, Martin would give them a quick demonstration, while Vince looked on in disgust. "It goes 'WAAAUUUUGH.'"

It was shortly after this doomed second show that Vince traded in his guitar for a synthesizer of his own. It was the spring of 1980, Gary Numan was a superstar, and though the true deluge of synthesized bands had yet to erupt in his wake, already the music scene was girding itself in readiness.

Even in Basildon, isolated from the heart and arteries of the British music scene by the town's own built-in ennui, electronic music was a national phenomenon. No longer ruthlessly capital-centric, the music industry had finally acknowledged—for the first time since the Merseyboom of almost twenty years before—that the provinces, too, had something to say.

Liverpudlians Orchestral Manoeuvres in the Dark, having flexed their muscles with the naive syncopation of "Electricity" and "Red Frame White Light," were in the Top Ten with the somber "Enola Gay." Manchester's Joy Division, still mourning the suicide of vocalist Ian Curtis, were nevertheless celebrating their first-ever hit, with "Love Will Tear Us Apart," a love song that drew heavily from Numan's lexicon of alienation. The Human League were gnawing at the fringes of the national chart with ever-increasing urgency—their latest single, the quirky "Empire State Human," had reached a respectable number sixty-two.

Why, Vince wondered as he fingered the keys of his factory fresh Moog, should Basildon, too, not have a voice?

Because, as even he conceded, there was nobody to give it one. Vince was neither a competent vocalist nor a comfortable frontman. When he dressed up for shows, he just felt silly, and though he was able to disguise his shyness while he still had a guitar to hide behind, now that he played synthesizer, there was no defense.

<49>

Briefly, Composition of Sound toyed with the idea of placing an ad in the Musicians Wanted columns of *Melody Maker,* looking for a new singer. But they were not comfortable with the idea. Although they had been together as a unit for less than a year, the trio was at ease with one another, understood one another's strengths and limitations.

"You can't possibly get on so well with newcomers who've been fixed up through ads as you can with somebody you already know," Martin remarked with an irony the group's subsequent history alone would appreciate. So although the band "desperately" needed a singer, they intended to take their time and wait for the right frontman to appear.

If a fourth member was going to gate-crash their party, then it would need to be someone they knew, and more important, someone they trusted. Which made it all the more improbable that Vince should single out David Gahan.

You Know That Sound That Goes "WAAAUUUUGH"? . . . .

Born in Epping on May 9, 1962, Gahan was close to two years younger than Vince and Fletch, although in terms of "life experience," he made many kids his age look like babes in arms—his latest prospective employers included.

Like Vince and Fletch, he'd experienced something of a religious upbringing—his mother's side of the family in particular was closely tied to the Salvation Army. Unlike Vince and Fletch, he had rejected it out of hand. When Dave and his older sister were packed off to Sunday school, they preferred to spend their time simply riding their bicycles around the neighborhood. "Then when we got back we'd say it was great."

Dave was five when his family broke up and his father left home. "I never heard from him again," Dave lamented years afterward. He was to spend much of the next quarter-century trying to find him again, ending an increasingly despairing search only when he found himself doing exactly the same thing to his family that Mr. Gahan Sr. had done to his own—walking out on his marriage and five-year-old-son to begin a new life in a different world.

The young Dave Gahan compensated for the loss of his father in the only way he could—by becoming what he describes as "a real wide boy with a chip on my shoulder, a real yob." Although he has claimed that "compared to my other mates, I didn't fit in very well," he led an active, if antisocial, social life. By the time Dave left school, he had already made three visits to juvenile court. His rap sheet included stealing cars which would then be abandoned and burned, vandalism, and spray-painting graffiti on walls.

Dave was fourteen when he got his first tattoo, from an old "sort of sailor guy named Clive," who set up his parlor on Southend sea front. Clive himself was something of a legend in the area, a grizzled bear of a man whose own body was a web of tattoos, including one that traced a dotted line around his neck, with the words "cut here." Without even understanding

<50>

why, the sheer nihilistic bravado of that statement impressed Dave beyond words.

Friends of his sister introduced Dave to other fleshly pleasures.

"She had a lot of really nice girlfriends, so I used to walk to school with a lot of nice girls. I was the young little brother they all needed to explore, so I had a lot of fun." Journalist Gavin Martin, recounting this conversation in 1993, could not hide his skepticism: "It's time to play that old game: I've-had-more-totty-than-you've-had-hot-dinners-before-you-were-even-born-kid." But Dave was not giving up his memories. "I learned pretty fast, I must say. I must boast."

And he did boast. By his early twenties, Dave was recounting memories that few people his age are able to treasure. "I was a soulboy, I've done it all, I've been everything," he once bragged. Even though he could have been no more than thirteen or fourteen at the time, he talked of regularly attending soul weekends and "hanging around with the crew from Global Village"—the notorious gay club beneath Charing Cross railway station. <5l>

Punk hit when Dave was fifteen and he threw himself into that with all the passion of the burgeoning cultural dilettante, flitting restlessly from scene to scene in search of the ultimate good time. He numbers himself among the tight knot of fans who followed the Damned, the anarchic punks who blended the adrenalined roar of the Stooges with the innocent guile of the music hall. When they split, in late 1977, he transferred his allegiance to the Clash, the snarling ball of vitriol whose earliest songs—"White Riot," "1977," "Career Opportunities"—were a call to arms for Britain's militant youth.

Dave admits that much of the Clash's ultra-political message sailed right past him. "I wasn't really into what they were singing about because I didn't really understand their first album. But I used to go and see them because I liked their attitude and the energy. They were brilliant. Coming away from all those gigs with your ears ringing, and telling all your mates in school the next day . . .''

Dave left St. Nicholas' in July 1978—although he claims he spent most of his last year playing truant anyway. He was not sorry to see the back of the place, and the feeling was apparently mutual. His very name was synonymous with trouble and truancy, and the stories of his working life that filtered back to his old teachers simply reinforced their own impressions.

Within six months of leaving school, Gahan had passed through an astonishing twenty different jobs. If he'd not been capable of settling down to his lessons, what chance did he have of sticking at anything else—even tasks as undemanding as selling soft drinks or bottling perfume? Even the long-suffering clerks at the Basildon unemployment office began to despair of him.

<52> Only when he was on display did Dave appear happy. He was a natural show-off, and his clothes reflected his night life, a blur of finery that at last pinpointed a possible talent. By 1980, when he first fell into Composition of Sound's orbit, Dave numbered among the lost souls who now haunted the London club scene, flitting between the increasingly painfully fashionable Billy's, Blitz, and Cabaret Futura, and the lesser-known but equally influential niteries that thrived on the capital's fringes: Scamps, Crocs, and more.

He still looked young, but he dressed tough; he had little difficulty insinuating himself into even these exclusive circles, and inspired by the clothes that he saw on display there, he applied for a place at Southend Art College, studying window design on his way to a possible future in the fashion industry. The first time Vince recalls truly noticing him, Dave was peacocking proudly through a crowd of local beer boys, greasy yobs for whom an even vaguely ostentatious outfit was normally an open invitation for a knuckle sandwich. Dave sashayed by unmolested.

According to one account of Dave Gahan's recruitment into Composition of Sound, he was first employed as sound engineer by that earlier Clarke-Gore union, French Look, then slipped into a similar role when Composition of Sound got under way. When the band began looking around for a vocalist, the flamboyant soundman was a natural choice.

The truth, as related by Fletch, is somewhat less glamorous. Through his and Vince's involvement with the local church, the band was permitted to take over one of the building's storage rooms as a rehearsal space. "The vicar used to just let us have the place. You just had to be nice and polite, and you weren't allowed to play loud."

With such comparatively luxurious surroundings at their disposal, Composition of Sound's rehearsals frequently turned into free-for-all jam sessions, with other musicians and bands welcome to drop by and join in. "We got Dave on the strength of him singing 'Heroes,' the Bowie number, at a jam session with some other band," Fletch recalls. "We weren't even sure that it was him we wanted, there were so many other people singing."

<59>

"In fact," Martin deadpans, "we're still not convinced."

Dave was invited to try out under less competitive conditions, and swiftly he gelled with the rest of Composition of Sound. Considering that he had never really contemplated singing in a band—looked upon it even now as just another laugh—he really was quite good.

Dave's arrival in Composition of Sound was the herald for the remaining members to make the last of the adjustments they deemed necessary before they were ready to face the world again. The most important, of course, was to change the group's name—no one particularly liked Composition of Sound, but they'd never come up with anything better.

Now Dave was suggesting a phrase he'd just come across on the cover of a French fashion magazine. "Dépêche Mode" translated as "Fast Fashion," although the group itself didn't know that at the time. "We just liked the sound of the words," Vince nervously admitted. "It could just as easily have been Depeche Mud"—or Dépede Moche, a subtle spoonerism with which the group's French detractors have long delighted in rechristening the band. It means "Dirty Pedophiles."

The band members also debated long and hard over the correct pronunciation of their new name. They settled, temporarily as it turned out, on "Depech-ay." "It's probably grammatically wrong," Vince admitted. "But we like it that way."

<54>

Chapter 4

Stop That

Clacking Noise

Now!

THE BAND TOOK their change of name seriously. It sounded new, exciting, modern; now it only remained for them to finish the internal redesign that would give them an image to match. As soon as he had saved enough money, Fletch sacrificed his faithful bass guitar for a third synthesizer. "We liked bands that used snyths," Vince reasons, "OMD, Human League, Gary Numan . . . that was the sort of stuff we listened to."

He denied, even as the newly named combo took its first steps outside the rehearsal room, that "we changed to make our sound more commercial, or because we thought it would be the fashionable thing to do." The songs with which Depeche Mode would soon be making their national breakthrough were the same songs they had started out with, "with the guitars and everything."

"To us," Martin reasoned, "the synthesizer was a punk instrument, an instant do-it-yourself kind of tool." He nodded in agreement as Andy continued, "You don't have to be a great musician to be allowed to play and get a message out, [and] that's what punk was all about, getting rid of the ego and getting right down to it. We certainly didn't know anything about music when we first started!"

It was not only for musical reasons that Depeche Mode packed up their guitars, however. With gigs becoming increasingly regular, the three musicians in the band had long since tired of cramming amplifiers and guitars onto the public buses and trains that were their only form of transport. They still ended up, as Martin put it, with Dave's mike stands wrapped around their heads, "but it was a lot easier than if we'd been loaded down with everything else."

<56> One thing that did not change was the band's refusal to recruit a drummer—and that despite the ever more evident shortcomings of a drum machine that was programmed to play only the most basic rhythms. "If a good drummer approached us, and fit in with the band, maybe we'd think about it," Dave conceded. "But we've never had much of a choice. There weren't any drummers in Basildon that would do, and besides, they need transport and a place to rehearse."

And rehearsal space was already at a premium.

The upsurge in the band's workload demanded a corresponding increase in the amount of time they spent rehearsing—every evening some weeks, four or five during others. Even the friendly local vicar could not accommodate them that often, so the proceedings shifted instead to Vince's garage.

It was a poor alternative. Even with all four band members wearing headphones, Vince's mother complained about the noise of the synthesizer keys, and the most productive rehearsal would eventually be brought to a close by an irate Mrs. Clarke poking her head around the door and demanding, "Stop that clacking noise *now!*"

Depeche Mode made its public debut with a show at

their old school, St. Nicholas' Comprehensive. For the group's three founder members, now veterans of a handful of performances, it was "just another show." For their normally hyper-buoyant vocalist, however, it was the most terrifying moment of his life.

Dave's only previous experience of public singing was in a Salvation Army Christmas choir when he was eight. Now, a decade on, he was sitting in a deserted school classroom, his face anxiously pale, and repeating over and over again, "I don't want to do it, I don't want to do it."

Martin, Vince, and Fletch did their best to rally him, with words and copious quantities of alcohol. After ten cans of lager, Dave's first-night nerves were finally reduced to a mild queasiness at the back of his brain, and thirty minutes of exhausting exertion later, the fast-sobering singer was on top of the world. "That was great! Let's do another!"

Toward the end of October 1980, Depeche Mode <57> landed a residency at the Top Alex, a Southend club which was hitherto the sole preserve of hard-drinking rhythm-and-blues addicts.

Once again the first show was nerve-wracking, as the group took the stage before the largest, and oldest, audience they had ever greeted, wondering how they could ever follow the club deejay's own repertoire of hard, fast R&B with a set that still revolved around pop classics, past and—though no one could have guessed it then—future.

"But we went down really well," Dave recalls. "They were all headbanging to our music!"

With the band's live reputation now building on a local level, the logical next step was to try winning some gigs farther afield. Depeche Mode had been together for just three months when they paid their first visit to a recording studio, laying down the three-song calling card that they would mail around the club and pub circuits.

All three songs were Vince's. Martin had brought a

couple of his own compositions along to rehearsals, "Tora! Tora! Tora!" and "Big Muff," but Vince was reluctant to loosen his hold on the group's creative direction. "Maybe once we're established, we can start branching out," he would explain. "But right now we need unity. We need an identifiable sound."

This unity was not the only thing that dominated a very primitive demo tape, even though two of the songs recorded that autumn afternoon—"Photographic," and an instrumental piece that Vince would later revamp for the theme to the U.K. television show "The Other Side of the Tracks"—were to remain in Depeche Mode's repertoire for the next year. (A third, long-forgotten title completed the collection.) Depeche Mode was still coming to grips with the intricacies of their synthesizers, still trying to figure out how to stop them from going, "WAAAUUUUGH!" Martin remains convinced that "all the songs on that first demo have the same sound to them."

<58>

Still, the power of the cassette was undeniable. Within a week of consigning the first batch of tapes to the mailstream, Depeche Mode was contacted by booking agents at two small but prestigious venues—the Canning Town Bridgehouse, a mock-Tudor pub in a distressed corner of east London's decaying docklands, and Dave's old hangout at Croc's, in Rayleigh.

The Bridgehouse was one of London's old-guard pub venues, renowned throughout the punk era as a welcome haunt for bands that might not otherwise have sat easily among the fire and brimstone of the Pistols generation.

In 1978 the venue opened its own record label, Bridgehouse Records, through which its most regular unsigned performers were guaranteed an outlet. Art-punx Warm Jets and Wasted Youth, power-poppers the Roll-Ups and Crunch—the clutch of would-be Mod bands who celebrated that year's May Day holiday with a full-scale Mod Ball—were all preserved in vinyl by the club.

The loyalty cut both ways. Among the Bridgehouse's headlined attractions that winter of 1980, nestling alongside such newborn headliners as TV Smith's Explorers and Paul Young's Q-Tips, Wasted Youth still marched toward their eventual destiny as Flesh for Lulu, and Roll-Ups guitarist Lea Hart plied his trade with ex–Bay City Roller Ian Mitchell.

Still, Depeche Mode's earliest Bridgehouse shows kept them far from even these notables, pitching them instead as support to a gentle stream of now largely forgotten club bands. The experience of working a disinterested crowd was invaluable, of course, but for Depeche Mode, Croc's was to prove a far more enjoyable outlet.

"The resident deejay there really liked us," Dave proudly relates. The deejay promptly offered Depeche Mode a residency at the Glamour Club, a regular Saturday-night electronics disco, and his faith began paying dividends right away. By early December 1980, Saturday nights were literally standing room only—there wasn't even room to dance.

Mikey Craig, bassist with Culture Club—one of the <59> succession of bands that would struggle to fill Depeche Mode's Saturday-night shoes at Croc's—remembers, "The age group there [was] about sixteen to twenty-two, and everybody [went] out of their way to overdress and get pissed on a Saturday night. You'd find a bunch of rockabillies, a bunch of skinheads probably, a bunch of New Romantics and Kid Creole look-alikes, all in the same place, which was really interesting"—and quite unique.

Britain was changing, and British pop was changing with it. Although its histories claim otherwise, Punk had never truly united the nation's traditionally warring pop clans. It had, however, calmed them a little, presented those who cared with a common enemy—the past; and a common cause—the future.

That future had now arrived, and with it a renewed splintering. Music was becoming more tribal than ever, dividing not only down cultural lines but subcultural ones as well, and as punk ebbed into the history books, nothing arrived to replace it—it would be another three years before even Prime Minister Margaret Thatcher could unite the separate factions of youth against her. In 1980, Punk and Skinhead, Two-Tone and Mod, New Romantic and Old Fart simply milled unwillingly together, rediscovering all the old flash points.

Those flash points flared every time the various groups met, at Croc's as often as anywhere else. Few Saturday nights passed off entirely trouble-free, and at least one Depeche Mode show, in November 1980, was scarred by a running battle in the car park outside.

But there was something strangely calming about the group's actual performances; something that, if not actively peaceful, nevertheless promulgated peace. For as long as Depeche Mode was onstage, even long-standing grudges and rivalries were forgotten. The most peculiar thing was, in other cities, other synthesizer bands reported the same phenomenon.

What set these groups apart was their apparent anonymity. Three guys playing synthesizers, a fourth gimpy dancing at the front—there was no room for posturing within such a lineup, no macho strutting and bare-chested belligerence, none of rock's traditional fighting talk. They threatened no one. Depeche Mode simply segued effortlessly between the Kraftwerk cuts on the disc jockey's turntable, just another excuse to dance.

<60>

And slowly a momentum was building around Depeche Mode, around those other bands in other cities. Away from the cults and cultures, divorced even from the club-clinging categories that overuse was already blurring, the likes of Depeche Mode, Soft Cell, and Blancmange were more than the second wave of Futurism, which some writers liked to tag them—were, in fact, the first wave of the 1980s, the bands that would break through without even the excess baggage of a post-punk birthright to weigh them down. That was something even Spandau Ballet, Duran Duran, Adam Ant, and the Human League could not claim.

All they needed now was a catalyst, something—or someone—with the vision to sense what was happening all around, and the means to present it to the public. From a deejay booth piled high with tapes, Stevo believed he could be that catalyst.

Depeche Mode originally rejected Stevo's invitation to contribute one of their demo tracks to the compilation of new music that he was busily planning. They were not even certain within their own minds of the "image" they were trying to project; the last thing they needed was for someone else to make that decision for them.

At the same time, however, they also realized that their inclusion on such a high-profile release would serve them infinitely better than anything they could muster under their own steam. Some Bizzare, as a label and a concept, was Stevo's antidote to the creeping disease of popular conformity. To be considered a part of that antidote was an honor Depeche Mode could not turn down. And Stevo, for his part, had no intention of letting them.

Although he continued deejaying on a regular basis, by the winter of 1980, Stevo was growing increasingly dissatisfied with the electronics movement. What started out as a musically exclusive mutual admiration society had now exploded into just another pop fad, characterized not by music but by clothing. Even the audience was suddenly *ordinary,* a seething mass of drably foppish humanity playing follow-the-leader on the dance floor each night. Stevo dreamed of giving them back an identity. And if they didn't want it, he'd just find different people who did.

As he pieced together his record, Stevo deliberately picked bands that did not fit in with the popular image of Futurism, at the same time ensuring that each, in its own way, blended with his—Depeche Mode, Blancmange, Naked Lunch, Jeff, Blah Blah, and the Loved One meant little outside of their own immediate localities, but that wasn't the point. All had potential, a couple—Soft Cell and the The—already threatened great things.

Hailing from Leeds, Soft Cell was an electronics-and-voice-fired duo that combined Suicide atmospherics with an almost Brechtian sense of cheap sexual drama; the Derby-shire-based the The was another synth-and-singing duo, the brainchild of a mercurial performer named Matt Johnson (whose other band, the Gadgets, was also scheduled to appear on Stevo's album, before being replaced by Depeche Mode). Between them, Soft Cell and the The defined the Some Bizzare ethos.

That, in many ways, was where Depeche Mode's apprehensions set in with a vengeance. Depeche Mode was, if not unique, at least a rarity among the Some Bizzare bands in that they made no deliberate attempt to rewrite rock history.

Other groups built their repertoire from the circuit board up—Soft Cell's self-released *Mutant Moments* EP was already being discussed in the same awestricken tones normally reserved for the latest Kraftwerk or DAF prolusion. Depeche Mode, by their own admission, worked the other way around altogether.

<62>

The vast majority of their repertoire had been written on guitar, to be played by guitars. The fact that they were able to restructure those songs to meet the demands of their new electronic lineup simply testified to their own strength of purpose. When Stevo announced to Depeche Mode that he intended naming the compilation after his embryonic record company—the *Some Bizzare Album*—Vince almost exploded. "But we're not a bizarre band!"

Unfortunately, the band was fast running out of suitable options. Stevo was not the only would-be businessman who was courting Depeche Mode; he was, however, the only one whose plans resembled something more than pipe dreams.

One evening at Croc's, Depeche Mode was unwinding at the conclusion of their set when a Rastafarian who had been watching appeared in their dressing room. He was moving to Lagos, he explained, and was looking for a suitable band to help him blow the Nigerian music scene wide open.

"But not any old group," he said. "It has to be futuristic, electronic, exciting. It has to be something the Nigerians have never seen before."

While Depeche Mode listened incredulously, the Rasta ran through his incredibly detailed schemes—which boiled down, Vince sputtered, "to having us put on space-monster costumes, and play electronic reggae music." The group unanimously turned him down.

More serious overtures came from Anton Johnson, a local business tycoon whose empire stretched from a supermarket chain to the chairmanship of the Southend United soccer club. His offer to finance the band's development, however, was coupled with what the group saw as an undisguised yearning to mold them as well, "to get his fingers into yet another pie," as Vince put it. He, too, was rejected.

Meanwhile, the group's own attempts to garner independent interest in their music were meeting with no more success than the suitors they themselves had turned away. The last straw came when Dave and Vince spent an entire day touring a dozen London record companies, quarter-inch master tape in hand, pleading to be heard.

<83>

"We used to demand that they play it while we waited in the office," Dave remembers, "and, of course, most of them would tell us to fuck off. They'd say, 'Leave the tape with us,' and we'd tell them we couldn't because it was our only one. Then we'd say good-bye and go somewhere else." After eleven consecutive rejections, tired and dispirited, the pair were all but ready to head for home.

But there was still one port of call left, the Kensington Park Road home of Rough Trade Records, the most brilliantly successful of all the truly independent labels that had sprung up in the past two or three years.

The label's catalog evidenced its spirit. Groups like the Raincoats, Kleenex, the Pop Group, and Monochrome Set were jagged doodles of sound on the postpunk landscape, furiously disdaining the conventions of traditional rock 'n' roll as they moved aggressively into almost free-form territory. Even as Vince and Dave walked into the office, they wondered why they bothered stopping by.

Rough Trade's staff, however, prided themselves on seeing bands for what they *were,* not—as was usually the case—for what they could become, or how they fit into the current scheme of things. The label was also accustomed to bands dropping by unannounced, clutching tapes and holding dreams. For the first time all day, Vince and Dave were invited to sit down, while their demo played.

"Rough Trade really liked the tape," Dave recalled. "But they didn't think we were really a Rough Trade band"—meaning, of course, that Depeche Mode's bouncy brand of catchy synth-pop would sit queerly on a label best known for the weighty muse of its other acts.

"However, they did think they knew someone who might like us. . . ."

<64>

Rough Trade, at that time, was still Daniel Miller's biggest customer. They distributed his Mute label releases, helped out with the necessary promotion, and even provided him a room to work from. And as luck would have it, Miller was in the office that afternoon.

Again the tape was threaded and played, but Miller's expression spoke volumes before he even opened his mouth. "He just looked at us," remembers Dave, "and said, 'YEEEUCH!' " Then he walked out.

"We just thought, Bastard."

Depeche Mode was fighting a losing battle. Regardless of their own agenda, heedless of the bright pop froth of their greatest songs, other people's conceptions would always prove louder than their own protestations. And when Basildon's local newspaper, the *Evening Echo,* caught up with the band in early December, the ensuing story hammered the final nails into the coffin of Depeche Mode's own sense of independence.

POSH CLOBBER COULD CLINCH IT FOR MODE! roared the

headline over Depeche Mode's first-ever news story, firmly reprimanding the band for *not* dressing the obvious part. All those other ". . . perfumed, ponced-up Futurist pop bands don't hold a candle to these four Basildon lads. They . . . could go a long way if someone just pointed them in the direction of a decent tailor."

"I used to wear plus-fours, soccer socks, and carpet slippers," Fletch later confessed. "Martin would paint his face half white, and Vince looked like a Vietnamese refugee. He'd tan his face, dye his hair black, and put on a headband."

Such ragged pantomime was now a thing of the past. Just as Stevo understood that if steered in the right direction, Depeche Mode could very quickly break out of their local-cult rut, so the *Evening Echo* sensed the potential that was locked up within the band, if only they would play the game.

The group's own protests were immaterial—they took the journalist's advice. "If you can't beat them, you can at least pretend to join them," Martin said with a laugh as he headed into the changing room, clutching his first frilly shirt. <65>

Boyd Rice remembers the first time he met Vince, at London's Bridgehouse: "He looked like Lucille Ball."

Depeche Mode's Bridgehouse gigs had little in common with their shows elsewhere. In Rayleigh and Southend, they were a known quantity, attracting their own army of acolytes to cheer them through their set. In the windswept shadow of an east London fly-over, there was little room for finery and foppishness.

But the enthusiasm with which Terry Murphy, the Bridgehouse's resident promoter, had received Depeche Mode's demonstration tape was swiftly matched by the venue's regular clientele. As Christmas drew closer, Depeche Mode ranked among the club's best-loved regular draws.

When Murphy offered them the opportunity to fulfill a similar function for Fad Gadget, the group leaped at the chance. Gadget was a known quantity, a guaranteed crowd-puller, the genius behind one of the year's most individual albums, *Fireside Favourites*. And he was managed by Daniel Miller, the man who had so recently written Depeche Mode off as "YEEEUCH!" "We'll show him what 'yeeeuch' really is!" Vince threatened.

Was it the warm glow of nostalgia playing tricks on the band members' memories that prompted Vince, Martin, Dave, and Fletch to describe that show as "the evening we knew something was going to happen to us"? Or was there really a hint of magic in the air that chill December night?

Gadget did indeed draw a large audience, and as Depeche Mode ran through their half-hour set, encoring as always with their increasingly mutated take on "Mouldy Old Dough," the band could sense the mood of the room changing. A knot of curious onlookers on the floor in front of the stage had swollen to a dancing melee, the hum of conversation and the clatter of glasses that had echoed from the back of the room had stilled. And even Daniel Miller, last sighted impatiently stalking the back of the room, disgusted to be back in the company of those awful, awful yeeuchs, was dancing a peculiar jig alongside the stage, and grinning wildly.

He pounced on the band the moment they came offstage, and it was as though he had never even heard them before, let alone pronounced harsh judgment from behind his office desk.

Over drinks, Daniel explained the Mute Records setup. Bands went with him not necessarily because they wanted to be superstars—Mute had not even sniffed a chart attack since the Silicon Teens—but because they wanted to be treated like human beings. He reiterated the mantra that had scared off so many other young hopefuls: There would be no big-money advances, no guarantees, no long-term "deals." Mute artists simply recorded a record, and if they liked the way things went, they recorded another. Then Fad Gadget came onstage, and the two parties went their separate ways, each promising to mull over what the other had said.

Daniel Miller was not the only person interested in

Depeche Mode, however. The Stevo connection had finally begun to work its magic, the electronics scene had coalesced, and as the new year of 1981 dawned, blanketing the south of England in the thickest snow it had seen in years, the phone lines between London and Basildon were red-hot.

In quick succession, Phonogram (distributors of *Some Bizzare Album*) CBS, and Island sent scouts out to see Depeche Mode perform; then "they all came in offering huge amounts of money, money you could never have imagined, and all sorts of crazy things, like clothes allowances!"

But, Dave admonished, that was all they offered—money.

"Suddenly that style of music came in, and they were all after us." The labels simply wanted to add Depeche Mode's name to their catalog, he continued. The first time Depeche Mode approached the music industry, they were rejected. Nobody was interested in them. Three months later, "everyone was interested and the majors were queuing up to sign us."

<67>

Displaying more business sense, and considerably more cynicism than their young years could ever have been expected to muster, Depeche Mode sat back and listened as the numbers piled up. Once or twice, they were even tempted simply to put their names to one of the many pieces of paper waved in their faces—to take the money and run.

But at the back of their minds, Daniel Miller remained the seductive unknown. He made no promises, offered no guarantees, but he pledged something far more important than money. "Daniel came along again and said . . . he could put out a record. If after that we didn't want to stay, we didn't have to," Dave remembers. "It was the most honest thing we had heard.

"The people he's got on his label, like Boyd Rice, really are out of order," Dave enthused. "He puts out a single even though he knows it'll only sell a thousand. He does it because he likes it." When Miller got back in touch, early in the new year, Depeche Mode made their minds up as one: They would join Mute.

It wasn't only Miller's honesty that appealed to them. There was something almost paternal in the way he talked, the way he laughed off his inability to offer Depeche Mode any kind of advance. It captivated Vince, Martin, and Fletch—but it convinced Dave. Even today, he is the band member most likely to describe Miller as a father figure—for it was he who had never really had one.

Miller responded in kind. Other Mute artists, he knew, were never going to set the charts on fire, and didn't really expect to. Otherwise, they would not have made the kind of records they made. They demanded the treatment that one would afford to any serious artist.

<68> Depeche Mode, though, were kids, and despite their determination, their unity and, yes, their common sense, they needed to be handled like kids—with care, affection, and a lot of time-consuming support. Miller wasn't simply taking a new band on board, he was also taking on a world of responsibilities, ranging from the mundane—chauffeuring them to gigs in his battered Renault—to the sublime.

Miller and Mute offered more than friendship and guidance, however. At a major record label, a band is virtually isolated from the machinations that are set up to propel them to fame. They will know their A&R man, of course, for it is he who will be walking them through the first stages of their career. They will meet their PR officer and hopefully strike up a rapport there.

But the pluggers, who physically take their records around to the radio stations and try to persuade the program director that *this time,* it *really* is the biggest hit ever; the promo people, upon whose ad campaigns a record can sink or sail; the distributors, charged with ensuring that the record reaches the shops—these people occupied a whole different world. Many bands didn't even know they existed. Daniel Miller promised to introduce Depeche Mode to them all.

"Okay. But can we see the contract first? Just check it over?" Vince spoke nervously, anxious in case his request should be taken the wrong way: *It's not that we don't trust you but...* "Our parents, you see," he added by way of weak explanation.

Daniel looked perturbed. "Contracts?"

"Yeah. You do have them with you, don't you?"

"Contracts?" Daniel repeated. He looked genuinely puzzled. "What sort of contracts?"

"Recording contracts . . ." Now it was Vince's turn to look confused. The man ran a record company and he didn't even know what a contract was . . .? "You promise this, we promise that . . ."

"I thought we'd already sorted all that out?"

"Yeah, but . . ."

"Well, if we're all in agreement, that's all we need." He put out a hand. "This is the only kind of contract I'm interested in." <69>

Depeche Mode put away their pens and shook.

Miller admits that the prospect of involving himself with Depeche Mode was as frightening as it was challenging, and not only on a personal level.

"I knew Depeche Mode had a lot of potential, but the big question was whether a company like Mute could get them into the Top 75. I just didn't want to commit them to me if I couldn't make them realize their potential, right from the start."

Booking time at Blackwing Studios, the deconsecrated Church of All Hallows that was now established among the best budget-priced studios in London, work began on Depeche Mode's debut single almost immediately.

Miller suggested, and the band unanimously agreed, that Vince's "Dreaming of Me" should be the A-side. Without laboring the pure vein of unadulterated synthesized pop that flowed through Depeche Mode's repertoire, "Dreaming of Me" had a strangely ethereal sense to it, an ambiguous musical maturity that—quite at odds with the rash of singles that would follow it—was the sound of Mute hedging their bets.

Miller was right to be cautious. Depeche Mode was as likely to be heralded as the new teenybop sensation as win the acceptance of the serious electronics buffs who comprised Mute's "regular" clientele. Boyd Rice had already admitted that he thought Daniel was making "a big mistake" in signing the band, and Miller respected his opinion, even if he did not agree with it. "Dreaming of Me" represented a comfortable middle ground between the two possible audiences, a chance for one to make up its own mind about Depeche Mode, without alienating the other.

Nowhere was this basic dichotomy more pronounced than when the band played Richard Strange's Cabaret Futura toward the end of January 1981. It was their central London debut, a showcase gig that was at last to unveil them to the capital's hip cognoscenti.

<70>

Even since its "discovery" by the music press, the Cabaret Futura remained a prestigious venue, perhaps *the* most prestigious in London. Strange himself was riding high in the critical estimation with his own *Phenomenal Rise of Richard Strange* album and one-man live show; the attention lavished on the Cabaret had even prompted his former record company to rush out a Doctors of Madness compilation album—less than three years after the band had disbanded, unloved and unsigned.

Another album, highlighting the Cabaret's live regulars—Richard Jobson, Kissing the Pink, and Positive Noise among them—ranked among the new year's most eagerly awaited new releases. For any artist invited to appear at the Cabaret, a new respectability was automatically conferred upon them—a respectability born of arty pretensions and experimentalist bravado. It was a strange place for Depeche Mode, with their distinct lack of pretensions and artiness, to play.

Yet still they engineered one of the most bizarre performances ever to grace the Cabaret stage. The sheer danceability of their music, the infectious get-up-and-go that spun crazily from their synthesizers, was belied completely by the band's presentation. Vince, Fletch, and Martin stood stock-still behind their instruments, grim-faced and dour. In front of them, Dave scarcely ventured as much as an animated bop. The Cabaret audience was cool, but that night Depeche Mode was cooler.

The accepted image of a synthesizer band, created by Kraftwerk but turned into a virtual art form by Gary Numan, was of total staticity—"the distant, lonely look and image," as Dave put it. "Because we play synthesizers, we're supposed to look strangely at people and not smile." That night, Depeche Mode acted the role with a passion. It was only afterward that Fletch admitted it wasn't an act at all, that Depeche Mode really wasn't the harbinger of a new age in studied indifference. "We just hadn't learned how to move yet!"

Neither had "Dreaming of Me." It was released in February 1981 to the same crop of guardedly enthusiastic reviews that normally greeted a new Mute release. But while a couple of disc jockeys did pick up on it—Peter Powell and Richard Skinner, over at the BBC's Radio One—the band's dream of making even the lowest reaches of the chart receded with every passing week.

<71>

Then, on the last day of March, each band member in turn was awakened by a frantic phone call from Daniel. He could barely speak, he was laughing so hard, and when he did finally sputter out his news, the group was as incoherent as he. "Dreaming of Me" had made it! And it only took two months!

"Dreaming of Me" eventually peaked at number fifty-seven. And though its chart life was scarcely more impressive than its chart peak—in and out in a mere four weeks—it proved to both Depeche Mode and Daniel Miller that their relationship was built on solid ground.

"If you can get a record that far," Miller proudly proclaimed, "you're capable of getting it anywhere. Provided the song is good enough, of course."

Chapter 5

Ugly Bands

Never Make It

THROUGHOUT THE SPRING of 1981, Depeche Mode gigged furiously—or as furiously as the band members' day jobs would let them. Martin was still turning up daily at the bank, modestly acknowledging the congratulations of his workmates; Fletch was an insurance clerk; Dave was still attending college. When Classix Nouveau, riding high on the chart with the technostomp "Guilty," and postpunk songstress Toyah Wilcox offered Depeche Mode the support slot on their forthcoming U.K. tours, the band had the ideal excuse to turn them both down. "Sorry, we can't get the time off work." In actual fact, neither tour had appealed to Depeche Mode. If they had to travel the country, they decided, it would be from the top of the bill.

"We got treated so bad," Dave complained of Depeche Mode's later support-slot apprenticeship. "The [headline bands] tread all over you, and to the PA blokes you're nothing. It's always 'Where's the support?' You're not even a name!"

Besides, Fletch continued, "I don't think tours play a major part in what we do. I think most of the people who bought our record have never been to a gig in their lives, and will never go to one. They'd rather see a picture in a magazine."

The "gainfully unemployed" Vince teased his workaholic bandmates mercilessly, all the same. The success of "Dreaming of Me" had proven that Depeche Mode really was a going concern. Now they had to take their success to the next plateau, but that could only be achieved if all four members were firmly behind it.

Dave was the first to quit. He had been sent to London for a short course of work experience, dressing windows at a major department store. Outside, a crowd of girls was gathering, watching him in wide-eyed wonder. Finally one of them spoke: " 'Ere! What you doing in there?" To them, he was already a pop star. And pop stars didn't hang around department-store window displays.

"The College were pretty good about me quitting," Dave reflects. "They sent me a note afterwards, saying, 'Congratulations on the success!' "

And, he modestly reflected, he had enjoyed some. Despite the band's continued reservations (and their recruitment by Mute), "Photographic" remained prominently featured on Stevo's *Some Bizzare Album* when it appeared in March 1981, and as the collection climbed to the outskirts of the British Top 50, it focused fresh attention upon its twelve contributors.

As Stevo had predicted, the critics' favorites were the The and Soft Cell; even in rough, homemade-demo form, Soft Cell's contribution to *Some Bizzare Album*, "The Girl with the Patent-Leather Face," oozed the same unquestionable, unstoppable class that would eventually establish the duo among the early 1980s' most consistent U.K. hitmakers. But Depeche Mode at least gave the northerners a run for their money.

"Photographic" was lifted directly from the band's demo tape, and reviewers hunting for another reason to recommend the compilation were swift to overlook the almost bumbling amateurism of Depeche Mode's recording, in favor of the sheer effervescence of the performance. And once again, the band found themselves in a gallant defense against the obvious preconceptions.

"We were never a Futurist band," screamed Fletch as *Some Bizzare Album* racked up its sales. He rejected attempts to pigeonhole the band "just because we use synthesizers." Their music wasn't Futurist, he insisted. "We don't fit into that at all."

They proved their independence by failing even to turn up at *Some Bizzare Album*'s launch night at the London Lyceum in February 1981, and that despite being billed to appear. According to Dave, "We were never even approached to play. It was only when we were advertised that we knew anything about it." Besides, he added, "We had no intention of doing it at all."

<75>

The group compensated its disappointed fans by appearing at Mute Records' own in-concert extravaganza, Mute Night Silent Night, in March—the first of two shows at the London Lyceum, six weeks apart, that saw Depeche Mode rise from third to second on the handbills. They also supported the newly revitalized Ultravox—with Midge Ure now wearing John Foxx's singing shoes—at London's short-lived People's Palace venue, and when Rusty Egan opened a new club, Flicks, in Dartford, Depeche Mode was the natural headliners.

Depeche Mode was also, finally, noticed by the mainstream music press. As the band waited backstage at the Mute Night show, they were cornered by *Melody Maker*'s Steve Sutherland.

Sutherland's enthusiasm was boundless. "Damn

near the most perfect pop group these two lucky lug'oles have sampled all season," he raved when the ensuing interview hit print. "[They] have a set full of knowing but naive, intense yet idiotically simple two-minute gems that stand quiff and earrings above the ever-growing pile of synth-pop fad followers. Suss enough to play by the rules, but brilliant enough to break them."

Words—and prophecies ("Watch them storm up the charts")—like Sutherland's matched Depeche Mode's mood exactly: an abrupt sense of brash new confidence that was immediately apparent in the band's latest studio work—a new single, Vince's "New Life"—and in a session for deejay Richard Skinner's influential Radio One evening show.

Under the watchful eye of producer Dale Griffin, once better known as Buffin, drummer with Mott the Hoople, Depeche Mode recorded four songs in one day: Vince's "Boys Say Go!" and "Photographic," and Martin's perennial "Big Muff" and "Tora! Tora! Tora!" With "between twenty and thirty" songs at his immediate disposal, Martin might, in any other band, have expected, maybe even demanded, to be the primary songwriter.

But as Daniel Miller once remarked, "He isn't the sort of guy to push himself," and prolific as Martin was, Vince was even more so. And at that early stage of Depeche Mode's career, he was also writing the most appropriate songs. The Skinner session alone evidenced the gulf in the two writers' styles: While Vince's contributions were dynamic pop, Martin's were more thoughtful—no less commercial, but noticeably less instantaneous. And in an increasingly cutthroat marketplace, the difference could prove fatal.

"New Life" entered the chart two days after the Richard Skinner session aired, on June 13, 1981. That same week, there were further new entries for the Specials—whose epochal "Ghost Town" would eventually top the charts—Ultravox, and Phil Collins. Smokey Robinson was number one, but the Jam and Michael Jackson were breathing hard down his

<76>

neck. Always competitive, the British charts were also at their most creative in years.

This time, though, Depeche Mode was well-equipped to meet the challenge, with a song that positively boiled with infectious enthusiasm—even if nobody knew what on earth it was about.

"Vince's songs are odd," puzzled Martin, "because they don't mean anything. He looks for a melody, then finds words that rhyme. He doesn't really search for anything. Some people search for a song that means something from the heart. Vince does it the other way round."

Dave got a firsthand taste of Vince's obliqueness as he walked home through the streets of Basildon one night. All the way down the road, he was conscious that he was being followed, and he was still deliberating over whether he should turn and run or stop and fight, when his stalkers suddenly burst into song . . . with the first verse of "New Life." "And even I had to wonder, What did it mean?"

<77>

Not that the record-buying public cared about that! Advance orders alone guaranteed "New Life" a Top 75 berth; within a fortnight, with another "Top of the Pops" appearance under their belt, Depeche Mode breached the Top 30. Three weeks later, "New Life" peaked at number eleven.

"It's really odd," Dave reflected as it became apparent that the Top Ten was to remain out of reach. "At first you think, 'God, imagine being on "Top of the Pops"!' But it all changes as it begins to happen. When we got into the lower reaches of the chart, we thought it was good for a while. But then we were asking, What was it worth unless we got into the Top Forty? We got there, and thought, Well, it's no good unless we're in the Top Twenty. And so on."

"Top of the Pops" itself was an eye-opener—albeit a "really boring" one—a far cry from the unmitigated glamour the show projects into ten million living rooms every Thursday night. To viewers, "Top of the Pops" serves up a nonstop diet of chart-toppers and contenders. To performers, however, it's simply interminable, waiting all day for a few minutes spent in front of the cameras.

"We were sitting around for twelve hours," complained Dave once the ordeal was over. "But we did get a chance to talk to the other bands—apart from Spandau. They were the only ones who wouldn't talk to us. They're getting a bit snobby." Or, perhaps, some listeners reasoned, a little nervous. Even without a Top Ten hit, in the race for the New Pop crown, Depeche Mode was coming up quickly behind all the favorites.

Depeche Mode's appeal to the record-buying public was the same as that which they exerted on other people who came into their orbit—they simply seemed so perfect. Their songs were short, sharp, and eminently singable. The band members themselves were cute, and while that in itself was nothing unusual, their looks had not gone to their heads. There was none of the studied posing of Duran Duran, the untouchable elitism of Spandau Ballet, the overdressed glamour of Adam Ant—Depeche Mode looked, dressed, and behaved like the boys next door, smiling for photographs, giggling when asked for their autographs. They were cuddly, and they were also very human.

<78>

Whether through design or accident—and both the band and Daniel Miller were still so new at the pop-star game that it is unlikely that it was anything but the latter—Depeche Mode had stumbled upon another of those niches that lie scattered throughout the world of pop stardom: the need for idols whose feet *could* be made of clay. And having stumbled upon it, the group now began to make it its own, equally guilelessly, equally innocently.

Depeche Mode's "Top of the Pops" performance was followed by an appearance on "Razzmatazz," a similarly Top 40–oriented show, but one that was aimed deliberately at the youngest pop audiences—the preadolescents who gave over their allowances as readily as they gave up their hearts.

It was a bold move, for both Depeche Mode and Daniel Miller, unequivocally severing the band's links with the world of "serious" electronic music even as it targeted that of pop fame and fortune. No longer sitting on the fence, Depeche Mode had made their choice, and as the spring of 1981 passed, it appeared more and more to be the only one that made sense.

The "Razzmatazz" audience loved Depeche Mode. That was apparent from the moment the cameras started rolling and a group of girls in the audience, having studied Dave's dancing during rehearsal, now mimicked his every move alongside him. Their antics were beamed out across the nation, and the die was cast. If "Razzmatazz" was the heartbeat of the teenage market, any band that made an impression there must be that market's lifeblood. Depeche Mode was "happening," and they were ready for the next step up the television ladder—a spot on the Sunday lunchtime magazine program "20th-Century Box." If they passed this test, the band congratulated themselves beforehand, they had it made.

Just a couple of months earlier, Spandau Ballet had appeared on the show, filmed live at one of their own, increasingly hectic gatherings at London's Scala Theater. Their segment was merely part of a lengthier look at the New Romantic scene, but overnight Spandau became the figureheads of a movement that, even after all the coverage it had received in the previous six months, a lot of people still weren't aware of.

Suddenly Blitz, and its Blitz Kid babies, saw every last ounce of exclusivity stripped from their bodies. When Spandau played aboard the retired warship HMS *Belfast,* in July 1981, their own audience was swollen by several thousand outsiders, all wanting in on this great "new" scene. Now those same thousands were casting around for similar thrills elsewhere. Depeche Mode, resplendent in their frilly shirts, pounding out their infectious pop, was an obvious target. And this time, the band didn't fight it.

Afterward, Depeche Mode claimed that they had "hated" their first-ever photo session, that they despised the frilly shirts and the thickly smeared makeup. But donning that look was no less calculated an act of self-promotion than agreeing to appear on "Razzmatazz" or, later, having their lives analyzed in the teenybop press.

Unlike so many other bands whose careers are directed from on high, dependent upon the whim of record-company executives who may never have heard them play, Depeche Mode's destiny was in their hands, and their hands alone. If they failed, they would have none to blame but themselves. But if they succeeded . . . They would worry about *that* later. The process they had begun just six months earlier, when they followed the *Evening Echo*'s advice, had reached its logical conclusion. Only instead of merely embracing New Romanticism, to many people, Depeche Mode now epitomized it.

In the future, any number of theories would be thrown around to explain Depeche Mode's apparent change of musical heart—how they slipped so gracefully from fiercely fighting the emergent fashion to accepting it wholesale into their lives. Possibly they were simply sick of kicking against the inevitable. Maybe they were challenging themselves, seeing how deep a hole they could jump into and still have a hope of getting out again. Or perhaps they just wanted to be pop stars.

Either way, by so unreservedly throwing in their lot with the New Romantic movement, Depeche Mode was guaranteeing itself a major slice of whichever chart pie was about to be carved up by the new wave of British pop stars. And though they continued to speak out against being so easily typecast, nobody was convinced.

"We must have done thirty interviews on the Continent, where they asked if we were 'Bleetz Keedz,' " Dave complained. The band would deny it, "then have them print that right next to those awful photos of us wearing frilly shirts and eyeliner."

He shrugged. It was important to look good, to be visual. Dave revealed that he himself designed the band's clothes, and had them made by a friend in trendy Kensington. "It's all part of a gig, to get dressed up—it gets the adrenaline

<80>

going. The gig really starts a couple of hours before you go on-stage, when you're getting ready."

That much was true. It was what they wore—the un-mistakable uniform of the new pop fad—that condemned Depeche Mode and, in the eyes of the musical elite who had hitherto regarded Mute as something more than a record label, condemned Daniel Miller as well. Any decisions made in Depeche Mode's name were arrived at with both his input and his blessing. Miller remained adamant that he would never stand in the group's way if they really wanted to do something, and that much was true.

But when the group was finally seen embracing a musical fashion with which they had previously been at such fierce, vocal odds, it was because Daniel believed they would outlast it—he believed it, and was willing to bet his record label's current success on it.

And so far, the gambit had succeeded. The only <8|> complaints he heard were the grumblings of a disaffected un-derground, who didn't understand how a label that so avidly supported Boyd Rice could then throw in its lot with a teenybop band. They didn't understand, either, that it was because of the teenybop band that Mute could continue to support Boyd Rice.

With its U.K. sales alone topping half a million cop-ies, "New Life" remained on the British charts throughout most of the summer of 1981—more than a decade later, no Depeche Mode single has bettered that fifteen-week run. In commercial terms, Depeche Mode could not have asked for more—Martin and Fletch were even able to give up their day jobs at last, with-out wondering where their next paycheck would come from. From the point of view of work, however, it was a mixed bless-ing.

In June the band returned to the studio to begin work on their next single, "Just Can't Get Enough."

It was a mistake.

With "New Life" still registering high in the chart,

the group was still brightly lit in the public eye, forever in demand for interviews and photo sessions. "We just couldn't concentrate on recording," Dave revealed. "The first time we did 'Just Can't Get Enough,' it was terrible. We got rid of most of what we had done, and recorded more tracks."

Visitors to Blackwing, eager to hear the new single, were instead regaled with the sound of the band relaxing; while Vince replaced Daniel at the mixing desk, and Dave took over his synth, Andy snatched away the microphone and led the group through impromptu renditions of "Simon Says," the Beatles' "You're Gonna Lose That Girl," and a collection of hymns. "Just Can't Get Enough" itself was to remain a tightly guarded secret for another three months—until "New Life" finally showed signs of slowing down.

Afterward, Dave admitted that he had never felt so relieved as he did when "Just Can't Get Enough" was finally released in September—a relief that was compounded when the single leaped instantly into the charts, just as "New Life" finally relinquished its grip and dropped out.

<82>

Depeche Mode celebrated the single's headlong rush into the Top Ten (it finally came to rest at number eight) with their highest-profile concert yet, a benefit for Amnesty International at London's Victoria Venue. There would be two shows—an evening performance for their working fans, and an afternoon matinee for the kids.

The shows—part of Amnesty's twentieth-anniversary celebrations—were something of a watershed for Depeche Mode and Amnesty alike. Although the organization had long enjoyed the often-voluble support of the music industry, Amnesty's only previous head-on meetings with pop culture were the 1979 and 1981 "Secret Policeman's Ball" music-and-comedy shows. Another five years would pass before the two again made so pronounced a union, and an Amnesty spokesman admits that for a long time, the human rights group viewed such blatant fund-raising activities with a certain degree of suspicion. In those pre–Band Aid days, pop music still had a bad reputation!

For Depeche Mode, too, the union broke a mold.

Punk, long dead and buried by 1981, had done more than politicize its listeners. It politicized British pop itself, to the point where every musician, it appeared, had an opinion to air—and a song to air it in.

New Romantics, however, cared little for politics. What made their movement—indeed, their entire existence— "special" was its absolute superficiality. The torn T-shirts and safety-pinned bin liners of punk were swept away in a backlash of gargantuan proportions, to be replaced by designer suits and matching ties. The spiteful spike hairstyles that had dominated the late Seventies were tamed and trimmed. The New Romantics behaved like musicians, but they looked like bankers.

In later years, these Blitz Kid butterflies would be the clay from which British Prime Minister Thatcher would try forging her "new society," a cult of self-aggrandizement built upon the principles of material again. And the first law of material gain, of course, was that charity began at home.

<83>

In linking themselves with Amnesty International, in pledging their day's earnings to the cause, then, Depeche Mode wasn't simply taking an unprecedented political stand— although that was remarkable enough. They were bucking the very tenets of their creed.

Dave tried to play down the dichotomy by denying—as usual—that it even existed. "Obviously, people who buy Duran Duran and Spandau Ballet records might buy ours as well," he explained for the umpteenth time. "But I think we're in a different market to all those bands."

He thought wrong. From the moment the band stepped out onstage, the two-thousand-capacity hall echoed to their impassioned screaming.

"Dave Gahan is astonished by the girls grabbing kisses, blushes glowing through makeup in a confusion of near terror," wrote *Record Mirror*'s Mike Nicholls, while even *Mel-*

ody Maker's Steve Sutherland, as staunch a supporter as ever, could see which way the wind was blowing. Depeche Mode, he wrote, was "so sweet [that] I worry, all malleable puppy fat equally at home over tea with your gran or snogging down the disco. Depeche Mode are a fantasy potential more-than-fulfilled, the Archies of the eighties." And because of them, "pop is no longer having to say you're sorry."

Hysteria became a way of life. When the band appeared onstage, at the Venue and elsewhere, they were bombarded with feminine gifts—everything from jewelry to items of clothing. The lines at the dressing-room door lengthened; *Melody Maker* once espied a line of over one hundred fans, ninety percent female.

<84>

"And if you ever come back," one was still bellowing as the band's van drove away at the end of the evening, "you can come round and see me and I'll make you a sandwich, and if you don't like sandwiches you can have a bun or a jam tart or a doughnut or ice cream or custard or cake . . . and when you dance onstage, you look as if you're SHAGGING!"

The only problem with all this attention, Fletch deadpanned, was that the girls were "all too young. The other night I looked out at the audience and felt as if I were playing in assembly in school!"

"You watch films of the Beatles and the screaming seems quite natural," Dave pondered. "But when people start screaming at you, it's really funny."

It was into this maelstrom that Depeche Mode was preparing to pitch their debut album, *Speak and Spell*.

Speak and Spell was a remarkable document and, to the people purchasing the album in sufficient quantities to blast it to number ten on the charts (and keep it on the listings for thirty-two weeks), a flawless record of the year's brightest new pop group. Its eleven tracks included all three of the band's hit singles, plus the very cream of the band's in-concert repertoire, all pieced together with a precision that again belied the band's inexperience.

Much of the credit for the record, of course, belonged to Daniel, despite his insistence on selflessly sharing a "co-production" credit with the band, and to engineers Eric Radcliffe and John Fryer.

It was Miller whose deft understanding of synthesizers re-created the sounds that the band heard in their heads, who designed the fresh arrangements that raised the individual songs so far above their ragged in-concert equivalents. And it was he who, convinced that Depeche Mode's most obvious appeal was the group's innate immediacy, was similarly convinced that the only way to preserve that mood was to work as quickly as possible. It would also ensure, of course, that the album would be ready for the lucrative Christmas shopping season. *Speak and Spell* was recorded in just three weeks in September 1981.

For the band's longtime listeners, the standout track on the album was "Photographic"—the song that for many fans <85> had started it all. Whether it stood out for good reasons or bad, however, was another matter entirely.

On *Some Bizzare Album,* "Photographic" was tentative, moody, mechanical; on *Speak and Spell,* the song itself waged constant battle with the technology that Blackwing Studios placed at Depeche Mode's disposal. And while Fletch confessed that "we've recorded 'Photographic' so many times now that we felt like doing something different on the album," he was also well aware that Depeche Mode's rise to proficiency left many of their earliest supporters, whom the band themselves called "the Originals," in the cold.

"They say we've changed things, that there are too many fiddly bits on the record!" Laughingly, he admitted that "the Originals even want us to release two sets of singles—one for the general public, and one for them, with the old sound." It was these demands that would, within a year, establish multiple-format—and multiple-mix—singles as a Depeche Mode tradition, to the point where every taste would eventually find something to satisfy it.

By those future standards, *Speak and Spell* was very utilitarian. Talented though Vince Clarke was, his earliest songs made the grade more on the strength of their joyous, synth-powered exuberance than any claims they might have had on durability.

On technical grounds, too, *Speak and Spell* became dated fast, a quaint reminder of a more innocent age. Again, within a year, the band members themselves would become unanimous in their condemnation of the record. "When I hear tracks from [*Speak and Spell*] I get embarrassed," Dave admitted to *NME* in 1983, "although at the time I thought it was great!" Reminded that the entire record was brought in for under twelve thousand dollars, he would laugh incredulously. "Maybe we should have spent some more."

But *Speak and Spell* was as much a victim of its timing as it was of its budget. The very equipment at the band's disposal was in a state of flux; out of date before hitting the shops, with new developments occurring almost daily, recording techniques themselves slipped from state of the art to state of the *ark* in less time than it took to tape a new single.

Neither was Depeche Mode the only band to be caught in this trap. Even Kraftwerk—the granddaddies of electronic pop—had arrived at a plateau of sorts, upon which their own music rested while the technology raced ahead once more. Dreaming of the day when more accessible studio technology would be available to "liberate people's creativity," as Ralf Hütter once put it, Kraftwerk now fell victim to their own powers of prophecy.

It was no coincidence that five years were to elapse between *Computer World*, in 1981, and its successor, *Electric Cafe*—five years during which the entire electronic landscape changed forever. Shortly before Depeche Mode began work on *Speak and Spell*, Boyd Rice, Fad Gadget, and the omnipresent Daniel Miller joined forces to record an album exclusively from sounds either collected from, or generated by, nonmusical instruments.

The process was slow, laborious, painful, and it simply piled insult onto injury that by the time the album came out, as *Easy Listening for the Hard of Hearing,* in 1983, the same record could have been constructed in half the time, with half the effort, simply by hiring a digital sampler—a piece of technology that had barely been available two years before.

If the masters themselves could not remain on top of the new music—or New Musik, as the usual handle-hungry journalists attempted to rechristen the movement—what hope was there for four lads from Basildon? Or anybody else, for that matter?

Without exception, not one of the bands that emerged on the keys of a synth in the early 1980s were to recapture anything like their initial successes, with most of them doomed to quick and early extinction. Those that were to survive into the post-nuclear dawn of electronic pop needed to prove their adaptability—and fast. <87>

It was ironic, then, that the most obvious signs of Depeche Mode's musical depth should have been the two songs that were not composed by Vince—Martin's now inevitable "Big Muff" and "Tora! Tora! Tora!"

Both songs, of course, were familiar from the Richard Skinner session and the band's live show. But whereas in the past they had simply rocketed by—pursued to the end by Vince's infinitely more catchy confections—on vinyl both were given time and space in which to grow, reflecting Depeche Mode's own ambitions more accurately than any number of Clarke-fired hit singles ever could. The fact that, at this point, the band alone appreciated its importance simply emphasizes its subsequent value.

Vince had been growing increasingly gloomy as the band's momentum gathered pace. The time he wanted to spend writing songs was devoured by other activities. Hours that should have been consumed in rehearsal or experimentation were instead spent waiting around drafty television studios.

On several occasions, as summer turned to fall, Depeche Mode conducted interviews as a trio, excusing Vince's absence by inflating his role within a band that had hitherto prided itself on stern democracy. He would be "away supervising other band business."

"Without Vince, we'd never have made it," Fletch confessed several years later. "He was on the dole, always pushing and pushing. He was very ambitious. We're not ambitious people. We're lazy people!"

But Vince was writing very few songs now, and conducting very little band business. He was also tired of pushing.

Everything had changed—the band, the band members, even Mute had exploded into prominence. From a tiny label specializing, as Dave once laughed, in singles that would be lucky to sell four figures, the company now had one of the hottest chart acts of the year, and a burgeoning catalog to boot. <88> Staff were being employed, some simply to answer the phone—a duty that Daniel Miller had once undertaken without even thinking about it. Now he was delegating responsibilities, and having started, he quickly began to redefine his own position within the Mute machinery. One day Martin telephoned Miller to ask about the band's latest T-shirts.

"Don't talk to me about that," Miller replied. "That's just a menial." Martin laughed it off, but it really wasn't that funny.

Many of Vince's frustrations boiled over in song, usually obliquely as was his style, but occasionally, and certainly no more than once on the album, in the most direct terms he could muster.

On the surface, the uncharacteristically brooding "Puppets" appeared simply to gloat over the bands that had grabbed the first major record deal that came along and were now suffering the reprisals even as they reaped the rewards. The inability to choose their own singles, the impossibility of defying the corporate machine—"you might think you're in control," warned "Puppets," "but you're not. Not really."

But there was a second agenda bound up in this, the darkest melody Vince had ever written, a realization that in their own way, Depeche Mode themselves were puppets, controlled by their burgeoning fame and dancing to its tune as obediently as anybody else.

The problem was, identifying the malaise was not the same as curing it, and that's where Vince was out on his own. When he wrote "Puppets," his frustrations were approaching the boiling point. Now they had passed it. Depeche Mode had the world at their feet. Vince wished he could simply kick it away again.

Instead, he did the next best thing. At the end of October 1981, with *Speak and Spell* still to be released, he announced he was leaving the band.

Depeche Mode was having a rare day off, a brief calm before the imminent storm of their first full British tour. Everyone would be relaxing at home, and Vince briefly considered simply convening an impromptu band meeting and dropping his bombshell on all three at once.

But no, that wasn't the way to do it. Instead, he decided to visit each band member in turn, tell them his decision, then leave. It was, he still remembers, a nightmare.

"They'd been expecting it. I'd been going through a gloomy phase, so they knew something was up. But I still had to go round to their houses and tell them. I knew they knew, but it was still horrible."

His reasons, he explained at the time, were simple. "I never expected Depeche Mode to become as popular as they did. And when they did, I no longer felt happy or fulfilled. All the things that come with success had suddenly become more popular than the music."

When the group first started, he remembered bitterly, "we used to get letters from fans saying, 'I like your music.'" A couple of hit singles later, "we got letters saying, 'I like your trousers.' Where do you go from there?"

For Dave, Fletch, and Martin, the immediate sensation was one of outright betrayal—coupled with a swift kick in the groin. There was, they knew, no point in arguing with Vince, or even trying to reason with him. He was a stubborn sod at the best of times. But they made the attempt regardless.

"There's no glamour. Nothing's really changed. We might have a few more pennies in our pockets, and when I say 'pennies,' I do mean pennies." Martin reiterated the words he had spoken so many times before, to journalists who asked him how his life had been altered by success. Somehow they seemed most appropriate. "But we have the same friends, the same places to go. You always think it would be great to have a hit single, but when it actually happens, nothing really changes."

Vince, however, was adamant. He conceded only two points: He would complete the U.K. tour that was scheduled to coincide with the release of *Speak and Spell,* and he would keep his departure a secret while the rest of the band plotted their next move. That wouldn't be too difficult—he'd been avoiding journalists for so long now that it was almost second nature.

‹90›

To coincide with the release of *Speak and Spell,* and to maintain the band's profile while they toured, a slew of press interviews was scheduled for the next two months, including several that would take place on the road. When the band offered Vince's excuses, not one journalist batted an eyelid.

Earlier that summer, shortly before Vince decided his destiny, Depeche Mode had been interviewed by tabloid journalist Rick Sky. It was not a particularly productive conversation; pressed to document the most exciting thing that had ever happened to the band, all Dave could muster was the night at Ronnie Scott's jazz club when the lights went out mid-performance.

"What did you do?" prompted Sky.

"We waited for them to come on again." It was hardly the sort of story that would transfix a nation as they munched their breakfast cereal!

Sky changed the subject.

"Do you think it's an advantage to be good-looking and in a band?"

Vince nodded. "Yeah, obviously it's an advantage in life to be good-looking." And Sky had his angle. When the story appeared, it hung beneath the banner headline UGLY BANDS NEVER MAKE IT. IF YOU'RE GOOD-LOOKING, THEN YOU'RE NUMBER ONE. Vince was mortified. "I never said that!" he protested. "That's not what I meant at all!"

The others just laughed. "Welcome to the real world!"

"It hit Vince hard," Dave laughed. "He didn't leave his flat for six weeks!"—and now he wasn't talking to the press. And while the hardest-bitten journalists felt a twinge of sympathy, the band reveled in their secret knowledge. They alone knew that Vince wasn't talking because he had nothing left to say.

Opening the fourteen-date tour was Blancmange, the synth duo that fate had salvaged from *Some Bizzare Album* and that was now edging toward a chart career of their own—within six months, "God's Kitchen" would emulate "Dreaming of Me" in scratching the chart's lower quarters; within a year, "Living on the Ceiling" would be a Top Ten hit.

For now, Blancmange was grateful simply to be heard, and uncomplainingly took their seats on the tour bus, politely ignorant of the gulf of brooding silence that now divided Depeche Mode. Vince and the others barely even spoke to one another the whole trip; instead, Dave and Martin spent as much time as they could with their girlfriends, Joanne and Anne, who had been brought along to man the merchandise stalls—and to keep an eye on their partners.

"He's allowed to receive them," Anne admonished the fan who was begging a kiss from Martin, "but he's not allowed to give them out."

The hysteria that dominated Depeche Mode's Lon-

don shows in September 1981 continued unabated throughout the country. Every show was sold out, even in those northern cities the band had never visited before.

The band members themselves were surprised—as each new metropolis came into view, one or another of the band would predict dark failure and violence: "Birmingham. They hate us in Birmingham. It's Duran Duran territory." Or, "Sheffield. Human League territory." . . . "Liverpool—OMD." Daryl Levy, Depeche Mode's road manager, regaled the bus with the story of how he was mugged in broad daylight the last time he was in Manchester. Every city hid new horrors—which could only be laughed off when another uneventful evening passed off in a cloud of adoration.

"We've done it!" Martin hissed to Fletch as the band fled another backstage battleground. "We're pop stars. . . ." And then he caught sight of Vince, silent, reserved, counting the days until he could pack it all in forever. "At least for the next few days."

<92>

The end of the tour loomed closer now, and with it, the end of Vince. The remaining trio had already made up their minds that Depeche Mode would continue—Martin was still writing songs, and the band had already run through a few of them. They were good as well; not as catchy as Vince's, admittedly, but what the hell—you can't be catchy forever! "We've got to grow up sometime," Martin said with a smile. It was just a shame, he reflected, that they had to grow up so quickly.

He wondered how much longer "all this"—and he gestured around the tour bus, smeared in lipstick graffiti and strewn with odd feminine gifts—would continue. One record? Two? How long before the fans got tired of waiting for another "New Life" and turned their attention elsewhere?

Back to Vince, maybe—he still hadn't informed them of what he intended doing next, beyond continuing to write songs, and maybe putting another band together: "A low-key band, something I can just do for fun, and get on with my life at the same time."

Dave, too, was locked in contemplation. Even with Joanne ever present beside him (she was now running Depeche Mode's fan club), he got a kick out of the adulation, reveled in the success that Depeche Mode had earned. Now Vince was kicking it all away—for what? So he could start again in obscurity? Wouldn't it be funny, he mused bitterly, if—even as Depeche Mode sank into obscurity—Vince remained a scream idol forever? Then he thought about it some more. "Actually, it wouldn't be very funny at all." But it would serve the bastard right.

Only Fletch remained unconcerned. For him, pop music was little more than a fun diversion, something to do in between school and adulthood. The most staunchly working-class member of Depeche Mode, Fletch was stamped with correspondingly staunch working-class ethics. He enjoyed what he did, of course, but he knew that he could enjoy whatever he did, whether it was chasing numbers across an accounting ledger, or <99> playing the very different kind of numbers that Vince, and now Martin, composed. He kept his thoughts to himself—he knew how much Depeche Mode meant to Martin and Dave. But if Depeche Mode ended tomorrow, he knew, "I'd just get on with my life."

The tour wound up on December 3, 1981, when the band was filmed live at the London Lyceum for the in-concert "Off the Record" television show. But the tour had climaxed a few days earlier, with Depeche Mode's triumphant return to Basildon, in front of a proud, adoring audience.

Before they went on, the band knew they could do no wrong—but they still made certain they did everything right, and were rewarded with a rave review in *New Musical Express:* "Depeche Mode, a technical drawing in pastel crayons, are home. [But] they did not act like heroes. They are to be embraced with affection, enjoyed for their enjoyment and the way they suggest enjoyment. Innocence is not as disposable as it may seem, and Depeche Mode are a warm breeze that whispers in your ear. It's good for you."

Nine days later, it was announced that Vince Clarke had quit.

"We didn't want to stay in the garage, and obviously the dream is to be successful," Fletch admitted as the bombshell dropped. "But we never thought it would happen—it just has. We've never struggled, and we haven't been gigging for years and years. When we first took 'Dreaming of Me' to our plugger, and he said it was amazing, we didn't believe him."

When Daniel announced that Depeche Mode would continue on without the man who wrote that song, nobody believed him, either.

Chapter 6

It Was Actually

Pretty Vile

THE SAME WEEK as Vince's departure was announced to a shocked music press, a classified
advertisement appeared in the back pages of
Melody Maker: "Name Band, Synthesizer,
Must Be Under 21." Applicants would be told
everything else later on—who the "name
band" was, of course, but also that there
would be no recording work, no chance of ad-
vancement, maybe even nothing more than a
few gigs in America in March 1982.

It was because of that imminent
American visit that Depeche Mode was so desperate to replenish their ranks. "Just Can't Get
Enough" had dominated Stateside college-
and club-circuit radio throughout the fall of
1981, but even more amazingly, *Speak and
Spell* had already made the U.S. Top 200! Import sales and radio play alone saw the album
attain a peak of number 192, a staggering feat

for an unavailable record by an unknown band. For Depeche Mode to make their American debut at anything less than full strength was tantamount to suicide.

But even as they awaited the first responses to their classified ad, the band remained adamant. They would not take the first remotely capable idiot to walk through the door; they would not be rushed or bullied into making a decision. Whether the new boy stayed for six weeks or six months, he had to be someone they could live with—and who could live with them.

For, as serious as they were about maintaining their musical equilibrium, Depeche Mode was also very serious about its own personal solidarity. It was difficult enough for them to put aside the concerns that had prevented them from advertising for a vocalist the eighteen months previous—and for a drummer all along. No matter what happened, they were not going to compromise those concerns—which had long since solidified into convictions—just for the sake of a quick trip to America.

<96>

The auditions threw up the usual array of would-be hopefuls: a handful of fans with a wide range of talents, but none that the band itself could use; twenty or so out-of-work musicians; and a couple of graduates from the school of hard knocks who might never have seen a synthesizer before, but "Hey, man, I'm a professional; I can handle anything." Either that, or they'd walk in and announce, "Synths are on the way out; what you really need's a guitarist."

Alan Wilder was one of the few who fit neither stereotype. He could play synthesizer, of course, together with virtually every other keyboard instrument Depeche Mode cared to mention. But when they introduced him to their repertoire, he simply looked politely curious. "I'd heard of Depeche Mode," he admits, "but I hadn't actually heard any of their songs. I wasn't that interested in the group at that time."

He wasn't under twenty-one, either. Born on June 1, 1959, Alan was a full year older than anyone else in the band.

But he was willing to lie if it meant a new challenge. And besides, the money was good!

Alan came from the occasionally affluent middle-class suburb of Acton, in west London. Like his two older brothers, he had a strong musical background; his parents had insisted on classical piano lessons for their youngest son, although when Alan left school in 1975, his abilities counted for little at his first job—making tea at a small central London recording studio.

Alan didn't mind. His ambition was to become a studio engineer, but he didn't hide his musical abilities, particularly once he realized that he was a considerably more accomplished pianist than many of the musicians who passed through the studio. Before long, Alan was appearing as an uncredited studio musician on a variety of recordings, and finally, he bowed to the inevitable. Accepting that "I was spending more time helping out on sessions as a keyboard player than <97> doing anything in the control room," he decided to throw himself into full-time musicianship.

None of Alan's early bands did anything: not the soft-rock Dragons, who worked the west London youth-club circuit; not Reel to Reel, who remained similarly locked to the local pub scene; not even Daphne and the Tenderspots, a vaguely New Wave–ish band that even released a single, the novelty-tinged "Disco Hell."

It all counted as experience, however, and toward the end of 1981, Alan answered a Keyboards Wanted ad placed by the Hitmen, a once highly rated band that had emerged toward the end of the 1970s, in the hope that amid the manifold themes and streams being thrown at the pop market, theirs might be the one that would stick.

It was not to be; guitar bands—as Gary Numan had proved—were out, and the Hitmen (whose brilliant young lead player, Pete Glenister, now records and tours with Kirsty Mac-Coll) were no exception.

Desperate to move with the times, the Hitmen augmented their lineup with a synthesizer, just in time for their second album, *Torn Together*. It didn't help, and by the time Alan joined, the Hitmen's lineup had been pared to a minimal three-piece—Glenister, vocalist Ben Watkins, and drummer Mike Gaffey. Their recording contract with CBS was nearing an end; the band members' own patience was similarly fraying.

"Ouija," the band's final single, was recorded without either Alan or the similarly newly-recruited bassist John Jay (from Depeche Mode's Bridgehouse contemporaries, the Ian Mitchell Band) taking part, and the pair had played no more than a handful of live shows with the band when Alan spotted that fateful ad in *Melody Maker*.

Later, Dave would joke that Alan Wilder looked more like a "real rock star" than anybody else in Depeche Mode. His short hair straggled spikily, his gaunt face bristled with a light stubble forced out by sharp cheekbones, and he arrived at the audition clad in a leather jacket and jeans. He looked odd standing behind a synthesizer; with looks like his, he should have been a guitarist, his instrument slung around his knees, furiously exorcising the Keith Richards–shaped demons that had so obviously determined his appearance.

<98>

But he only needed to hear a melody once before he was playing it, even improving upon it. When Martin, Dave, and Fletch agreed to offer Alan a place in the band, Dave joked that if it didn't work out, he could have their jobs as well.

The group offered Alan the most generous terms they could—a six-month trial basis that would see them through to the recording of their second album. In the meantime, he would be starting work immediately, as Depeche Mode set about promoting their first post-Vince single, Martin's "See You."

Recorded shortly before Christmas 1981, it was a beautiful song, riding with what remains one of Martin's most exquisite melodies, not to mention one of his earliest—"See You" was among the first songs Martin ever wrote.

But would beauty be enough? Vince's departure did

more than deprive Depeche Mode of a bandmate, it also robbed them of what the public perceived as their number-one asset, a man who could find chart hits in his breakfast cereal. Even though the band tried desperately to downplay his importance, insisting—as Fletch succinctly put it—that "we always let Vince take care of things because the rest of us are quite lazy," few outsiders even tried to conceal their skepticism.

Strangely, the ambivalence that Depeche Mode wore when they faced the outside world was not altogether a simple brave front. For all their resentment and fears, and the awkwardness that was to sour the band members' future personal relations with the errant Vince, confidence within the band was high—particularly after Alan announced that he, too, could write songs.

"I think we should have been slightly more worried than we were," Martin concedes today, and although he exaggerates his own optimism when he opines, "When your chief songwriter leaves the band, you should worry a bit"—as though Vince's departure was water off a duck's back—the speed with which the group regained its composure certainly justifies his belief that "if we had panicked, we probably wouldn't be here today."

The history of rock 'n' roll is littered with apparently fatal departures turned into triumphs by the sheer doggedness of the people left behind.

When Peter Gabriel quit Genesis in 1976, nobody ever expected the group's *drummer* to step down from his riser and take over vocals himself. When Ian Curtis's death robbed Joy Division of both their vocalist and their chief songwriter, few people even imagined that New Order would rise unassisted from the rubble.

AC/DC without Bon Scott, Van Halen without David Lee Roth, Black Sabbath without Ozzy Osbourne—each of these ruptures deprived a band of an intrinsic member of their hit-making machinery. But each continued on, often toward even greater successes.

<99>

But there were some sobering corollaries, too—Mott the Hoople without Ian Hunter, the Sex Pistols without Johnny Rotten, the Sensational Alex Harvey Band without the sensational Alex—all of them shadows shifting uncomfortably beneath their own careers' sadly setting suns. And while Vince was nowhere near as visible as those other absentees, still he was indelibly associated with the Depeche Mode sound.

In the weeks before "See You" was announced as Depeche Mode's fourth single, the word went out that Vince had not quit altogether, and would be remaining on board as songwriter alone—the Brian Wilson of the Eighties.

The notion did much to calm both press and public speculation about the group's future, and that despite it being nothing more than a Daniel Miller joke—albeit a particularly brilliant one. "See You" was a near-perfect pastiche of the legendary Wilson's own band, the Beach Boys—beautiful, innocent, and littered with the soaring harmonies that made classics out of "Good Vibrations" and "California Girls." If this was the sort of song Martin Gore had up his sleeve, a lot of people could breathe easy again.

In actual fact, Vince did offer Depeche Mode one new song, to tide them over until they found their feet again. They turned it down, and Vince retaliated by taking "Only You" into the charts himself, just three months after "See You."

While reading through the Musicians Wanted columns in the local newspaper one week, an ad caught Vince's eye: "Female Singer looking for rootsy blues band." He called the number; it was answered by Alison Moyet, the strangely named "Alf" who had once powered the Vicars through those old Van Gogh nights.

At first, Vince simply needed someone to sing on a demo he'd just completed; Daniel Miller had called, asking Vince to continue recording with Mute, and if Depeche Mode didn't want "Only You," maybe Daniel would. According to Miller, Vince simply told him he'd got someone from Basildon

<100>

to sing the song for him. "It could have been anyone. It was a real surprise to hear *that* voice!"

Moyet did have a magnificent voice, but what was strangest was the way it gelled so effectively with Vince's music—which had nothing whatsoever to do with the "rootsy blues" she had so recently been searching for. Miller himself reckoned that "with her voice, *anything* could be going on in the background, and she'd [still] sound great." Allied to Vince's effortlessly memorable melodies, the combination was irresistible.

For a few weeks, it even appeared as though Dave's most spiteful fears were about to come true—the effervescent "Only You" soared to number two on the U.K. charts, and suddenly Yazoo—as the couple called themselves—were the name on every tongue, superstars-in-waiting.

But Yazoo was always going to be a very different group than Depeche Mode. Vince's own experiences, and Moyet's deep rhythm-and-blues-based roots, ensured that—and added fresh fuel to the fires of Depeche Mode's resentment as they did so. Was that the real reason why Vince left the group? Because he was tired of their sound, not their success?

According to Vince, the aftermath of the breakup was, in many ways, even worse than the breakup itself. "It wasn't amiable at all. There was a lot of bad feeling on both parts. It was about a year before it finally died down, and until then it was actually pretty vile."

The success first of "Only You," then of "Don't Go" and "Nobody's Diary," only exacerbated this animosity. Throughout a year during which Depeche Mode would be struggling to make the Top Ten, Yazoo hit the top with almost spiteful regularity. *Upstairs at Eric's,* the duo's debut album, made number two; *You And Me Both,* its follow-up, went one better. And when the British music industry tallied up the greatest successes of 1982, it was Yazoo's brilliant consistency that ensured a two percent share of the singles market for Mute, a ranking that saw the label equal to, or even outstripping, the performances of A & M and Island, both long-established majors. Depeche Mode's contribution to that success was scarcely worth speaking of.

Yet 1982 began with such promise. Depeche Mode were the cover stars of the first *Face* of the year; "See You" was winning surprisingly encouraging reviews, clocking up sufficient advance orders to guarantee the band a berth on "Top of the Pops" before the record even hit the shops. Alan made a triumphant live debut when the band played a semisecret gig at Croc's in January, and less than a week later, he was the acknowledged star of the band's next television appearance, the BBC's live "In Concert" show.

Depeche Mode's decision to play "In Concert" ranks among their most courageous moves ever; there can be very few bands that would choose to introduce their latest member via a forty-minute prime-time television special, particularly when that latest member has only been with the group for two weeks!

But there was a method to Depeche Mode's apparent madness. Well aware that Vince's departure had caused many people to simply write the group off, they needed to prove that Depeche Mode still functioned. "In Concert" would both confound the band's premature coffin-bearers and reassure their fans.

Nevertheless, as they readied themselves for the broadcast, at the BBC's historic Paris Studios, Depeche Mode was aware that more eyes would be upon them that night than at almost any time in their career. Would they, *could* they, survive Vince's departure? And if they could, in what form? A pop cabaret act stretching out their twelve months at the top into a long and embarrassing career? A bold but ultimately doomed self-regeneration that would make a couple more records, then fade back into oblivion? Or something else entirely?

Throughout the "In Concert" broadcast, Depeche Mode appeared in total control. *Speak and Spell* still dominated the band's repertoire, but it was "Tora! Tora! Tora!" and "Big

Muff" that produced the most convincing performances. "See You" won a tentative live debut, its complex harmonies challenging Dave to vocal extremes he had seldom even attempted onstage, while "Now This Is Fun," its ragged B-side, was given a convincing depth that its vinyl counterpart never threatened to match.

For everybody mulling over Depeche Mode's future, however, the most reassuring moment came when the band introduced a brand-new song, "The Meaning of Love." It was a little sloppy, as befitted a song that Martin had only just recently introduced to rehearsals, but as *Melody Maker* remarked, "A handful of gigs will pull the fresh stuff as taut as the favorites." It was indicative of Depeche Mode's newfound confidence that they would begin playing that handful of gigs in New York City.

Of all the emotions running through the band members' minds as they boarded the plane to New York, it was the Stateside <103> impact of *Speak and Spell* that most concerned them; the need both to live up to the welter of anticipation that had gathered around their visit, and to prove that they actually deserved the colossal head start they had over Britain's other transatlantic exports.

Without exception, the bands regarded as the leaders of the pop pack at home—Duran Duran, Spandau Ballet, and Orchestral Maneuvers in the Dark—were still awaiting their first Stateside successes. A Flock of Seagulls, the bizarrely groomed band that would eventually become synonymous with the so-called Second British Invasion, was still just a funny name on the nascent MTV; even Human League, with the U.K.-chart-topping "Don't You Want Me Baby" under their belts, had yet to make an impact. The song wouldn't commence its conquest of the American charts until after Depeche Mode had returned home. Depeche Mode arrived in New York for two shows and a series of interviews fully aware that the aspirations of an entire generation of British pop groups rode on their shoulders.

The intention of this initial visit was simply to introduce Depeche Mode to the people who had taken them this far. In the wake of *Speak and Spell*'s import success, Daniel Miller had shrewdly licensed the North American rights to the band's recordings to Sire, now part of the immense WEA group—itself steeped in indie history—and a full domestic release was now scheduled for March 1982.

Even so, Sire cautioned, the best they could hope to do was consolidate a burgeoning reputation. "America isn't like the U.K.," the band was warned. "Simply showing your faces on the coasts doesn't cut it. You have to work your asses off, play every club in the country and then some. Nationwide visibility is the name of the game." Depeche Mode just looked at one another and groaned.

Their expectations sank even further when the group was introduced to the American press. In interview after interview, Martin complained afterward, the key question was "Why don't you use guitars?"

<104>

"Some interviewers got very pushy about it. There was a real rockist attitude, 'Springsteen is God,' that kind of thing. They couldn't *believe* we'd want to be an all-electronic band."

Martin's attempts to lighten the conversation by bringing up his own favorite bands only further worsened matters. Acts like Sparks, T. Rex, and Gary Glitter—household names in Britain, where they had enjoyed a slew of major hits throughout the early/mid 1970s—meant little or nothing in America; they were, in fact, often regarded as disposable pop for the bubblegum generation.

References to David Bowie went no further. Once the crowned prince of British glam rock, Bowie was now living out a confused half-life between a slow-death musical career and a nonstarter theatrical sideline. With his *Let's Dance* megasmash still twelve months away, Bowie's own glorious pop past had barely filtered into the American consciousness.

And as for Kraftwerk . . . The German group had

done nothing in America since "Autobahn," and the critics rolled their eyes in despair. The hottest band that Britain had to offer, aligning itself with a half-decade-old one-hit wonder. Maybe Springsteen really was God!

If the critics were harsh and uncomprehending, however, the concerts themselves were unquestionable triumphs. Quite coincidentally, Duran Duran was in New York at the same time as Depeche Mode, but while they entertained three hundred curious stragglers at the Peppermint Lounge, the doormen at Depeche Mode's two Ritz gigs were turning that many *away*!

The band was still on American soil and already a second visit was being scheduled for May, with headlining shows in Canada in Toronto and Vancouver; and—instigating the love affair that remains the key to Depeche Mode's modern American popularity—California, with near sell-out shows at San Francisco's Kabuki Theater and Pasadena's Perkins Palace. <105>

Sometimes, the band mused as they flew home, America was the most welcoming place on earth. But other times, as Martin complained, if the critics they'd already met were anything to go by, "even releasing records seemed hardly worth the effort."

Immediately upon their return from the U.S., in early March 1982, Depeche Mode launched into a fifteen-date British tour. "See You" was still climbing the chart; ticket sales were as strong as they ever were with Vince. For the time being, the very momentum of the band's early hit singles was sufficient to carry them through the first months of the divorce.

"The only things we have to worry about," Martin laughed to *Record Mirror* journalist Sunie, "are really stupid things." A friend of Fletch's had gone into a local record store the week "See You" was released, and found it already languishing in the bargain bins. The group spent the next week wondering if maybe the shop knew it wasn't going to chart, "so they've stuck it straight into the rack."

Only when "See You" debuted at number forty in

the week of the band's "Top of the Pops" performance, jumped to thirty-one, and then drove directly into the Top Ten while the band was in the U.S.A. did they agree—the shop had just made a mistake.

Once again, the British tour was set to end in London in late March, with two nights at the Hammersmith Odeon, then the most prestigious venue on the country's live circuit. The real climax, however, came a few nights after that, with a secret gig at the dingy east London pub where the Depeche Mode story started, the Bridgehouse in Canning Town.

A recent, routine visit by the local fire inspectors had revealed that the Bridgehouse's attention to safety precautions did not meet basic legal requirements. Unless the necessary, very expensive renovations were made within a matter of weeks, the Bridgehouse would be forced to close its doors as a live venue. In an area where established live venues were already scarce, the loss of east London's best-known club would be catastrophic.

As soon as they heard the news, Depeche Mode contacted promotor Terry Murphy and they were booked to play the pub on the final Saturday of March 1982. At the band's own suggestion, advertising was restricted to word of mouth alone, but that was sufficient. The line began forming at the Bridgehouse doors in the early afternoon; by the time Depeche Mode took the stage around ten o'clock that evening, the pub was jammed solid, and the Bridgehouse was saved. Just to make sure, the band added their own fee, over one thousand pounds (around $2,500), to the door takings.

Alan Wilder's six-month trial period was due to end shortly before Depeche Mode returned to the Blackwing studio to begin work on their second album—refreshed after taking their first proper holidays in almost two years. Dave and Joanne took two weeks in Greece and came back raving about the almost absolute absence of any nightlife they found there. "It was great! I didn't have to think about music at all!"

<106>

Music, on the other hand, was all Alan thought about, and when Depeche Mode reconvened at the end of July 1982, they were as conscious of his single-mindedness as anybody could be.

Unlike many of the bands whose live show relies on prerecorded tapes, Depeche Mode was never content to simply adapt their studio recordings to the new environment. Rather, they would laboriously rerecord their backing tracks, exaggerating certain elements of the original version, playing down others. It was—and remains—a time-consuming exercise, especially as the group's own ideas became more adventurous, and though the band members took it seriously, it was not one of their favorite chores.

Alan, however, delighted in the task. Even today, his bandmates describe him as the only truly musical member of the group, and his talent and enthusiasm even resounded through the tapes he prepared from the band's *Speak and Spell* <107> material. Long before Martin, Dave, and Fletch informed him that they wanted him to remain with the group on a permanent basis, at the end of July, Alan was fairly certain he'd gotten the job. Which made the band's next decision all the harder for him to take and, perhaps, for them to deliver.

Alan had been wondering why no one had yet given him the precise details of the upcoming studio sessions, but convincing himself that the others simply assumed he knew, he waited until virtually the last minute before asking what time he should turn up at Blackwing.

Martin shuffled his feet awkwardly. "Actually, you don't really have to."

"What's that supposed to mean?"

"We won't be needing you. We don't want you to record with us."

Fletch chimed in. "Or to tell anyone you've joined the group properly."

They tried to explain; they still weren't yet ready to

fully open their ranks to the newcomer. Although Alan was welcome to drop by the studio to watch, his presence as a musician was not required.

Alan was furious. "I thought we'd got over that! You've only just asked me to join the band—are you kicking me out again already?"

"It's not that. . . ." Fletch, Dave, and Martin looked uncomfortable, but they were determined all the same. Patiently, they explained that despite "See You," despite their live successes, Depeche Mode still had something to prove—to themselves, and to "all the people out there who still reckon Vince was the brains behind the group."

Introducing Alan into the studio would simply allow their detractors even more ammunition, "like we couldn't cut it on our own, so we had to bring someone else in, a proper musician"—the only one in the group. They were determined that no one would ever have the opportunity to accuse them of that.

<108>

Alan was scarcely able to conceal his rage, but he accepted the band's will, even went along with them when they asked that he keep his full-time recruitment in the group a close secret. But he swore that it would be different next time.

Although Martin was fully aware of the dangers of complacency, the success of "See You" had long since allayed any fears he may have entertained regarding the suitability of his own songwriting. Even before "The Meaning of Love" made it to number twelve in April 1982, the band members were boasting of the group's newfound studio freedom.

"We've done a reggae song, with horn sounds on it," Fletch proudly boasted, while Martin joked easily about "hardening" Depeche Mode's sound. "We were going to do a mean B-side; it started out with a bass line and fast drums, like a DAF thing." Unfortunately," he continued, "it didn't work. We thought we'd have this one *mean* track . . . but in the end, we put some bells on it."

Work on Depeche Mode's second album was undertaken at a considerably more leisurely pace than the hurried schedule that had created *Speak and Spell.* But it was also harder work. In many ways, the group was not yet ready to record a new album; songs that might pass muster in concert still required a little more sharpening. "We were just thrown into the deep end and had to shove together a pile of songs that were written over a very long period of time," Martin complained. "It was a mishmash."

Daniel, Eric Radcliffe, and John Fryer were again on hand to lend all the assistance the band could need, but there was only so much that they, even with the best will in the world, could do. It was not the band's music that was at issue, it was their identity. In refusing to allow Alan to take part in the sessions, the group had effectively cut off one of their own limbs—just months after the most successful transplant they could have hoped for. If there was less enthusiasm ricocheting through the studio while the band worked, it was because everybody knew Depeche Mode had made a mistake—and were now too proud to rectify it.

<109>

"People were letting us drift," Dave remonstrated. "There was a lack of enthusiasm." In later years, the band became as fervent in their disregard for *A Broken Frame,* as the album was destined to be titled, as they had been to its predecessor.

Yet Depeche Mode was in reality broadening its musical base. Tracks such as the dirgelike "Leave in Silence," the sinister "Shouldn't Have Done That," and the ambitious "My Secret Garden"—a lengthy piece which the band broke up into three separate songs—evinced a musical maturity, which even the clumsy borrowing of Bowie's "V2 Schneider" riff during "Further Excerpts from My Secret Garden" could not hamstring.

Only occasionally did Martin allow his pen to hark back to earlier triumphs, and even there, simply to sketch the outline of a song that Vince would have turned into a full-blown epic. "A Photograph of You" was almost cripplingly naive in its presentation, bereft on vinyl of its in-concert energy. "The

Meaning of Love" was simply crippling—musically and visually.

Depeche Mode had only produced one video during Vince's time with the band: the somewhat stinted performance that accompanied "Just Can't Get Enough" on MTV and led, in turn, to the song's eventual success on American college-radio stations.

Since then, they had begun to take more notice of the field although, uncertain of exactly what they wanted to do, they relied instead on the judgment of others. It was not necessarily the wisest choice.

Renowned today for his work with the Cure, and justly regarded among the best directors in the entire field of video, in 1982 Tim Pope was still carving out his reputation, primarily through his work with Soft Cell. Because he specialized in almost literal translations of a song's subject matter, it was the perfect union—Marc Almond's evocative lyrics simply spat out images, and when Pope came to grips with Soft Cell's "Sex Dwarf," the ensuing video did indeed involve dwarves . . . and sex . . . and Marc Almond wielding a bloodied chainsaw around a slaughterhouse.

Applying the same principles to Depeche Mode, however, was never going to yield the same results. The video for "See You," for instance, was set in a photograph booth in a department store; it was cute, but little more than adequate.

"The Meaning of Love" did not even meet those standards, as it was saddled with a video so mawkish that it might have been single-handedly responsible for Depeche Mode's future condemnation of their earliest clips.

"When those films turn up on television, as they occasionally do, we get a bit embarrassed," Dave admitted, and in his mind there would appear the image of a baby playing with his building bricks, while his parents fight in the same room. Then the bricks fall, and when Mom and Dad turn around to see what's wrong, the baby is smiling and the bricks have spelled

<||0>

out the title of the song. The parents embrace as the record fades out.

It was, Martin agreed, "really, really sickly. I know at the time our music was a bit like that anyway, but I think we were doing it more tongue-in-cheek, and that never came across in the videos." After "The Meaning of Love," he was adamant, Depeche Mode would be considerably more careful of the video concepts they agreed to.

But "The Meaning of Love" was to mark the end of another era as well, standing today as the last inescapably saccharine single Depeche Mode would record, one final, joyous, ride on the merry-go-round of innocence, and the last time any music critic could, in all honesty, complain that "the lead melody line is musically identical to their last hit," as *Sounds'* Valac Van De Veen did, or mourn Vince's absence one more time, as did *The Face*'s Johnny Mono. Cruelly reviewing Yazoo's "Only You" in the same breath as "The Meaning of Love," Mono concluded, "Depeche Mode could learn a lesson from this. . . ."

<111>

"Martin can still write . . . lightweight poppy songs," Dave explained, but now it was time "to try something totally different, just to see if we [can]." In August 1982 Depeche Mode released "Leave in Silence," a cut from the forthcoming *A Broken Frame* and arguably the first truly significant record of their career.

No less than the riots of 1981, the Falklands War—Britain and Argentina finally coming to blows over a territorial dispute that had simmered for close to a hundred and fifty years—was to prove a defining moment in British musical history.

True, it was not to forge a vast repertoire of songs that, by their very existence, defined the mood of a nation, but Britain was not the United States, and the Falklands War was not Vietnam. Besides, the war did not last that long; by the time the best antiwar protests made it into the shops—Spear of Destiny's "Mickey," TV Smith's "War Fever," Fad Gadget's chilling "For Whom the Bell Tolls"—the fighting was already long over. Students of cynicism alone could ponder the true state of Britain's pop mind-set during those six weeks of war; the biggest hits of the period at least lent themselves to some ironic contemplation—"A Little Peace," "Island of Lost Souls," "Run to the Hills," and—prompting memories of past territorial disputes—"This Time We'll Get It Right."

Neither was the conflict to wreak permanent change across a complacent military. There was no draft for young England to dodge, no daily delivery of sad black body bags to be beamed into a nation's dinnertime viewing. Except for those people personally bound up in the fighting, on the home front the Falklands were an ideological battleground, fought between those who believed that any piece of British soil, no matter how near to the end of the earth it was, remained sacrosanct, and those who dismissed the principles of Empire as the last surviving offspring of a world that had died decades earlier.

It was these ideologies that "Leave in Silence," written at the height of Prime Minister Thatcher's personal war fever, sought to address.

Ostensibly, the song detailed the demise of a long-term romance, painting its death throes in tones of dark resignation: "We've reached our natural conclusion," sang Dave: "I hate being in these situations that call for diplomatic relations."

But it was not a love that had shattered, as most people blithely assumed, it was a tradition. The Falklands War was essentially a war of sovereignty between two nations whose claim on the disputed territory was no more binding than history (in Britain's case) and geography (the islands lay less than two hundred miles off the Argentinian coast) demanded.

In an age that had already witnessed the partial dismemberment of every significant empire on the planet, that was already racing toward the shattering of the Soviet Union's political commonwealth, the notions put forth by the Falklands War weren't simply outdated, they were positively, literally Victorian. In recognizing this fact, in admitting that the antagonists in this century-and-a-half dispute had been "running round in circles all year," Martin was calling for the only *sensible* solution to the conflict: Both sides should go home quietly . . . leave in silence.

" 'Leave in Silence' was a risk because it wasn't catchy," Dave boasted. You had to hear it several times before it really began to make sense. He agreed that there were other songs the band could have released "which could have gone straight into the charts and been really successful, but it just didn't seem right." "Leave in Silence" faltered at number eighteen that summer of 1982. As the band had reminded themselves in the wake of Vince's departure, "You can't just carry on releasing stuff every few months, and having hits with something catchy!"

Such sentiments caught many of Depeche Mode's fans off guard; their detractors wrong-footed. The little boys were growing up, no longer the "banal inno-paps" that *NME* journalist Paul Morley once dubbed them, nor the funny-haircut purveyors of "bland inoffensive pop music" that punk poet Attila the Stockbroker condemned in his poem "Nigel Wants to Go and See Depeche Mode" (a track from his 1982 *Ranting at the Nation* album). The question, of course, was whether the band would be allowed to grow up.

<113>

For all intents and purposes, it was the old, old story, the tale of the simple pop group that moved out of its familiar neighborhood and dreamed of taking its audience with it. That in itself was just cause for censureship; the journalists and musicians of the early 1980s had been the teenagers of a decade before, watching aghast as their favorite chart acts—the Sweet and Slade, T. Rex and the Bay City Rollers—began spouting off about "artistic credibility" and how they wanted their music to be taken "seriously."

Suddenly the melodies that swept your heart away were replaced with impenetrable dirges, serious and credible to be certain, but to an audience that just wanted to have some fun—utterly devoid of character or taste. Anyone comparing "Leave in Silence" with "Just Can't Get Enough" could not fail to have seen history repeating itself with a vengeance.

The difference was, Depeche Mode was about to turn tradition on its head, to succeed where those former giants had fallen on their faces. Within a year, their betrayal of history would be both complete and, apparently, permanent. A decade after that, journalist Stephen Dalton wrote in the British magazine *Vox*, "No wonder the Depeche lads are huge in Europe and America," because there, "their inescapably naff brand of Essex electro can be enjoyed out of context and their self-reinvention as pervy pop sex lords taken at face value."

"Britain is the only country we've got a history in," Fletch agreed, "because in the first two or three years [when] we produced our worst records, we were at our most famous and at our sickliest. We smiled in every photo, we were in *Smash Hits* every week, and people still remember that. They think we went from that to doom and gloom, so there's two extreme views of Depeche Mode in England. We're either pop, or doom and gloom. Actually, we're both." Commercially, Depeche Mode was to become masters of their destiny. Critically, at least at home, they were the ultimate victims of their own success.

Paul Weller, the outspoken former vocalist with the Jam, led the charge against Depeche Mode when he became *Melody Maker*'s guest singles reviewer the week "Leave in Silence" was released: "I've heard more melody coming out of [an] arsehole."

On another occasion, the female trio Bananarama was asked to judge Depeche Mode's latest on a radio show. "Wimps!" was their considered verdict. Bow Wow Wow, Malcolm MacLaren's latest managerial enterprise, echoed the same sentiments, and Fletch bristled with only half-humored outrage. "Bow Wow Wow? I'd take them on any day."

<114>

The Glitter Twins.
Ian Hooton / Retna Ltd.

Dave—a New Romantic through and through!
Adrian Boot / Retna Ltd.

Martin models the grunge look, five years ahead of the world.
Adrian Boot / Retna Ltd.

Alan relaxing …
Tim Bauer / Retna Ltd.

Fletch on tour.
Tim Bauer / Retna Ltd.

Left: Another hotel, another chandelier.
Lisa Haun / Retna Ltd.

Below: Depeche Mode making their "Top of the Pops" debut, 1981.
Michael Putland / Retna Ltd.

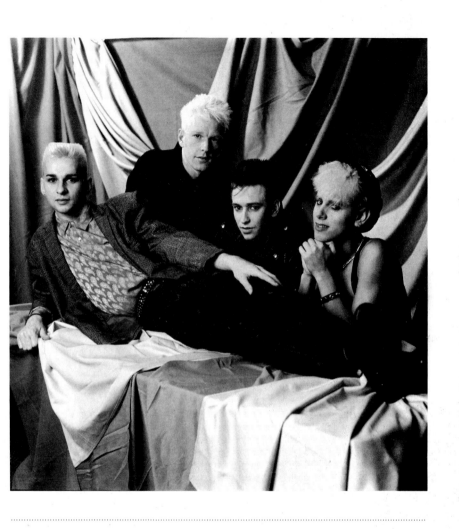

Get the haircut right (again!).
Andy Freeberg / Retna Ltd.

Left: Dave onstage— "What, here?"
Gary Gershoff / Retna Ltd.

Below: By the mid-1980's, the band's stage sets were growing increasingly elaborate.
Gary Gershoff / Retna Ltd.

Above: The *Violator* tour press conference.
Steve Granitz / Retna Ltd.

Right: Martin onstage—the dresses come later.
Gary Gershoff / Retna Ltd.

Your own personal Jesus, 1993.
Cam Garrett / S.c.u.d. Studio

Reach out, touch faith—1993.
Cam Garrett / S.c.u.d. Studio

Chapter 7

Get the Haircut

Right

A BROKEN FRAME was released in October 1982 to advance sales of half a million—sufficient to earn Depeche Mode an instant silver disc, and to guarantee another series of full houses when the band returned to the road. "Brief, cunning, certain, [the album] is as much as anything an assertion that the Mode is no headless chick," wrote Paul Morley in *NME.* "They could have got silly, withdrawn into ditties or got all weepy. But they have kept their head . . . the wandering of Vince has not harmed the Depeche balance."

It had, however, dented their public profile, as Fletch admitted when he complained, "Our success was overshadowed by Yazoo's." By the end of 1982, the biggest chart failure Yazoo had experienced was when "The Other Side of Love" scraped no higher than thirteenth place. *A Broken Frame,* on the other hand, stopped short at number eight; "Leave in Silence" stalled at eighteen. In terms of chart performance, Yazoo was way ahead, "and a lot of people really think we resent [them]," Fletch continued. "A lot of people in the general public still think Vince was the brains behind the group."

At least part of *A Broken Frame*'s brief, then, was to scotch such sentiments, a task it was quite capable of accomplishing. More important, however, it was to prove that the dark power of "Leave in Silence" was not a fluke.

"That song kind of summed up the whole of the second album," Dave remarked, and he clearly took a peculiar pride in the record's failure to bust the Top Twenty wide open when he revealed, "The radio didn't see it as a single; they saw it more as an album track." It was still important, he continued, for Depeche Mode to have hit singles, but "we want to get [even deeper] into the album-oriented market. Bands like Echo and the Bunnymen and Simple Minds do well in both charts. We just want to produce a really fine album that will hopefully establish us as a major act."

<116>

As usual, the group toured Britain in the immediate wake of the album, with double dates at Hammersmith Odeon again the inevitable closing point. Mute recorded the second of these shows, on October 25, 1982, and over the next year, excerpts from the concert were to dribble out on the B-sides of Depeche Mode's twelve-inch singles.

All twelve tracks proved journalist Paul Colbert's prediction earlier that year, that given time, the new songs would fit the stage show as snugly as the old ones. Indeed, the maniacal exuberance of "Just Can't Get Enough," "Boys Say Go," and "New Life" lay harshly at odds with the depth of the more recent material, as though at regular points in the concert the band would suddenly realize, "We're getting too heavy! Quick, let's have some fun!"

It was a problem that was to become even more pronounced before Depeche Mode grew much older and, acknowledging their own musical shortcomings, the band knew there was only one way to resolve it—by taking the step they should have taken almost six months previous.

Shortly before Christmas 1982, a Mute press release announced that Alan was joining Depeche Mode as a full member. He would be making his recorded debut in the new year, with the band's next single, "Get the Balance Right"; not only that, but he would also make his first appearance as Martin's songwriting partner—the instrumental B-side, "The Great Outdoors," was a joint Wilder-Gore composition. The possibility that without these concessions Alan might have simply quit the group in frustration was not acknowledged.

In print, Alan took his lengthy apprenticeship lightly. "I was touring and doing TV with them, but . . . somebody in their position doesn't bring in somebody new in the first week who might turn out to be a complete arsehole." Having proven that he wasn't that, he said with a smile, it was only natural that he would eventually take his place in the group. The <117> lie rankled, but it was finally at an end. The expertise that Alan had already brought to Depeche Mode's live sound could now explode in the studio.

"Get the Balance Right" (or—still dwelling on the band's original look—"Get the Haircut Right," as Depeche Mode's foes delighted in retitling the song) was to prove a pivotal release, both musically and in terms of Depeche Mode's back catalog.

Just seven years before, in October 1976, Polydor Records had introduced the concept of the twelve-inch single to the U.K. pop market (they were long-established within the disco/club scene), with a limited-edition reissue of the Who's "Substitute." Since then, twelve-inchers had become a staple of the industry, so taken for granted that even the presence of extended or remixed versions of the seven-inch cuts rarely impressed people.

As avid record buyers themselves, and aware that a lot of the people who bought singles weren't necessarily interested in hearing their favorite songs stretched interminably out in the studio, Depeche Mode instituted a program that has now itself become integral to the British singles market: deluxe twelve-inchers that are issued in strictly limited quantities and often offer a different selection of tracks than the regular twelve-incher. The limited "Get the Balance Right," for instance, included the first of the previous October's Hammersmith Odeon recordings.

But this revolution in packaging was not the new single's greatest accomplishment. Although "Get the Balance Right" was, even by Depeche Mode's recent standards, a challenging release, it was lyrically that it truly took on a whole new character.

The ambiguities of "Leave in Silence" were left behind; "Get the Balance Right" was a plea for tolerance, whose message was embodied as boldly in the lyrics as in its title. Neither was the single blessed with an instantly catchy tune—like "Leave in Silence," "Get the Balance Right" demanded more from the listener than a simple ear for a nice pop song.

Nevertheless, it was instantly recognizable Depeche Mode —*Melody Maker*'s review even puzzled aloud over "the debate between consistency and similarity . . . The second it started, I knew who it was."

But it was *Sounds*' Johnny Waller who captured the mood of the song better than any. "Depeche seem to have fallen from grace with the critical cognoscenti," he accurately pointed out. "But this is exactly the sort of single they do better than everyone else—a sweeping ditty of a melody, with clever arrangements and subtle little noises underneath."

Depeche Mode's audience evidently agreed. "Get the Balance Right" smashed into the British charts at number thirty-two, their highest new entry ever. The band breathed a collective sigh of relief—returning from a handful of European tour dates, they were waiting for their luggage at London's Heathrow Airport when they heard the news. "So despite predictions of their downfall," an accompanying journalist, *NME*'s

Mat Snow, wrote afterward, "Depeche Mode are still ahead of the game."

Two trips to Europe, on either side of Christmas, were only the first leg of Depeche Mode's latest live itinerary. The Far East and the United States also beckoned, a lengthy outing whose grueling routine flew in the face of Fletch's continued insistence that Depeche Mode did not enjoy touring.

He complained, with surprising honesty, that unlike most so-called rock stars, he actually lost friends while he was on the road, "because I'd return and have nothing to talk to them about. Touring became my life, and when people asked what I'd been doing—'well, we flew to Spain and appeared on TV. . . .' " Bitterly, he revealed that "the biggest thrill I'll ever feel was when we went into the charts at [number] fifty-five for the first time."

The only real benefits he could pinpoint from being on the road was the rapid improvement in his Space Invaders video-game skills and the chance to take a close-up look at the machinations of organizing a major band.

<119>

He studied every area—the vast acreage of paperwork that needed to be completed before the band's equipment could pass through customs; the ease with which a traveler could pass from millionaire status in one country to virtual beggar in another; and the assurances Depeche Mode would have to give when another foreign visa department discovered Dave's teenage rap sheet and balked at allowing him into their country. A decade on, Dave was still pleading with journalists, "Don't bring that up again! I have enough trouble getting in places as it is!"

Reading over Daniel's shoulder, Fletch studied the contracts that bound Depeche Mode to different labels and distributors abroad, double-checking the figures that had already been verified by Mute's accountant, questioning anything and everything that didn't make sense. To the occasional fan who blustered his or her way into Mute's west London offices, the visiting Fletch barely even merited a second glance. He was just another horn-rim bespectacled clerk, with a ledger under one arm and a ballpoint behind his ear.

It was Fletch—carefully scrutinizing every request for interviews which came in, studying local maps in search of new ways of killing time—who tried to ensure that the burden of touring was lightened, or at least alleviated as much as possible. But still there was only the occasional break in the monotony of traveling and playing.

In the United States, where Depeche Mode returned in March 1983, the band's burgeoning cult reputation was cemented with their first American full house, at the Beverly Hills Theater, and by a meeting with the staff of KROQ, the largest "alternative" radio station in the Los Angeles area—already devoted Depeche Mode fans.

In Portugal, where "Just Can't Get Enough" had proven one of 1981's biggest hits, the band was feted as international superstars. And in Germany, careful booking had ensured that the band would be headlining Frankfurt's Kongresshalle in the same week as the annual Frankfurt Music Fair. Aside from the hour or so while he was onstage, Martin spent every available moment touring the vast exhibition hall with Daniel Miller, trying out the new keyboards and synthesizers.

In terms of simple tour madness, however, nothing could eclipse the Far Eastern leg of the outing. The days when Japan alone guaranteed a fanatical reception for visiting Western pop groups were long gone. Western music was sweeping the entire Pacific Rim, and while Depeche Mode was simply one more in an ever-increasing number of bands that added the likes of Thailand and Hong Kong to their tour itineraries, the reception they received was that of an all-conquering trailblazer—complete with a genuine riot!

Frustrated by the long wait for Depeche Mode's aircraft to touch down at Hong Kong's Kai Tak Airport, cramped and discomforted by the local police's patent impatience with

<120>

their chanting and screaming, several thousand fans finally exploded. Whole sections of the airport were closed off while the police applied the billy club to fan club, and when Depeche Mode did finally land, it was into a debris-strewn battleground, from which howling ambulances still streamed urgently away. And still there were sufficient fans left to mob them!

But it was Thailand that left the deepest, darkest, impressions upon Depeche Mode. The band was booked into a hotel in the very center of Bangkok, but any intentions they had had of tasting the local nightlife were abandoned the moment they caught sight of the first child prostitute being led upstairs by a businessman old enough to be her grandfather.

"All the women over there [are] prostitutes." Martin was disgusted. "That's the only way they can make money. And of course, the businessmen love it." He suggested that the next time somebody wanted to spout the beauties of capitalism, they first go to Bangkok and see its effects firsthand.

<121>

"But they probably still wouldn't understand it," he said with a sigh. Like the foreign businessmen who had apparently reduced an entire culture to the level of a sexual service economy, those sort of people "tend to treat others as though they're *nothing.*"

All the band was affected. "From the age of about ten," Dave reasoned, "I can remember things quite vividly that just didn't seem right. [But] then you see things that are poorer than you've ever seen—people begging and little kids coming up to us with disgusting, dirty clothes hanging off them, showing themselves or holding their hands out for food. When you experience that, you begin to understand what a lucky position all of us here are in."

Even as Depeche Mode flew back to Britain, Martin was scribbling furiously, desperately trying to purge his mind of Bangkok's demeaning bitterness. Slowly, and with Dave, Alan, and Fletch contributing their own observations through conversation and suggestion, the theme of Depeche Mode's next album began to coalesce.

For two or three years now, a handful of British music journalists had been nudging their editors in the direction of a new musical form leaking out of the art community.

Several of the bands involved already had British record deals; Daniel Miller, for instance, had done much to pioneer the scene with his adoption of Boyd Rice and DAF, both of whom utilized cacophony in their drive to follow Kraftwerk's pioneering combination of electronics with "found" sounds—the roar of passing locomotives, the clatter of the foundry—a roar that, to audiences raised on the gentle electronics of Faust and Tangerine Dream, represented musical Armageddon. Hijacking the name of Throbbing Gristle's old record label, the new movement was quickly dubbed "industrial music."

But the Mute stable was merely the tip of a fast-flowing iceberg, and one that, it swiftly transpired, had already circumnavigated the globe.

<122>

Stark and tuneless—and to the untrained ear, unshackled by the remotest sense of melody—Australians the Birthday Party and Jim "Foetus" Thirwell had already made considerable inroads into the rock 'n' roll consciousness, with Thirwell and Birthday Party vocalist Nick Cave even joining forces with Soft Cell's Marc Almond in a one-off band called the Immaculate Consumptives.

Now there was another Australian noise machine to reckon with. SPK took their name from the Socialist Patients Kollektiv, a group of West German mental patients who, inspired by the Baader Meinhoff Group, attempted to form their own terrorist group and died while making their first bombs in their hospital room.

SPK was similarly extreme, and sometimes equally careless. At one show in San Francisco, a member of the audience was accidentally set on fire while SPK was demonstrating a flamethrower onstage; at another, also in San Francisco, they reduced the crowd to a vomiting mass by noisily eating raw sheep's brains during their show. In both instances, the audience reaction was as integral to the musical performance as any sounds generated by the band members themselves.

Other bands, readily identifiable by their onstage paucity of conventional musical hardware (and frequently, Teutonic-sounding names), followed, but by far the most important were Einstürzende Neubauten, the Berlin-based conceptualists the meaning of whose name simply echoed their sound: collapsing new buildings.

While not completely espousing traditional instrumentation, Einstürzende Neubauten's calling card remained a dense wall of pounding, screeching, roaring, pieced together from loudly amplified power drills, hammers, and anvils. To the uninitiated, the band's live performances were akin to spending an evening in a blacksmith's forge, knowing the blacksmith had just downed a ton of angel dust.

Early in 1983, Einstürzende Neubauten staged their self-explanatory Metal Concerto at London's Institute of Contemporary Arts. Many of the onlookers were simply curious, lured into earshot by the band's continued flirtation with the music press; now, deprived of the visual reassurance of guitars, drums, or keyboards, a full house had its every last preconception about music torn asunder by the Germans' furious assault on an arsenal comprised of metal sheets, hammers, and machinery. <123>

In the crowd that night was Martin Gore. "The power and excitement of it was brilliant!" he raved afterward— so brilliant that he was already contemplating how to use "the ideas in a different context, in the context of pop." Melody, as Dave continued to assure Depeche Mode's fans, "has always been very important to Martin."

At the same time, though, he shared Martin's need to "gravitate to the experimental side. We've always been interested in sound, and as the technology goes on, we'll move with it."

Highlighting the continuous upgrading of the band's

instrumental lineup—an extravagance funded both by their records and Martin's and Alan's insatiable curiosity—Dave claimed that "a lot of the time we actually are the first people to use the technology as it comes out!" Einstürzende Neubauten's Metal Concerto simply signposted the direction in which Depeche Mode could take that technology. Tied to Martin's current musical preoccupations, there was no end to the possibilities.

Exploration was the key to the recording sessions that tied Depeche Mode to London's Garden Studios throughout the summer of 1983. But though they were certainly referring to the example of that latest wave of industrial bands that so influenced Martin's recent writing, Depeche Mode's most immediate inspiration remained the ubiquitous Boyd Rice, and in particular, the now two-year-old *Easy Listening for the Hard of Hearing*—or "new sounds from old sources," as Daniel Miller once offhandedly described it.

<124>

Depeche Mode strayed from Rice's original vision in just one department. Rice had concentrated on creating sounds alone, building rhythms and textures, but very little else. Depeche Mode returned music to the equation.

They were also able to lighten the noisemaking workload through the use of the Synclavier, the digital sampler that had barely been developed when *Easy Listening for the Hard of Hearing* was constructed.

For many people, the sampler was simply another fancy toy, something that could lift prerecorded sounds from one source, render them unrecognizable (or thereabouts), then transplant them elsewhere. Now, the sampler's most vocal acolytes proclaimed, it was possible to have Robert Plant, Jimi Hendrix, and the London Symphony Orchestra all playing on the same record—without there being more than two people in the studio, one to work the machine, the other to run down to the record store to pick up the records.

Daniel and Depeche Mode wanted to take the possibilities even further. Taking natural or found sounds, Daniel Miller was able to completely reprocess them through the Synclavier, twisting the original tones and textures to create entirely new noises. Running water, anvils, and creaking doors were all utilized during the sessions, and rendered totally unrecognizable in the process.

"When we first ordered the Synclavier," Daniel Miller remembered, "we already knew all about it and had loads of ideas as to what we could do with it." One of those ideas involved exploring what Miller calls "the psychological effect of recording sounds in their own acoustical space, and using them without adding any artificial reverb."

Frequently he led the band outside the studio, to tour London's East End in search of new sounds to sample. Neighborhood construction sites fast proved a particularly fruitful hunting ground. On one occasion, the band was happily recording the sound of things banged against a fence when an <125> overvigilant watchman burst onto the scene. The ensuing sound, according to Alan, went "CREEESH—OY!"

Similarly productive was a site that was dominated by a disused railroad station, pocked with piles of junk metal stacked up inside vast, otherwise empty workshops.

"One day," Miller explains, "we grabbed a stereo tape recorder and sampled a bunch of things—old metal, bottles breaking, things running into walls—then brought the sounds back to the studio and put them into the Synclavier." Many of Dave's vocals would also be recorded in those barren workshops, "again without any enhancement other than the natural reverb of the room."

"You can take the purest voice in the world," Alan enthused, "and fool around with it digitally until it's the most monstrous, evil sound. Or you can take a moose fart and make it beautiful."

"I look at a lot of other people that use sampled sounds in disappointment nowadays," Dave condemned.

"They just seem to hire a Fairlight [the first synthesizer to facilitate sampling], sample a few orchestral sounds, and that's it. It all seems really boring."

Depeche Mode intended that entire tracks should be constructed from sampled sounds alone, often without any kind of artificial studio enhancements. As their third album took shape, it was clear that the band was not only pioneers in the use of the Synclavier, they were pioneering its multitudinous functions and abilities as well. "If you're going to spend that amount of money hiring a piece of equipment," Dave reasoned, "why not explore it?"

It was only in later years that he conceded that "maybe we were trying too hard . . . sampling too much and trying to give a message without thinking so much of the structure and the point of the song. Musically, some of [what we were doing] was very forced." He barely needed to add that Daniel aside, none of the band actually knew how to work the machine. "The manual's very thick," Martin simpered.

<126>

Work on what was to become *Construction Time Again*—a name suggested by the industrial clattering of so many of the tracks—stretched throughout the spring and early summer of 1983, with the first weeks spent collecting samples, building up a library of sounds to which the band could refer during the actual recording process.

Throughout, two overriding themes dominated the band's thinking: the cacophonous metallics of Einstürzende Neubauten, and the jacket design that photographer Brian Griffin had already begun—a shirtless worker whose raised hammer, it seemed, intended to smash the mountain peak that rose alongside him.

"But not to destroy," Alan explained. "Because he's a worker, it's to rebuild it—it's positive. That was the overall idea of the album, to be positive." That, he continued, was why the band chose the title *Construction Time Again,* "not *Destruction.*"

The image of the worker was a loaded one, nevertheless, redolent of socialism, even—in a Britain four years into
Margaret Thatcher's belligerently capitalist rule—communism.
In any other society, Martin and Alan's mantric "Work Hard"
would have been regarded as a shining example to a work-shy
youth. In Britain in 1983, it was described as a left-wing mani-
festo—a frightening preconception in an increasingly frightening country.

The notions of selfish gain that were so presciently
epitomized by the first wave of New Romantics had blossomed
with almost frightening rapidity. An entire national infrastruc-
ture was under attack by a government whose own lust for
money appeared determined to send Britain spiraling into the
same state of degraded servitude as the women of Bangkok
were in.

The country's free National Health Service, for more
than thirty years the envy of the world, was no longer free, as
the government froze subsidies and slapped the shortfall on the
public. The welfare system, set up to provide for the poor and
needy, was poor and needy itself, crippled by soaring unemployment and slashed benefits.

<127>

Public services that past administrations had nation-
alized—from the power and telecommunications industries to
the ship and aircraft manufacturers—were now teetering on the
brink of a massive privatization scheme. And the Labour Party,
the official opposition, was so racked with internal strife that it
had all but ceased to function, at least in the eyes of the elector-
ate.

Crushed when the country went to the polls in June
1983, Labour's humiliation was suddenly representative of all
coherent anti-Thatcherite sentiment. People simply gave up
fighting—and that included even the musical voices that were
once raised so loud against her.

In 1980 the English Beat railed against Thatcher's
then newly elected government with the furious "Stand Down

Margaret." They greeted the 1983 election with a remake of Andy Williams's "Can't Get Used to Losing You"—with no ironic pun intended.

UB40 took their name from the identity card issued to all recipients of unemployment benefits, and had a hit in 1981 with "One in Ten," titled after the percentage of the working population then in possession of those cards. Their latest hit was the silky "Red Red Wine."

The Specials, whose "Ghost Town" had provided such eerie accompaniment to riots that rocked the nation in 1981, had splintered; so had the Jam, the aggressively influential trio whose songs once pioneered the concept of a working-class consciousness for the 1980s. Their heirs—Jerry Dammers's Special A.K.A., Paul Weller's Style Council—remained politically active, but for them, the enemies were now almost fatally specific. Dammers's "Racist Friend" and Weller's championing of the Campaign for Nuclear Disarmament (CND) both addressed crucial issues, but neither addressed *the* crucial issue.

<128>

It was to be 1985, two years hence, before Weller, together with the likes of Billy Bragg, Madness, and Alison Moyet (now a solo artist, following the 1983 dissolution of Yazoo), linked arms with the Labour Party itself, and formed Red Wedge, the first actively political pop movement of the 1980s. In the meantime, it was as though the two greatest reflections of any modern nation's state of mind—its pop stars and its politicians—had taken a vow of mutual disinterest.

Construction Time Again shattered that vow. "When we decided on the theme for the album," Alan informed *NME* writer X. Moore (himself a member of the socialist band the Redskins), "the first word that came up was 'caring,' and that's the main idea behind it." Dave added, "Martin, Andy, and me all come from working-class backgrounds and that's starting to reflect in the lyrics."

Construction Time Again was not a specific call for rebellion. When Martin wrote, "All we need . . . is universal revolution"—in the album's closing track—"And Then . . .," he didn't intend for everyone to take up arms; rather, he was calling for "a change of attitude. That's what's needed. People's attitudes have got to be changed.

"You've got to look at the world to change things—attitudes in the world, poverty in the world." He insisted that when Depeche Mode sang of socialism, they didn't mean the "English socialism" of Orwell and all—"we mean 'International socialism.' " And the songs on the new album "aren't so much political as songs of common sense."

The misconceptions piled up regardless. Backtracking from *Construction Time Again,* suddenly, previous Depeche Mode album jackets took on new, hitherto unnoticed socialist overtones—the predominantly red *Speak and Spell,* the sickle-wielding peasant woman reaping corn on *A Broken Frame.* The notion of Depeche Mode as long-term harbingers of a new political consciousness was difficult for many critics to accept, but you could not argue with the evidence of your own eyes . . . could you?

<129>

Certainly a Belgian television producer felt that it was an open-and-shut case, taking *Construction Time Again*'s implied message so literally that when the band arrived at TV studios, they were presented with an enormous haystack upon which they were expected to perform. Around them, red flags fluttered in the breeze, and an army of peasants stood ready to wave hammers and sickles at the cameras.

The band was stunned. "We can't do *that!*"

The producer looked surprised. "Whyever not?"

"Because . . ." the band was sputtering. Why *couldn't* they do it? "Because!" With the best socialist will in the world, the imagery around which they were expected to cavort was simply too strong, too loaded, too *clichéd!*

They tried to explain, but the producer simply looked bored. "Oh, it's okay." Gesturing at the arrayed hammers, sickles, and red flags, he shrugged and, confusing the band's musical simplicity with intellectual inanity, he continued, "It doesn't have the same meaning over here!"

Dave, recounting the incident months later, was still in shock. "You've got twenty-foot red flags behind you, and all these heroic peasants, and they expect you to believe it doesn't have any meaning! Unbelievable!"

Depeche Mode's outlook had nevertheless changed considerably since the days, less than two years previous, when Dave blithely boasted to visiting journalists, "We don't have political views . . . I don't think." Musically and visually, *Construction Time Again* was a rallying call to Britain's hitherto voiceless, disaffected masses.

Arguing that "it's more important to sing about something of substance than sing about nonsense," Dave believed *Construction Time Again* worked because "it wasn't hard-hitting or trying to ram messages down people's throats, it was a social awareness that just came out of noticing what was happening in places we were visiting. If you're in a band in our position, you're in a very strong position to write about those things, so why not do it?"

<130>

He laughed; he was well aware that "a lot of people just expected us to sing about nonsense," and Depeche Mode was singing about things that are important. "But we're doing it subtly. If you're coming out as a hard force and really screaming about it, I think it scares people."

The first of the new songs to escape the studio, however, was not subtle. With its genesis in the band's visit to the Far East earlier in the year, and their firsthand experience of the havoc that unbridled capitalism can wreak on developing and developed nation alike, "Everything Counts" was a barely disguised condemnation of all multinational businesses—including those lining up to purchase majority shares in Britain's industrial sell-off.

"The grabbing hands grab all they can," the velvet vocals intoned in the song's opening minute. "Everything counts in large amounts." Such sentiments clashed vividly with the hint of autobiography with which the lyric opened: the simple handshake that had sealed Depeche Mode's own contract with Mute.

Where "Everything Counts" differed from the plethora of similarly intentioned "anthems" that past years had seen foisted upon the listening public was in its very delivery. Other artists all but built their careers around their beliefs—the Clash, Paul Weller, Gang of Four, and Billy Bragg were all, more or less, so enslaved by their own long-standing and much-publicized politics, that their words were almost disregarded by the listening public: Ah, they're just being *angry* again.

When Depeche Mode raised their voice, they brought new weight to the equation, and though Dave tried to convince X. Moore that "with ['Everything Counts'], people cotton on to the tune and the beat and later they listen to the lyric and hear something more," in reality, the song's intentions were evident from the first—were, if anything, amplified, "because people don't associate us with those sort of sentiments at all."

<|3|>

But when Moore asked whether Depeche Mode would allow itself to be associated with any of the political movements that were forever courting the rock establishment—CND and the antiracist lobby included—Dave simply shrugged resignedly. "Maybe we would. But most times we wouldn't even get asked."

Besides, by the end of 1983, Depeche Mode's political stance had already been overshadowed by a group of actors from the left-wing theater group 7:84 (named, in 1974, for the 7 percent of the population who controlled 84 percent of Britain's wealth).

The Flying Pickets became the first band ever to top the British charts with an a cappella song. But it was nothing less than savage irony that demanded that the song to give them such a resounding success should be "Only You"—the same Vince Clarke–composed "Only You" that Depeche Mode had turned down just two years before.

Chapter < 8 >

We've Still Got a Long Way to Go Before People Will Be *Proud* to Have Depeche Mode Albums in Their Collection (*or*, We Hate Everyone Under Twenty)

CONSTRUCTION TIME AGAIN was the most intricate project Depeche Mode had yet attempted, so intricate that it swiftly outgrew the twenty-four-track Garden studios where the band was working. Tempers were fraying, patience was running out. When engineer Gareth Jones suggested that the entire proceedings be relocated to Berlin's Hansa Mischraum studios, home to what was then the only commercially available fifty-six-track mixing desk in the world, the band jumped at the chance.

Ever since David Bowie immortalized it on his 1977 *Heroes* album, Hansa has been regarded among the world's most influential studios. It stood just five hundred yards from the Berlin Wall; through its windows, the musicians and their crew could see the patrolling border guards watching them through binoculars, their Kalishnakovs slung across their shoulders. According to Bowie's producer, Tony Visconti, the atmosphere of the studio was "so provocative, so stimulating, and so frightening that the band played with an incredible amount of energy, because . . . I think they just wanted to go home!"

It was this sense of menace and oppression that Depeche Mode wanted to capture, the claustrophobia that would bring a new dimension to the music they were recording. And that, in turn, was a conscious effort to finally raise the band out of the teenybop milieu that, incredibly, many people still insisted on placing them in.

It was embarrassing, all four members concurred, to be performing a song like "Shame," its resigned acceptance of the world's wrongs as affecting as any bleeding-heart condemnation of starvation and deprivation, in front of an arena full of screaming girls—to still, after all this time, be answering questions about their favorite color. To the serious "rock fan," Depeche Mode's reputation still stunk—and they knew it.

"We've still got a long way to go before people will be *proud* to have Depeche Mode albums in their collection," Fletch sighed wearily, and despite the generally encouraging (if not altogether understanding) reviews garnered by *Construction Time Again,* the band members remained unhappy.

On the surface, measured by both its critical reception and its chart performance (it reached number six in the U.K.), *Construction Time Again* appeared to have registered the crossover hit Depeche Mode was yearning for, spinning off a major hit single ("Everything Counts" also hit sixth place), at the same time establishing the group as one that could compete in the album market.

But the accompanying tour, which carried the group through the fall of 1983, proved that far from abating, Depeche Mode's teen following had swollen even further.

Part of this, the band members conceded, was Depeche Mode's own fault. Acknowledging that "we're suc-

<134>

cessful, but we're not hugely successful," Alan admitted to *Record Mirror* that the group still worried that "if we took a year off, we'd come back and nobody would remember us." So Depeche Mode ensured that they remained in the public eye, turning up on British television's predominantly children-oriented Saturday-morning variety shows in spite of their own belief that such things were an embarrassment.

They complied when a sixteen-year-old fan wrote to the television program "Jim'll Fix It," through whose auspices youngsters had their dreams come true, asking to meet them. They went along with the teen press's requests for printed impressions of their lips. They smiled and simpered for the cameras. "It'd be nice not to have to do that sort of thing," mused Martin, but as Fletch pointed out, "We do like to sell records, so we have to go through with all that . . ." No matter what the cost.

<135>

And if Depeche Mode's lyrics were becoming increasingly world-weary and mature, that just added a new dimension to the equation—suddenly, Depeche Mode was the "thinking screamer's band," and the relative failure of their next single, "Love, in Itself" did not deflect that strangely backhanded compliment.

Described by *Melody Maker* as drawing a "final line [with] its apparent rejection of so much pop," the single struggled to reach even a lowly number twenty-one—a long way from the lofty Top Five peaks that Vince Clarke was now scaling with Assembly, a one-off project that paired Depeche Mode's old songwriter with Feargal Sharkey. Martin laughed when the subject came up in conversation. "Good old Vince— he always did know what the kiddies wanted. We don't have a clue!"

But that didn't stop them screaming. In Germany, home to so much of their recent inspiration, *Construction Time Again* finally sent Depeche Mode racing across the line between stardom and *super*stardom—with all the aches and pains that entails.

In Munich, a drunken Austrian businessman recognized Depeche Mode in a hotel bar, and immediately picked a fight because he didn't like their haircuts. And when the Frankfurt-based experimentalists KMFDM—their name originally an acronym for the somewhat bombastic Kein Mittleid für die Mehrheit, "No Pity for The Majority"—asked their audience for their own interpretation of the initials, the band's own favorite was "Kill Motherfucking Depeche Mode."

"You can see something's happening, that we're building," Fletch remarked shortly before the German release of *Construction Time Again.* "We can see ourselves getting bigger every time we come over here to play." Now they were at the level where even the gossip columnists knew who they were, and they became fair game for the most scurrilous rumors as well.

<156>

When Depeche Mode refused to be interviewed on Germany's "Bravo" TV pop show, the program's sister magazine immediately circulated the rumor that at the end of every performance, Dave was carried offstage, taken to a separate dressing room, and kept supplied with constant fluids.

It was, Martin swore, a cruel exaggeration. "When we're on tour, which is generally very boring, we—or *some* of us—tend to go out every night, have a lot to drink, and generally have a good time. Going out *is* enjoyable, drinking *is* enjoyable, and collapsing *is* enjoyable." Depeche Mode just happened to be doing a lot of all three, and Dave proudly confessed to single-handedly downing a bottle of brandy on either side of each show. "But being *carried* offstage? I can hold my drink better than that!"

It was *Bravo* magazine, too, that concocted an interview in which Depeche Mode claimed to hate everybody under the age of twenty—"which made us very popular with their readership," Fletch sarcastically explained.

That particular breach was obviously repaired fairly swiftly, and *Construction Time Again* went on to dominate the German charts for over a year. More important, however, the band's live performances were both enthusiastically *and* respectfully attended. For the first time on a major European stage, Depeche Mode was able to hear itself play, without first having to filter out the keening of several thousand howling scream-agers.

Germany also provided the group with some new visual images. The "Everything Counts" video was shot in Berlin, under the supervision of director Clive Richardson, at that time enjoying a wave of phenomenal success with his work for Siouxsie and the Banshees and the now fully chart-integrated Blancmange.

The video was remarkably simplistic, but it remains among Depeche Mode's most enduringly popular—and strangely controversial. Several scenes included shots of a shawm, the Chinese oboe whose sound was re-created—through the Synclavier, of course—on the record. The moment the video aired, Martin revealed, "people wrote to us to say they felt cheated that we hadn't spent three months learning how to play the shawm!"

The complaints highlighted an ever-broadening gulf between bands like Depeche Mode, who had so fully embraced the new musical technologies, and the "old guard"—musicians who were, for want of a better word, *real* musicians, versed in the intricacies of guitars, drums, and bass.

For them, the advent of sampling spelled considerably more than the opening up of new audio frontiers. They felt threatened, and understandably so, by the ease with which a machine could now replicate any sound, including that of other instruments. Reacting with a fury that the music press—jokingly at first, but with increasing sincerity as time passed—compared to the Luddites of industrial-revolutionary Britain, many musicians formed a loose coalition whose stated aim was best illustrated by the stickers that suddenly began appearing on flight cases and amplifiers: Keep Music Live.

At a grass-roots level, several venues got so heavily behind the movement that synthesizer bands were all but banned from many traditional rock venues.

The Musicians' Union itself took a firm stance behind the traditionalists. Among the many samples Depeche Mode intended using on their forthcoming album were a series of percussive notes that they obtained by inviting a noted drum collector along to the studio and having him play a single beat on each one.

"There's no doubt that he understood what we were doing," Alan complained. "Then he sent us a bill for sampling fee, consultancy fee—God knows what else. He'd been talking to the MU, who'd obviously convinced him that what we were doing was totally immoral, and he charged us six times the amount we'd agreed."

<138>

With the self-righteous shortsightedness of the true acolyte, Martin and Alan furiously defended Depeche Mode's use of sampling—and everybody else's. "We'd be quite happy for people to nick our sounds and sample them." Alan admitted that Depeche Mode had already lifted a drum beat from a Frankie Goes to Hollywood single, and added it to one of their recent twelve-inch remixes.

"I don't think you can stand in the way of technology—you've just got to have the ideas and the imagination to put it to original use."

Which is what Depeche Mode had done with the shawm. It was such an esoteric instrument, Martin reasoned, that it was highly unlikely the band would ever use that sound again. What, then, was the point of learning to play the thing, simply for the refrain of one single song?

His opponents responded with equal zeal—today the shawm, tomorrow the guitar, and the next day, entire records. The argument was not even one of "musical purity"—the traditional stick with which the allegedly "unemotional" synthesizer was beaten. It came down to the preservation of an entire livelihood. Why should any band bother employing a session guitarist when they could simply feed a guitar sound into a computer and re-create the same effect in a matter of moments?

And what would happen to the session man then? He'd be on the scrapheap, just another archaic craftsman to turn up on television documentaries, demonstrating how to spend three weeks doing something by hand that a machine could do in three minutes. The sentiments that Queen had invoked on their earliest albums—proudly proclaiming, "No Synthesizers!"—had unexpectedly exploded into the common consciousness.

Moving with the tide, several hitherto synthesized bands did begin experimenting with other instruments—the Human League, for instance, reintroduced guitars to their lineup.

<139>

Depeche Mode, however, was not budging; indeed, Martin went out of his way to provoke further ill feeling when he appeared on German television with a guitar slung around his neck, miming to the samples that Daniel Miller had programmed into "Love, in Itself." With sidesplitting irony, the performance was to be aired immediately before a guitar duel between Pink Floyd's Dave Gilmore and Bad Company's Mick Ralphs.

"Rock musicians say you can't express yourself with a synthesizer," Martin argued. " 'Soulless' is the word [they use]. But what is there in whacking a guitar? Every heavy-metal riff is near enough the same anyway." It wasn't that musicians were not as good as machines, he laughed. But machines were certainly better than musicians.

The only area in which Depeche Mode conceded that their reliance upon synthesizers left them at a disadvantage was visual. Despite some quite astonishing onstage lighting trickery, Martin admitted that he could see "that people are maybe a bit bored watching Depeche Mode prancing around three synthesizers."

But on the other hand, "I wouldn't want us looking like every other rock band!" The solution to this dilemma, carved out during the group's winter 1983 return to Berlin, was to create a whole new stage setup, one that would add fresh fuel to the fire of man-versus-machinery. Daniel Miller and Gareth Jones were already ensconced at Hansa, completing Fad Gadget's latest album, *Gag;* while Depeche Mode awaited their turn in the studio, Martin's imagination ran riot.

The images that danced in his mind were of a stage on which the band members themselves became little more than samples, acting out routines dictated by their surroundings. Before that could be unveiled, however, Depeche Mode needed to create an appropriate musical environment.

<140>

Depeche Mode's latest Berlin sojourn coincided with the final leg of their European tour, a frenzy of German shows that led right up to Christmas, and the opportunity to run wild in the studio was as therapeutic as it was creative.

"It had got very difficult to do something different [onstage] every night," Dave admitted. "My mind used to drift sometimes and I'd forget the words!"

He would have no such trouble with the song the band was now working on for release in March 1984 as the band's next single. Reveling in an almost demonic simplicity, "People Are People" was nothing more or less than a plainspoken call for unity and equality—which made it all the more ironic that while his bandmates worked on what Martin was describing as "a song about all sorts of differences between people, not just racism," Fletch was coming dangerously close to blows with Daniel Miller.

Fletch's position within Depeche Mode had become increasingly nebulous over the years. He had never played a defining role within the band's creative process, had never really wanted to. While first Vince, and now Martin, prepared the actual songs; while Alan arranged them and Dave—simply by singing—interpreted them, Fletch often found himself simply an intermediary between three often overpowering egos, a deciding vote when opinions were split, a voice of reason when tempers flared.

It was a comfortable position, an extension, in many ways, of his continued involvement in the band's business affairs. Fletch was unconsumed by the musical passions that fired his bandmates, and the flashes of fury to which he occasionally gave vent were rarely inspired by musical frustrations. So when they erupted, people remembered them.

This particular evening, Martin and Fletch were goofing around in the studio, "trying out self-defense on each other," as Martin guiltily imparted. The game was not particularly rough, but of course it involved much flailing of limbs and unconcerned leaping about, with little apparent regard for the thousands of dollars' worth of equipment that stood around the room.

<|4|>

Daniel, reentering the room from an errand somewhere, took in the scene in a moment and exploded. But while Martin contritely left the scene, Fletch stood his ground, barking his own anger. Swiftly Alan and Dave moved to defuse the situation, but afterward, neither could forget what they had seen: Fletch, his face red with rage, one fist drawn back to strike Miller; Daniel, white-faced and trembling, ready to reply in kind.

The incident was trivial, but it spoke volumes, not only of the tense rivalry that was slowly building between Daniel and Fletch—the unwilling manager and his unwitting rival—but also the pressures that surrounded Depeche Mode as a whole.

Although Martin was adamant that they were no longer the eager-to-please puppy dogs who once "just did anything that came along, the first video script, the first TV show," he was constantly aware that whatever Depeche Mode did would come in for the most intense scrutiny. It was, he commented privately, almost as if people wanted the group to fail, but enjoyed seeing them succeed because it made the waiting just that little bit more enjoyable.

"We don't fit people's preconceived notions of a 'serious' band, and a lot of people don't like that. So they are always looking for cracks, signs that we're still the funny little things we used to be."

He elaborated on this shortly after the release of "People Are People" ("and spiders are hairy," as the *Bury Free Press* reviewer cynically added).

"When people say you're a serious band, they think you don't have a good time anymore, that you walk around all the time with your cheeks sucked in, things like that. But we don't. We're still exactly the same."

The group's secret, if such it was, was Mute Records' setup. Over the previous three years, Mute had grown into one of the most successful independent companies of the early Eighties. Even though the label's hits-to-releases ratio had dipped in the past twelve months, thanks largely to the 1983 demise of Yazoo and its only-partial replacement by Vince's Assembly, Mute's 1.4 percent share of Britain's still-lucrative singles market was bettered by only one other contender in a field now overflowing with independent labels: Stiff Records, home to Madness, Kirsty MacColl, and Tracey Ullman.

<142>

But success did not go to the label's head. Daniel continued to people his release schedules with the bizarre and the brilliant (an Einstürzende Neubauten anthology; a single pairing Fad Gadget with the Birthday Party's Rowland Howard; and another that matched Nick Cave's growl with Elvis Presley's finest hour, a seething version of "In the Ghetto"), continued to treat his artists like human beings first, sellable product a very distant second.

In the past, it had been common practice among even the most established record companies for new bands to be eased into circulation gradually, each new single racking up a wealth of fresh experiences that would eventually be applied toward making an album—the same process, of course, by which Depeche Mode learned their trade.

By the early 1980s, however, singles had simply become things to be pulled from an album and flung into the marketplace, which in turn meant that many new acts were recording LPs before the general public had even heard them play! The results, all too often, were cruelly inevitable—a killer single surrounded by eleven passable B-sides. And then, if the bands did not attain certain commercial standards within a set period of time—and retain them for the rest of their days—they would be dropped, just another unknown casualty in the bargain bins.

Even after the successes they had already garnered, Depeche Mode knew that a "conventional" label would have fought furiously against the growth they had exhibited over the past year—would have pointed accusingly at the band's declin- <143> ing singles performances and suggested, politely, of course, that maybe Martin should write something "a little more catchy."

The almost wholly percussive "People Are People," of course, fit that bill so comfortably that many outsiders suggested that the band had finally gone too far even for Daniel Miller's liberated presidency. Martin was swift to scotch that rumor—and several more, besides.

"Through being with Mute, we were given a chance to develop in our own time, without being manipulated." And that meant both manipulated musically, and in terms of "product"—that cruelly artless term that the 1980s had developed to describe a band's output.

In the year since Depeche Mode first began experimenting with limited-edition twelve-inch singles, the marketplace had exploded with similarly intentioned gimmickry. Picture discs, shaped vinyl, and the like now flowed from every direction, and unquestionably played their part in increasing a new release's profile—so much so that by the early 1990s, the compilers of the U.K. charts, the Gallup pollsters, announced that henceforth no more than three permutations of a single release would be reckoned into their calculations.

Depeche Mode, unwitting pioneers of this alarming new fashion, now prided themselves on remaining outside of it. Mute, as Martin proudly put it, never pressured them into "giving away posters or free singles or anything like that." When the band remixed a single, "We [made] sure it *is* something that gives value for money."

"People Are People" certainly met that criterion. Danny Baker, writing in *NME,* adjudged "the foot-wide version" of the otherwise "puerile" song "a miraculous transormation, the nearest anyone's yet come to the perfect arc-welding of pop and industry, funk and factory."

And even better was to come. "People Are People" was among several tapes Depeche Mode handed to producer Adrian Sherwood so that he might remix them in his own inimitable fashion. ("Just Can't Get Enough," "Photographic," and an unreleased track called "Death Wish" were also included.) The ensuing twelve-inch singles defied even Depeche Mode's reputation for adventure.

<|44>

For four or five years now, Adrian Sherwood had reigned supreme as Britain's premier underground dance producer, his On-U Sound studio pioneering the application of solid-dub techniques to other musical disciplines. But even at his finest—Judy Nylon's 1982 album, *Pal Joey,* for instance—Sherwood remained little more than a cult favorite, and a shadowy one at that. According to legend, Depeche Mode themselves barely met Sherwood—"He just disappeared into the studio with the tapes." He emerged with "Are People People?"—an unrecognizable deconstruction of the year's most easily identified hit.

Of course, the dominant instrument on "People Are People" was the Synclavier, but the sounds it regurgitated were again far removed from standard rock 'n' roll soundtracks—an airline stewardess running through the pre-takeoff safety drill; a bass drum hit with a piece of metal "to give it more attack," as Martin explained; and an acoustic guitar plucked with a German coin.

"We made a conscious decision to become harder musically," Alan explained to *Record Mirror,* and this time, even the inclusion of some gently tinkling bells could not derail the band. "So we thought, What sounds really hard and nasty?—and of course we decided on metal." And while some observers gleefully reboarded the old anti-Mode bandwagon—painting the band with the new, if somewhat oxymoronic accusation, "a smoothed out SPK"—*NME*'s Don Watson offered the band a perfect defense.

"Anyone who has heard SPK's continuing deterioration is aware that they are struggling towards the form of commerciality that Depeche achieve with the grace of second nature," said Watson. And not the other way around—a point which "People Are People" proved perfectly. In Germany, the single clanged, hammered, and banged its way straight to number one, remaining there for the next three weeks.

In the United States, "People Are People" became Depeche Mode's first-ever Top Forty entry, tearing up to number thirteen on the back of MTV's adoption of the song's characteristically vivid video, filmed aboard the floating museum on the World War II battleship HMS *Belfast,* with images of moving anchor chains and capstans synchronized with the harsh metallics of the backing track.

The single's success even prompted Sire to release a new Depeche Mode album, a compilation of album cuts and twelve-inch singles titled after the hit. It, too, became the group's biggest U.S. hit yet—albeit a lowly number 166—and to American reviewers whose working knowledge of the group went beyond the essentials presented in the accompanying press releases, the twin successes vindicated three or four years of championing; to those who had hitherto written Depeche

Mode off unheard, as one more set of sallow teabags ("Why don't you use guitars?"), it was a moment of critical redefinition.

Britain, too, clasped "People Are People" firmly to its heart, giving Depeche Mode their highest-ever chart entry (number twenty-two), their fastest Top Tenner (the very next week), and their biggest-ever hit—within a month of release, "People Are People" was sitting at number four.

Ahead of it, only the combined weight of Shakin' Stevens, the Thompson Twins, and Lionel Ritchie's unstoppable "Hello" kept Depeche Mode from rising any further, a feat made all the more remarkable by the band's refusal to make more than one live appearance in the U.K. during the single's lifetime: a one-off gig in Birmingham, filmed for broadcast by BBC TV's "Oxford Road" show, in April.

<166> But if "People Are People" was surprising, its B-side, Alan's "In Your Memory," was even more so. Its harsh melody line was almost theoretical, carried wholly by Dave's voice in strict opposition to the direction taken by the backing track. As a one-off excursion into almost purely percussive territory, it was a fascinating exercise, but for Depeche Mode themselves, it was a creative cul-de-sac. It was supremely ironic, then, that while they retreated, the field was left open instead for their most enduring rivals, Duran Duran.

Over the past year, Duran Duran's fortunes had fluctuated almost as wildly as Depeche Mode's, and for many of the same reasons. Eager to pull away from their own teenbait reputation, Duran Duran had launched into a brief and remarkably unsuccessful flirtation with the same kind of muted maturity as Spandau Ballet—now purveyors of achingly lush ballads. But while Spandau Ballet enjoyed their biggest hits yet, Duran Duran was rewarded not only with the lowest-selling singles of their career to date, but also with their most unsuccessful album yet, the aptly titled *Seven and the Ragged Tiger*.

Reinventing themselves at the speed of thought,

Duran Duran bounced back overnight: "The Reflex" possessed a metallic harshness a million miles removed from either the accepted or the expected Duran Duran sound, and gave the group its first number one in over a year. Emboldened, the group leaped out next with the epic "Wild Boys," a musical tangent that could only have been suggested by Depeche Mode; did, in fact, openly borrow many of their techniques.

Depeche Mode, however, was in no mood for battle. By the time "Wild Boys" hit the streets that fall, Depeche Mode's Berlin sessions had thrown up the song that, released as a single in August 1984, was to define Depeche Mode's own new stance—and leave their competition in the dust once again.

A study of sexual domination, twisting from bedroom to boardroom, "Master and Servant" rode in on an a cappella falsetto, as breezy as any intro in Depeche Mode's canon. It was only as the lyric unfolded over a crashing soundtrack of dragging chains and cracking whips (actually Daniel Miller hissing and spitting), that the veneer of pure pop sweetness fell away.

<147>

Not for the first time, Depeche Mode had shifted the pop goalposts, but the musical discomfort to which they had hitherto subjected their more impressionable listeners was nothing compared to the deliberately unequivocable shock treatment of the lascivious "Master and Servant."

Stunned, even shocked by the song, watching journalists described Depeche Mode, dramatically, as "the most subversive pop group around." "Master and Servant" would have made a dangerous choice for release even by an established pop dissident. Coming from a band that would be promoting their product in the teen-scream press, it was unheard of.

Discussing Depeche Mode's first attempts to break the teenybop mold, Alan admitted that "we're in the position where we know we're going to get a certain amount of airplay just on the strength of reputation," and although neither Depeche Mode nor Mute had any compunction whatsoever about releasing "Master and Servant" as a single, the day that the BBC's Radio One called the office demanding a copy of the lyrics was a fraught one.

Nineteen eighty-four was the year in which British pop was given a major lesson in morality after Frankie Goes to Hollywood's "Relax" was banned from daytime BBC airplay because of the supposedly explicit sexuality of its lyrics. "It's not what they say," a BBC spokesman admitted, "it's the way that they say it."

"Relax" went on to become the year's third-biggest single, a direct consequence of the ban. Few things arouse the British record-buying public's curiosity so quickly as being imperiously forbidden to hear a certain record, and immediately the warning bells began ringing through a red-faced BBC.

<148>

This was not, after all, the first time that a major hit had resulted from a radio ban. As far back as 1964, Twinkle's "Terry" rose to number four after the BBC rejected its ghoulish depiction of a fatal motorcycle accident. A decade later, an English deejay named Judge Dread enjoyed a staggering run of ten Top Fifty hits without *once* getting his distorted versions of popular nursery rhymes past the vigilant censors! Indeed, in a bizarre twist on Depeche Mode's belief that they were guaranteed radio play on the strength of their reputation, Dread was guaranteed *not* to receive any, for the same reason. His first-ever "clean" single, "Molly," was also outlawed!

In the post-Frankie dawn, the BBC finally woke up to a fact outside observers had long believed true (and which statistics certainly proved): that a ban actually heightened a record's profile. From now on, it was decreed, no record would be banned. If the BBC didn't like it, they simply wouldn't play it—a fate that already befell upward of four hundred new singles every week of the year. There would be no fuss, no publicity, and, it was hoped, no more dirty-minded pop groups going out of their way to be shocking.

According to Dave, the BBC's concerns over the suitability of "Master and Servant" were held by just one staff member, albeit a senior one. It was fortunate, then, that he was away on vacation during the week the final decision over the song was taken. With perhaps just a hint of knowing irony, Dave explained to *Melody Maker*, "The girl who took the decision agreed with us that it's [a song] about love and life, which of course it is." And in case there were any lingering comparisons to be made between "Master and Servant" and Frankie's "Relax," he added, " 'Master and Servant' is a bit more subtle than 'Relax,' but then it's got a very different point to make. . . ."

Mining that same sense of irony, Martin continued, "It wasn't that big a fuss. If you call yourself a pop band in England, you can get away with murder!"

With its innocence now proven, "Master and Servant" lost no time in racing into the U.K. Top Ten. (It also breached the American Top 100.) For the band, however, the performance of their latest single was of considerably less im- <149> portance than the fate awaiting their next album, *Some Great Reward*.

According to Martin, *Some Great Reward* was the first album the band members were unanimously "really proud of," and though he acknowledged that "we went over the top really, and it cost us," in terms of both time and money, in terms of production and presentation, *Some Great Reward* was a flawless effort.

It even became a favorite among hi-fi-showroom employees, the sheer depth of sound putting their equipment through paces that challenged even Pink Floyd's *Dark Side of the Moon*—the grandfather of stereo-demonstration records. Indeed, *Some Great Reward* remains the first *true* Depeche Mode album—the first on which the band had fully absorbed the experiences and experiments that, on earlier recordings, were obviously as novel to them as they were to the audience.

"What makes *Some Great Reward* a good LP," declared *NME*'s Don Watson, "is a scattering of irony and a search for diversity in the sound." There was a fresh honesty, too, to the lyrics; without abandoning the often-overt politics of *Construction Time Again,* Martin's latest songs honed in on considerably more specific targets, and retained a sense of the ridiculous as well.

Buried amid the epics of social, sexual, and religious imagery, which were the album's most obvious point of entry, a self-indulgent humor smirked slyly through the gathering gloom, derailing the darkness with what Fletch described as "things that you'd hear people saying in Basildon, but not so much elsewhere. Most of them are quite humorous, but people don't get them—particularly if they're not Basos [local slang for Basildon's natives]. "Things like 'the world we live in and life in general' [a quote from "Somebody," reprinted on the album's jacket]. People really seem to think we're serious when we write things like that." It was an easy mistake to make, for elsewhere

<150>

on the album, Martin's questioning, questing earnestness shone like a beacon.

Nowhere was this more pronounced than on the closing cut, "Blasphemous Rumours."

In pure musical terms, "Blasphemous Rumours" was simply a reprise of the "People Are People" formula, a childishly simple lyric coupled with a powerful sentiment. But whereas "People Are People" had struck many people as perhaps *too* simple (a fate that also awaited Culture Club's "War Song," a ditty whose transparent debt to Depeche Mode's songwriting technique was on many people's lips that fall), "Blasphemous Rumours" boasted a power that wholly transcended its lyrical frailty.

Above a melody that was unquestionably as gorgeous as any Depeche Mode song since "See You," Dave related two anecdotal tales: a sixteen-year-old, "bored with life," who attempted suicide, but survived unscathed, and an eighteen-year-old who underwent a religious rebirth just days before a road accident consigned her to die on a life-support machine.

Both cases were true, and the twisted irony that linked them left Martin to draw just one conclusion: "I don't want to start any blasphemous rumours, but I think that God's got a sick sense of humor." The shit hit the fan even before Mute announced that the song would be Depeche Mode's next single.

"So many unhappy things have happened," Dave argued in the song's defense, "that I just feel [the teachings of organized Christianity] can't all be true." It wasn't an antireligion song—"It's a statement of how everybody must feel at one time or another."

The rumor circulated among Depeche Mode's fan club that the song was, in truth, inspired by the suicide of one of Martin's own closest family members, but the song's real genesis lay in an experience both Martin and Dave have lain claim to in different interviews.

<151>

Attending church, lyricist and vocalist alike remembered how the service always included the reading of a Prayer List for seriously ill parishioners, "and the one at the top always died," Dave said with a smirk. "But still, everyone went right ahead thanking God for carrying out his will," Martin added. "It just seemed so strange."

The response to the song, of course, was swift and—somewhat ironically, in the light of standard Christian teachings—unforgiving. Within weeks of *Melody Maker* citing "Blasphemous Rumours" as "a prime candidate for official censure," Mary Whitehouse, the self-appointed moral watchdog of Britain's media; the Independent Broadcasting Authority, her government-appointed counterpart; and the notorious *Sun* tabloid newspaper all raised their voices in condemnation of the song.

The Church itself took the rare step of speaking out against the song. "If we can say God so loved the world that He sent His only son," a Basildon priest sputtered indignantly to the Southend press, "if He did that, He cannot have a sick sense of humor."

We've Still Got a Long Way to Go

Still affecting calm, Mute approached the BBC to find out what their stance would be. The response was not particularly reassuring—the broadcaster simply pointed out that not *every* new single could be played on the radio. Mute was left with no misapprehensions whatsoever concerning the single's potential fate.

But Depeche Mode remained adamant that "Blasphemous Rumours" was to be their next single, and in the ensuing battle of moral rectitude and commercial responsibility, there could be only one winner—compromise. The band's traditional policy of reserving their B-sides for more experimental, non-album tracks was halted; instead, "Somebody" was culled from *Some Great Reward,* and the new single was presented as a double A-side.

"Somebody"/"Blasphemous Rumours" reached number sixteen, a poor showing by recent Depeche Mode standards, but more than reasonable for what were already two-month-old album tracks. Even more surprising, the BBC's original hesitance had completely disappeared, and in September, Depeche Mode performed "Blasphemous Rumours" on that grand old bastion of pop respectability, "Top of the Pops."

Afterward, the band told *The Face,* there was "a barrage of complaints and a reprimand for [TOTP producer] Michael Hurll." But the single continued to sell, so maybe, Depeche Mode mused, "Blasphemous Rumours" really did strike a responsive chord in its listeners' hearts. Either that or people simply bought it for its catchy chorus.

Whatever its audience's motives, there was still something both poignant and powerful about "Blasphemous Rumours" climbing the British Top Thirty at precisely the same time British television brought the world its first footage of the dreadful famine that had stricken Ethiopia—a predominantly Christian nation.

A year earlier, Alan had reminded *New Musical Express* that "if the world stopped spending all the money it spends on arms for just two weeks, you could feed the starving

<152>

millions for two years." There was little consolation for him to see his sentiments now repeated word for word, on TV and in tabloid alike. And a decade on, it still appears strange that of the dozens of pop and rock groups that Bob Geldof recruited for his Band Aid (and later, Live Aid) project, Depeche Mode was conspicuously absent.

Their undeniable status among Britain's chart elite notwithstanding, the band's reputation for "social awareness" was second to none—certainly it was higher than that of such flash-in-the-pan participants as the one-hit wonder who allegedly responded to the invitation to "do something for Ethiopia" by asking, "I didn't know I sold records in Ethiopia!"

Yet public politics (or the lack thereof!) were only part of the Band Aid criteria. Private politics, too, played an inestimable role, and whether Depeche Mode's absence from the Band Aid roster was a conscious snub or not, it remained wry justification of the off-the-cuff response Dave offered journalist X. Moore when asked whether the band would ever pledge itself to a political movement: "I don't think we'd even be asked."

<153>

Depeche Mode salved their pride by condemning the events of the next six weeks—the chart-topping "Do They Know It's Christmas" and "We Are the World" celebrity megabashes, and the Live Aid television circus—as little more than a brilliantly executed marketing device.

Almost every band involved in the London and Philadelphia Live Aid concerts experienced a massive surge in record sales, an inevitable consequence of appearing on so gigantic a stage in front of so many viewers, and Martin spoke for many observers when he asked, "If all these bands really care so much [for these causes], they should just donate the money and let that be it. Why can't they just do it without all the surrounding hype?"

His cynicism, however, disguised a certain bitterness. For all their success, for all their progress, too, Depeche Mode were still considered outsiders. The question that re-

We've Still Got a Long Way to Go

mained to be answered as the band entered its sixth year was whether they intended to remain there.

Asked that question, Depeche Mode kept their own counsel. Only Fletch showed a flicker of interest. He had discovered a new hobby, he imparted, one even more enthralling than Space Invaders. It was a board game called Risk, and its object was to achieve total world domination.

<154>

Chapter 9

For God's Sake, Stop Putting Out Records!

THE YOUNG MAN walking through customs had gone out of his way to appear instantly noticeable, and the excise men were not about to disappoint him. A quiff of hair, bleached painfully blond, exploded from a single point on an otherwise shaven scalp, as though, someone observed, it were toothpaste oozing through a hole in his head. He wore too much makeup, his nails were painted a chipped black, and he wore a matching leather dress. Once they'd overcome their initial shock—and customs officials have seen so much, it's not too easy to shock them—two guards swooped.

"Would you step this way, please?"

The apparition stopped and looked at them through hooded eyes. Definitely too much makeup. "Is there a problem?"

"We'd just like you to step this

way." They gestured toward a pair of cubicles at the back of the hall, screened from the general public's view. Then, as a third official approached, a broad, bearlike woman whose love for her job clearly took second place to her love of strip-searching weirdos, the guards halted.

"Just one thing, though. Would you prefer we used the men's cubicle? Or the women's?"

The apparition simpered sweetly. Martin *loved* it when they asked him that question!

When the first photographs appeared of Martin wearing a tiny leather minidress, stepping up to the microphone to perform his solo vocal debut, the aching "Somebody," it raised few eyebrows. Recent years had seen "gender-bending"— as perfected by Boy George, Marilyn, and Pete Burns—reach chart-topping proportions. One more cross-dressing pop star, even one who decked himself in leather and wrote black odes to S&M, made little difference either way. The way in which Martin disported himself, however, did.

For a start, there appeared to be no point to it. He wasn't the band's front man; he spent most of each show hidden away behind his banks of synths. Neither, with only the most obvious exceptions, did his clothing match Depeche Mode's mood; if anything, it distracted from it. If Martin's manner met any kind of agenda at all, it was obviously a very well-hidden one. And that was the key.

Boy George, Burns, and those others then riding their frock-tails were first and foremost showmen, their glittering flamboyance that of the gaudy vaudeville stripper—titillating but ultimately harmless. They spoke of unknown pleasures, in dress and demeanor, but that was as far as they took it—a simple visual tease. Never did they pledge consummation.

By refusing outright to discuss either his sex or sensuality, by leaving it to others to interpret his actions, Martin brought a whole new dimension to the equation—a dark confusion that drew close to pure androgyny, but fell short, likewise, of making promises he couldn't, or wouldn't, be willing to keep.

<156>

"I've always admired Boy George a bit, and anyone who takes that stance to [such] an extreme," Martin told *The Face.* "We are in a position where we can influence to a certain extent—not to get everyone wearing a skirt, but it does open people up to that sort of thing slightly, especially if they're some of the macho types who like our music."

Later, Martin would deny that he wore the dress for anything but fun, but in 1984 the impact of his cross-dressing phase struck deeply, and it was not simply transvestites and bondage freaks who felt grateful to Gore for bringing their life-styles to prominence—and, by his band's own respectability, conferring a certain respectability upon them in turn. For pop fans in general, Martin was the culmination of Boy George's two-year-long tease.

It was George who took adolescent sex out of the backseat of the car and served it up on "Top of the Pops," but it was Martin who promised to show how it worked. And how-ever unwillingly (or otherwise) he did so, he made a bigger im-pact on a pubescent audience only just beginning to come to terms with their own bodies' needs and functions than anybody since David Bowie first made little boys wet their theater seats.

In an age when sex was served up to a nation's teeny-boppers in the form of vacuous teenage/teenaged idols, neatly sanitized, smart and smarmy, or through the vivacious slutti-ness of Madonna, then still struggling to shake off the disco image that initially created her, Martin Gore cut across all the barriers with nothing more than a backless dress, a contagious hookline, and the suggestion of the ability to back everything to the hilt.

To an audience almost actively encouraged to be ashamed of its feelings, he touched upon the raw nerve, the hungry energy, and the inability to channel any of it. It didn't matter whether ultimately Martin would become as untouch-able as any idol past or present. However fleetingly, he was the figurehead, and his promise was of broken taboos, not broken hearts.

For God's Sake, Stop Putting Out Records!

According to Dave, Martin's flirtation with women's clothing took shape over a considerable period of time. It was certainly not the abrupt outburst that many reviewers conjectured. As far back as Depeche Mode's first tour, Martin would talk of going onstage topless, while the rest of the group teased him for being in love with his body.

Then, one night, as Dave and Martin sat quietly talking, Martin revealed how much he enjoyed looking into a mirror just before he went onstage, and simply marveled at the sight—"Look what I'm getting away with tonight." Now, as Dave thought back over the last three years, he could trace the progression.

In old band photographs, it was always Martin who wore the makeup, and if the rest of the band encroached on his territory, maybe applied a dash of rouge and eyeliner themselves, then Martin would just slap on more. From leather trousers adorned with a pair of handcuffs, to leather trousers with a skirt on top, "he then sort of extended to just wearing a skirt."

His latest outfit, an off-the-nipple black lace slip, was found hanging on the band's tour bus one evening.

Backstage before shows, Alan, Dave, and Fletch would simply stare at him in horror. "Martin, you can't fucking wear that, man! You've got to take that off!" And Martin would just shrug and laugh. "Watch me."

On the rare occasions when outsiders did question him on the subject, Martin's reaction would be much the same: "It's no big deal." Pressed further, however, and he'd point to another of his song lyrics, "Something to Do," and its unremitting examination of small-town boredom—bring him something to do, he pledged, and he'd "gladly put your pretty dress on."

But few people did ask. "Everyone just accepts it without a thought," he said with a smirk. "They probably all think I'm a poof, anyway. But I don't think that matters in the music business."

<158>

Not in the music business, perhaps. But in Basildon, Dave couldn't help but remind Martin, "I didn't half get a lot of stick over that!"

There again, the skirt was positively modest compared with Martin's outfit the night "Somebody" was recorded. Fletch was dismissive about the song, describing it as "not *just* a love song, it's a real moon-in-June lovey-dovey love song. Martin's in love again, see?" For Martin, however, "Somebody" was considerably more than that.

After more than five years together, Martin and his long-term fiancée, Anne, had split up. The love between them had long since been replaced by the complacency bred by familiarity; according to Fletch, Martin was no longer able, or even willing, to accept the terms under which the relationship existed.

He left Anne, and left Britain, too. Now he was living in Berlin, and he had fallen in love again, with a German girl named Christina. It was to her that he dedicated "Somebody." She had, in the words of that other song, brought him something to do; now he was living up to his end of the bargain. <159>

But the dress didn't work in the recording studio. "Somebody" was such an honest song, he reminded the band, that it required an honest performance. Raw emotion demanded a raw performer.

"Some people tend to think that love songs shouldn't be treated seriously," Martin explained. "That it's only if you're writing about social problems that a song becomes serious. But the point is to see something that's important and write about it, even if it's only important to yourself." Then, stripping off all of his clothes, Martin announced that he would be performing the song naked in the Hansa studio cellar. His only concession to modesty was that Stefi Marcus, one of the assistant engineers, should be sent outside, "to check the connections."

Dutifully, if a little puzzled by the request, Marcus

left the room, checked the connections, then returned. She had no idea what Martin was planning to do; Martin had no idea she would be back in the room so soon.

Both had their peace of mind shattered the moment she reentered the studio and emitted a tiny scream at the sight of the full-frontal Gore, lost in the throes of his solo vocal debut. Seated at the piano, Alan simply grinned and kept on playing; afterward, Dave remarked that if the rest of *Some Great Reward* had been completed as swiftly as "Somebody," "we might actually stand to make some money from the record."

The rest of Depeche Mode viewed Martin's relocation to Berlin, and the changes that followed it, with patient calm. Just months before he broke up with Anne, Martin laughingly reminded *Melody Maker* that though Basildon was not "the center of the world," it was very hard to get away from. "Vince Clarke moved to Walton-on-Thames and even that was too far away! He's thinking of coming back to Basildon."

<180>

Berlin, Dave sniggered, was even farther, in every sense of the word. It was another world entirely, a world peopled by the colorful late-night denizens of the all-night clubs and bars. No one is certain which came first, the decadence or the decadents, but by the early 1980s, Berlin—once the political capital of Germany—was the counterculture capital of Europe: the gay capital, the drug capital, the avant-garde capital.

Its best-known clubs were the weird ones: Romy Haag's notorious, eponymous drag club, and the infamous Twenties transvestite theme bar, Lutzower Laupse; the tiny gay clubs that pocked Motz and Keiststrasse; Minks, the white neon, white-tiled basement, which even its regulars knew as "the Toilet." It was all a long way from Basildon; a long way, too, from the cream of London's nightlife—Le Kilt and St. Moritz, the Embassy, and so on. Martin adored the place.

"He's just being the way he always wanted to be," Dave reasoned. Martin and Anne had been going steady since they were at school, so "he missed out on his teens, missed out on just going out, seeing different girls every night and getting drunk all the time. He's living that now. It's not a bad thing—everybody should go through that phase."

"Adding psychiatry to his list of accomplishments," as *NME* writer Danny Kelly jokingly noted, Dave continued, "he has totally changed. Martin says that he hates going into the street and feeling normal. As soon as he gets into a normal situation, he gets scared. Personally, I think he's just doing all the things I did when I was sixteen. All that stuff about boredom is exactly the attitude I went through; I went to clubs with people much older than myself. I wore tons of makeup and dresses too. . . ."

But not every day, not on the streets, and certainly not in foreign customs halls.

Depeche Mode visited a lot of customs halls as 1984–85 unfolded. They had, to their not-altogether-concealed disgust, settled comfortably into the single-album–tour–new-single routine, the lot of every band whose appeal was now too great for them to still be struggling, but still too small for them to start taking interminable breaks between records.

<161>

A U.K. tour that included four long-since sold-out nights at the inevitable Hammersmith Odeon (and a show in Liverpool that was recorded for future B-sides and bonus tracks) was followed by another full-scale European outing. And after that, it was off to America. As he studied the itinerary, even the normally indomitable Dave felt exhausted.

"The fewer gigs you do on a tour, the more you enjoy yourself," he complained to *Melody Maker*. "There are a few days off, but the gigs are mostly back-to-back—when we do get a day off, it's always a Sunday in Hanley. Have you ever been to Hanley on a Sunday? You look at a couple of antique shops, you wander about thinking, What the hell can I do? You go back to the hotel and watch a couple of videos. It's awful!"

But work could provide an escape if they let it, and as Depeche Mode headed out on the road, the very logistics of this latest tour were more than enough to occupy them.

For God's Sake, Stop Putting Out Records!

The stage show they had conceived the previous year in Berlin had finally reached fruition. Working with designer Jane Spiers, the band designed a moving stage set, fully re-creating a factory scene, complete with sliding screens and scaffolding and suspended metal sheeting. Superficially, there was much in common with Einstürzende Neubaten's live setup, as the band members themselves admitted. But they remained adamant that these new comparisons between Depeche Mode and the pure industrial bands—like the old ones had been!— were both irrelevant and inadequate.

"We use a lot of metallic sounds," Martin explained, "but so do a lot of people, from Bowie onwards." The difference, as Martin had frequently pointed out in the past, was that Depeche Mode was using those sounds in the context of pop songs, musically, and now, visually. "Hitting bits of metal is very visual," he continued. A band like Depeche Mode "needs something else," he admitted, "and when we've got something more visual, we look more confident."

Also bound up in the introduction of all this hardware to the stage, however, was a conscious effort on the band's behalf to escape the hitherto hurtfully accurate accusations that a Depeche Mode live show was considerably more "show" than "live."

In the decade since 10cc had almost apologetically taken prerecorded vocal tapes onstage to help perform their international hit "I'm Not in Love," the concept of prerecording backing tracks had become perfectly acceptable. Cabaret Futura owner Richard Strange, at the height of his *Phenomenal Rise,* had dispensed with a live backing band altogether, and gone onstage alone, with his TEAC tape player in full view of the audience. Depeche Mode, with so much of their set preprogrammed into their instruments, did not go to quite the same extremes, but like so many other electronic bands, they were close.

Now, however, there was—as one reviewer cynically

put it—always someplace new to run, something new to hit, and in Martin's case, something new to wear!

The tour reached the United States in March 1985. It was short—fifteen shows spread over close to three weeks—but if Depeche Mode was suggesting that they didn't need America, those cities they did visit were sending a very different message back to them.

It was the group's first time over since March 1983, but although their record sales (the flukish "People Are People" aside) continued insisting that Depeche Mode was still a cult attraction, from the moment tickets for the fifteen shows went on sale, it was evident that something far larger was afoot.

The gigs concentrated, of course, upon those areas where the band's support was already proven: the Northeast, California, Texas, and the Chicago-Detroit region. But still, nobody could have predicted the response. The L.A. Palladium <183> show sold out within fifteen minutes of tickets going on sale, halving Billy Idol's previous sales record. Another Southern California gig, at University Hall, was so oversubscribed that the promoters were forced to shift it to the much larger Irvine Meadows. Within thirty minutes, all seven thousand tickets had gone.

The mid-1980s were a time of great change in American musical attitudes. Bands that had hitherto been regarded as mere eccentric cults—R.E.M., the Smiths, New Order, and the Cure—were now playing to larger and larger audiences, even as their records, ignored by radio but feted by the still-curious MTV, began creeping higher up the charts.

It was obvious which direction the wind was blowing, and in a few select areas, promotors began leaning the same way. Suddenly, they realized, stadium rock—previously a pelvis-thrusting, guitar-howling, head-shaking riot of codpiece-clad heavy metal—was no longer the preserve of the bands that made the most noise and could lead the loudest singalongs.

Now you could be thoughtful, introspective, calm, and still entrance a crowd the size of a small Midwestern city.

Where these new bands differed from those that preceded them—Duran Duran, Culture Club, A Flock of Seagulls, and so forth—was in their refusal to write their songs by the rules. And while they may initially have capitalized on exaggerated American notions of "English eccentricity" (Robert Smith's finger-painting makeup owed little to any notions of either beauty or balance, but was in many ways a logical progression from Boy George's look of sluttish androgyny), they also had the advantage of a lengthy personal history, previous albums, previous tours, previous videos, all adding up to a solid basis on which the future could be built. If that basis could somehow be harnessed to their own advantage . . .

<164>

When Depeche Mode arrived in America in March 1985, these notions were still tenuous at best. Even the Cure had yet to follow up their initial, lowly chart successes with anything better than a Top 200 berth for the recently issued *The Top*. In Depeche Mode's case, having a year-old hit single counted for little more. As with those other groups, the most important task ahead of them was to prove their own worth, to provide America with a genuine *reason* to take the romance to the next plateau.

In 1987, both the Cure and New Order had best-selling greatest-hits packages on the market, and were reaping the attendant rewards. Depeche Mode had taken the same route two years earlier. With no plans to release a new album in 1985, Depeche Mode was considering releasing a greatest-hits album for the British and European markets long before Sire suggested that America, too, might be interested in such a collection—an acknowledgment of the band's own belief that the previous year's *People Are People* compilation was little more than a stop-gap filler.

Depeche Mode, for their part, agreed. What better way was there of reminding people just how much success the band had attained over the past four years? Plus, it also gave them the opportunity to preserve on album their most recent single, "Shake the Disease"—a release that had otherwise slipped on and off of the U.K. charts with barely a murmur.

After the successes of the previous twelve months, the song's comparative failure had hurt Depeche Mode more than they would ever admit. Especially when that failure was compounded by official concerns that its title was somehow distasteful, in the wake of recent AIDS-related headlines.

Another new single, the gorgeous "It's Called a Heart," followed "Shake the Disease" onto the album; again, it was a lesser hit than it deserved to be, but that, at least, was understandable. It was released within a month of its appearance on the album, too soon even for its ultimate chart position to be included within the compilation album's sleeve notes, and with *The Singles 1981–85* rapidly shaping up as one of the year's most popular stocking fillers, who could blame the public if they did not buy the same song twice in one week?

<165>

The mood of retrospection created by the hits compilation (aptly retitled *Catching Up with Depeche Mode* in America) was continued with *The World We Live In and Live in Hamburg,* a seventy-five-minute no-frills video of one night from the band's last tour, released simultaneously with the album.

The first tentative step on a video journey that would culminate four years later with the spectacular *101* movie, *The World We Live In* was also the band's first attempt to express themselves as something more than the shadowy idols behind one of Britain's biggest pop groups. *The Singles 1981–85* was the first Depeche Mode album ever to feature the band's portrait on the cover; the ritual shattering of this past anonymity, on video and vinyl, was itself indicative of the band's growing confidence.

Yet *The World We Live In* was a disappointing outing, particularly—as *Melody Maker* pointed out—considering Depeche Mode's reputation as a band "who [has] strived to break down convention with each new record release." The excitement of Depeche Mode's live show, undeniable in the flesh, simply did not translate to the small screen.

But it was all the band's following could expect for the time being. When *NME*'s Danny Kelly caught up with Depeche Mode in October 1985, the group was clearly reveling in the unaccustomed luxury of taking so long away from the duties of a pop star.

They smiled at the thought of their old partner (but renewed friend) Vince Clarke setting out all over again, this time as one half of Erasure, and seeing his first single, "Who Needs Love Like That?," fail to even crack the Top Fifty, and more than one observer laughingly suggested that maybe Martin should write them a song.

Dave found time to marry his childhood sweetheart, Joanne, and while he, Alan, and Fletch admitted that "yes, we are very dependent on Martin's ideas," a flagrant mood of stark independence had crept into Depeche Mode's camp. Alan was contemplating a sideline solo career, busily toying with the name Recoil, while rumor—unfulfilled but tantalizing all the same—was hinting that Dave, too, had finally tired of playing Roger Daltrey to Martin's synthesized Pete Townshend, and might be stepping out on his own as well.

<166>

Scornfully, the threesome had dismissed Martin's notion, mooted earlier (and separately) in the *NME* interview, of dressing the rest of the band in the same dresses as he wore, but Kelly's attempts to draw the band into a considered discussion of how far apart from his bandmates Martin had apparently grown—reawakening, perhaps, the specter of Vince Clarke's considered withdrawal four years before—came to naught.

"Their worst fears," Kelly wrote afterward, "[have] proved unfounded. Martin [hasn't] become a coke-encrusted axe murderer and his songs [are] not suddenly peopled with smack-wrecked bluesmonster shamen." Instead, he revealed, Martin continued to talk, quietly and characteristically vaguely, of all that he was trying to achieve in his music. The most telling moment, however, came when Kelly invited Martin to "smash through the self-imposed restraint" of Depeche Mode's records.

"I want to reflect life's boredom," Martin answered slowly. "If you take things to absurd extremes, you're not really reflecting life. Real life is not extreme, so we're not, and nor is our music." The suggestion that Depeche Mode *deliberately* made "less than riveting records" was surely the work of a pop star who still considered himself to be off-duty.

In actual fact, Martin was now hard at work demoing the songs that would comprise Depeche Mode's next album, with the rest of the band due to join him in Berlin in the new year.

Once again, the band was booked into Hansa. "It's Called a Heart," their most recent single, was recorded in England, at Martin Rushent's Genetic Studios, and for a time, the band was considering making the entire album there. But the sheer technical majesty of Hansa once again proved irresistible.

But *Black Celebration* was never going to be an easy album to make. As usual, Martin had a very fixed idea of how he wanted the new record to sound, but his muse was apparently working in direct opposition to his dreams. Several of his most recent compositions were in dire need of serious revision, simply—he complained—because "they were too bright or summery or poppy."

The rest of the band's ideas, too, were often at violent odds with Martin's. Usually, the songwriter would cave in to the opinions of the majority, but he did so with increasing reluctance.

"Martin's sometimes not entirely happy with what's happened to his demos . . . in the studio," Dave confessed, with just a twinge of guilt, and while he and Alan agreed that Martin was "the kind of bloke that doesn't say much . . . until after it's released," the songwriter's frustrations were evident nevertheless.

<187>

"Flexible," Martin's skiffle-flavored knockabout B-side to "Shake the Disease," addressed both this rage and Martin's own attempts to come to terms with it. "Is it a sin," he asked, "to be flexible?" And later, playing his own devil's advocate, he simply pondered the inevitable process of democracy—open the window to debate, "and another idea flies out."

The problem was, as the four-month-long recording process stretched on into the spring of 1986, it was not only ideas that were sailing into oblivion. Depeche Mode's very fabric was beginning to tear.

With the benefit of hindsight, the pressure points were scarcely worth discussing, incidents no more serious than when Fletch and Daniel Miller had almost come to blows during the making of "People Are People." Less than a year after, Alan was unable even to recollect any frictions beyond "the problems . . . all groups have."

<168>

According to Dave, however, the cumulative effect bordered on catastrophe. "The intensity was just too much to handle," he insisted. "Friction within the band was at its highest ever." Arguments shattered the calm of the studio, not just daily, but hourly.

Independently, all four band members flashed on a letter that had recently arrived at their fan-club offices from a clearly distraught mother. It read simply, "My child is obsessed with you. For God's sake, please stop putting out records!" Throughout the band's first month in Berlin, her wish came very close to being granted. "If we were ever going to break up the band," Dave warned, "it would have happened then."

The theme that had dominated the band's most recent press encounters—the notion of artistic growth versus commercial success—lay closest to the heart of these frictions. Was it possible for any band to continue progressing as artists while retaining the kind of support that most truly progressive artists simply could not imagine? So far, Depeche Mode had proven that it was possible, but how much farther could they take it?

"We started rationalizing," Alan admitted; having progressed, as journalist Danny Kelly put it, "from A to somewhere past C," did the band need to continue on to points D, E, and F in that order? Or could they leap illogically on to point J or even L, and hope to take their audience with them?

On the one hand, the band's growth over the last few years proved that their audience *was* more than willing to allow them a great deal of creative latitude; on the other, however, the fading sales of their singles indicated that maybe enough was enough. And while Dave admitted that "musically, I don't think we go far enough," he also confessed that he enjoyed being Dave Gahan, universally recognized vocalist with top pop group Depeche Mode.

The nature of Depeche Mode's relationship with the music press, particularly in Britain, only complicated matters further. If the new Depeche Mode album did not represent a major step forward, in both sonic and spiritual terms, the logical assumption would be that the battle had been fought—and that Art had been slain by Artifice.

<169>

The corollary of that predicament, then, was to throw caution to the wind and go all-out for uncompromising denseness—in which case, they could be living on the streets by Christmas. Depeche Mode's success should have insulated them against "bad press"; instead, it had simply heightened their awareness of it. Many times in the past, the band had argued that if a record did not meet their own standards of satisfaction, they would not release it. But as *Black Celebration* gathered shape amid the grim shadows of Berlin, even that simple equation had become corrupted.

New ideas were discussed not on their own merits, but on those that others might perceive them to have. An awareness that a certain sound had already appeared on someone else's record sent them scurrying to defend themselves against accusations of plagiarism, even on the occasions when that particular sound was precisely what the music called for.

At times, the cycle seemed impossible to break. Constructing the vocal choir that underpins "It Doesn't Matter Two," a simple matter of sampling one choral note and then replaying it through the keyboard became the drawn-out process of sampling *every* single note—a chore that could just as successfully have been accomplished by hiring a real choir for the afternoon, and simply having them sing the required part live.

"It gives you a more realistic feel," excused Alan. "We try to take a bit more care to push our ideas further and make them a bit more realistic."

But he was also aware that the vast majority of the group's listeners would not even be aware of that. To them, sampling was the shattering sound of the Art of Noise—spiraling sound bytes and tape loops into a convoluted infinity resolved only by the recurrent melodies that were allowed to permeate the chaos—and "19," the vivid, vibrant collage with which disc jockey Paul Hardcastle hauled sampling technology into realms even Depeche Mode had yet to consider.

"19" was simplicity itself—a potpourri of news broadcasts, real and imagined, set against a turbulent backdrop that owed more to keeping a finger on the digital delay button than anything else. But it was devastatingly effective, an aural revolution that was to pave the way for further, even more audacious acts of vinyl recycling over the next few years.

In the grasp of such performers as the Justified Ancients of Mu (the JAMs), the sampler not only negated the need for live musicians, it rendered original music itself redundant. All you needed was a sizable record collection and the imagination to splice its highlights together into one coherent, danceable track.

Compared to what Hardcastle, the JAMs, and so many other emergent pioneers were accomplishing, Depeche Mode wasn't so much behind the times as moving in a different timestream altogether. To Depeche Mode, the sound of a saucepan being hurled down the stairs was worth a thousand borrowed drumbeats and sound bytes, but somewhere, the defining line between perfectionism and obsession had become well and truly obscured. Depeche Mode was losing faith not in its music—for Martin was now consistently writing the best material of his life—but in their ability to do that music justice.

Frustrated, angry, confused—even once they had come to terms with one another's expectations—the band members continued to search for an outlet. That restless energy could have gone in any direction—into the still-rumored solo projects, into furious slanging matches. Instead, it was channeled into the cause of the conflict itself—the new Depeche Mode album.

The very act of recording became a battleground. The power drill that launched "Fly on the Windscreen," the idling motorbike that underpinned "Stripped" . . . once, Martin had talked simply of making "harder-sounding" records. Now he dreamed of making a positively menacing one, a record that was to be swamped in self-doubt and disgust.

<171>

The romantic songs, such as they were, were powered by negativity; the loveless sex of "It Doesn't Matter Two" (so-titled to distinguish it from the similarly titled opus on *Some Great Reward*), the apologetic self-loathing of Martin's solo "Sometimes"—each, in a way, was a little time capsule, reiterating the images and emotions unleashed by the most painful recording sessions of the band's career.

"A Question of Time" even found time for what some observers absurdly speculated was a touch of guilty autobiography. The song's protagonist was unquestionably involved in a relationship with a minor. But was it an individual child? Or an auditorium filled with them? During an interview with the *L.A. Times,* Martin was asked if he had ever considered the effect his visions of darkness and disgrace might have on an impressionable mind, particularly one that had never previously contemplated such notions.

Martin replied with a chuckle and an offhand jest about corrupting the world. But "A Question of Time"—an unlikely but surprisingly successful choice for a single, close to a year after the album's June 1986 release—had already addressed that issue, and answered it as well. What sort of pop star filled his audience's heads with death and despondency? One who wanted to "get to you first," before the real world laid its hands on you and made you "just like the rest."

If there were any comparisons to be made, they pointed in the direction of the Cure, another band that had remedied its personal disabilities with an album of almost religious intensity, the austere majesty of *Faith*.

For that band, however, the catharsis had failed. *Pornography,* the Cure's fourth album, crushed even its predecessor, *Faith*'s, gothic desolation, and by the end of 1982 the Cure had effectively disbanded. It was to be another year before leader Robert Smith had exorcised sufficient demons to be able to contemplate his pop-machine rebirth.

<172>

The only difference now between the Cure and Depeche Mode was that Depeche Mode was able to halt their descent before they touched rock bottom.

Black Celebration was by no means exclusively an exercise in dark piety and sinister machinations, of course. Once again, Martin had reserved one song for himself; once again, it was the most tender on the album.

"A Question of Lust" approached infidelity not from the point of view of jealousy, anger, or pain, but as something that was simply insignificant when compared to the strength of the two parties' own relationship.

The failure of "A Question of Lust" to climb higher than number twenty-eight on the U.K. singles chart owed as much, the song's supporters argued, to its almost harrowing honesty as it did to the general public's rejection of such a beautiful piece of music. Even before Berlin-based producer Rico Conning constructed his elaborate Old and Newtown remixes of the track, few simple pop songs had ever so deliberately rewritten the genre's traditional formulae.

In their own minds, however, the band's backs were already against the wall; there was nothing to be lost, then, by pushing against that as well. Previous Depeche Mode albums had moved boundaries; *Black Celebration,* as a piece of music, was to move mountains.

The album's centerpiece was a song that had hitherto passed by unnoticed, lost on the B-side of "It's Called a Heart." "Fly on the Windshield" was a contemplation of the last moments before an unspecified death, the insects spattered on the windscreen of the title reminders that "we could be torn apart tonight." The premonitions of both physical and psychic disaster redolent in that verse was to permeate *Black Celebration* long after "Fly on the Windscreen" had passed on.

This dark side to Depeche Mode, accepted (and, typically, made light of) in Britain, received particular attention in the United States, especially as the band made its triumphant way across country following the album's release. The *L.A. Times* review of the group's sold-out concert at the Great Western Forum in July 1986 dwelt on little else, and in questioning <173> the group's own motives, perhaps it also called into question those of the group's fans.

That was the impression the *Times* letters editor was left with, once he finished sifting through the storm of protest that the review had unleashed—by which time he, too, was agreeing with the reviewer's original point: How is it that a group whose viewpoint is *so* far removed from the teen-pop stereotype has an audience that so blatantly fits that billing?

"We do notice that when we become popular in a country, the average age of our audience tends to go down," an incredulous Martin once remarked. It had happened in Germany, where the group's original electronics acolytes were ruthlessly trampled beneath the hooves of screaming youth; it had happened in Britain, where the plaudits of their initial signing to Mute were forgotten the first time Depeche Mode appeared on "Top of the Pops." And though he tried to rationalize it, arguing that many groups find their older support fading as their popularity increases, that did not explain the phenomenon that Depeche Mode was experiencing.

For God's Sake, Stop Putting Out Records! . . . . . .

The dichotomy was that, in those earlier instances, Depeche Mode had accepted the need to make certain artistic sacrifices. To sell records in Europe, particularly singles, the teen-oriented press was important. True, many bands were getting by quite nicely without pandering to the "favorite color"–type interrogation, but they, for the most part, were older acts: Simple Minds, Echo and the Bunnymen, the Psychedelic Furs, and U2 all exploded from the punk/New Wave milieu before Britain's teen press regained its post-punk equilibrium.

Depeche Mode broke through amid a host of bands that did actively pursue teen recognition; indeed, for all their protestations, Depeche Mode themselves pandered to that same crowd as adroitly as any Boy George or Simon LeBon.

In the United States, however, Depeche Mode erupted with a different pack altogether, drawing into their orbit an audience who really could differentiate between SPK and DAF, and who were considerably more prone to earnestly debate the hidden meanings in Martin's lyrics than they were his favorite fish dish.

The band's unique self-sufficient managerial situation, the handshake contract that still bound them to Mute, these factors only endeared Depeche Mode to the cognoscenti of America's rock underground. So did the band's obvious distaste for corporate manipulation; when Sire flipped the "Stripped" single—which Depeche Mode had spent three weeks perfecting—to take advantage of its B-side, "But Not Tonight" ("a throwaway thing which we did in a day"), appearing in the *Modern Girls* movie soundtrack, the band's displeasure was evident even before the movie bombed.

Depeche Mode neither courted, nor allowed themselves to be courted by, America's teen press, yet already their name was being bandied around the pinup stakes. And despite the knowing sneers of their peers and Martin's resigned "It's unfortunate really," they tapped into a market that few—if any—major league bands had ever even dreamed of.

"Don't believe for a second the old maxim that the

<174>

kids 'don't listen to the words,' " wrote the *L.A. Times*' Chris Willman in perhaps the most perceptive of all examinations of Depeche Mode's burgeoning Stateside status. "In this case, at least, the evidence is . . . that the [band's] massive popularity is in large part *because* of the dour themes. No more getting morose with Sylvia Plath for this generation of plaintive high schoolers. Nowadays you can ponder the cessation of all existence [a reference to 'Fly on the Windshield'] *and* dance to the rhythm of life at the same time."

The mailbag that greeted the *L.A. Times* review of Depeche Mode's 1986 Forum concert backed Willman's words to the hilt. For past generations, the letter writers were unanimous—pop escapism was just that, a hopeless voice rising from the waterlogged Woodstock stage suggesting that "maybe if we all think real hard, we can stop the rain." "Yeah—right," sneered one correspondent. "Remember Altamont."

<175>

Depeche Mode offered no spiritual solutions, no bright light at the end of the tunnel. Instead, they addressed the issues that society itself was not ready to discuss openly—not specifically, perhaps, but with razor-sharp accuracy nonetheless. They sang not only of love and life, but also of its corollaries, hatred and death. Particularly death.

In 1986 America's murder rate rose to a four-year high of over twenty thousand ("Death is all around"). Accidental deaths topped seventy-five thousand, with more than two-thirds of them attributed to automobiles ("We could be torn apart"). In the urban areas where Depeche Mode's chief support rested, creeping even into the safety of one's own home, it was as though everybody knew someone whose life had been snuffed out during the previous twelve months ("lambs for the slaughter").

"The unprepared parent visiting a Depeche Mode arena show in expectation of . . . another evening of communal pop frivolity may well leave unsettled by the sense of dread that has replaced puppy love in these young minds," Chris Willman continued. Then he added his pen to the dozens that had already commented on the hideous incongruity of Dave Gahan exhorting a barely pubescent choir to "join in the chorus of this next one, I think you all know it, it's called 'Blasphemous Rumours'!" And the crowd would obey—gleefully, gloriously—because in America in the mid-1980s, God *did* have a sick sense of humor. Either that, or He didn't exist at all. For many, the former conclusion was still the most comforting.

"I think most of the people who know the songs *do* understand them," Martin reasoned. "But when they come to the concerts, it's a kind of celebration. They've listened to the records at home, but when they come out, they just want to enjoy themselves. And we encourage that."

There were many people, however, who disagreed. Although their protests never took on the fanatical organization of the various pressure groups that did unite against pop's "corrupting influence" throughout the mid-1980s, many people did <176> loudly voice their concern about Depeche Mode's lyrical and musical imagery being foisted on an audience who should never be asked to contemplate such weighty issues.

But *why* shouldn't they? And even more important, was Depeche Mode's contemplation of the unthinkable that great a deviation from pop's already proven course?

Even at the pinnacles of success, pop music has always drawn heavily from the inspirations of morbidity. "Just as listening to Robert Johnson scream the blues provided catharsis to earlier generations," declared *Keyboard World*, "Depeche Mode's throbbing loneliness and confusion . . . reassures a younger generation that they are not alone."

But the equation went deeper than that, touching upon the very reasons for society's often hysterical reaction to this catharsis.

In 1993 Depeche Mode's Mute label colleague Boyd Rice joined with Rose MacDowell to record an entire album's worth of songs about death and despondency, all dating from the 1960s and early 1970s, and including several that had been colossal hits on one side of the Atlantic or another.

John Leyton's "Johnny Remember Me," Terry Jacks's "Seasons in the Sun," Marianne Faithfull's "This Little Bird" had each, in its own way, suffered the slings of adult disapproval—Twinkle's "Terry," detailing a motorcycle accident, had even been condemned by the British lord Ted Willis as "sick . . . dangerous drivel." But, replied journalist David Hall a full twenty-one years before Depeche Mode came in for a similar drubbing, "isn't it a fact that everyone symbolizes their life or their age with what happens around them at that age? In this case, we have young people singing . . . genuine songs dealing with a genuine problem. Isn't it true that teenagers do get killed on motorbikes, and therefore they should be able to sing about them on record?"

"Terry" was banned nevertheless. Then, as now, the "cure" for society's ills was to outlaw the symptoms instead of the disease, for what could be more diseased than a culture that takes its entertainment so seriously that the culture acts upon its <177> suggestions? Besides, it is often easier to *tell* people that everything's all right, than it is to make sure that everything really is all right in the first place.

Depeche Mode was never alone in fighting for the right to speak out for (or about) what they believed. But in 1986 they were still unique. Most people fought their battles from the sidelines of cultish obscurity. Depeche Mode fought theirs from the frontlines of success, preaching to the *un*converted. And the speed with which tickets for the band's 1986 American tour established fresh box-office records proved that the unconverted were enjoying the sermon.

The Great Western Forum show came at the tail end of Depeche Mode's most successful American tour yet—the perfect companion, then, for their most ambitious stage show ever.

The stage itself was constructed largely from inflatable plastics, which could simply be inflated with helium before each show, then deflated and folded away at the end—a far cry from the tons of iron tubing and wooden boards Depeche Mode had once dragged around with them. Now the heaviest items in their entourage were the smoke machines that pumped out the billowing clouds through which a barrage of colored searchlights cut like lasers.

Hollow risers allowed the band to tuck plug boards, leads, and even roadies out of sight. There was a special matted floor that allowed Dave to run around the stage without, as had happened in the past, losing his footing and falling down. As designer Jane Spiers and the band members ran through every facet of the set—loosely modeled on Leni Reifenstahl's designs for the 1936 Munich Olympiad—they were prepared for every eventuality.

Or so they thought. The only thing that went wrong was the one they had otherwise taken for granted—a stage curtain that needed to simply drop to the floor at a specific time in the show.

<178>

"It's a very dramatic effect, but when it goes wrong, when it's only half-dropped or something, it's very funny. Half the stage is covered, and half is out in the open." Alan paused in mid-thought. "When you're on the road, there are so many things that remind you of *Spinal Tap!*"

It was shocking to hear a member of Depeche Mode comparing his own adventures with those of the archetypal dumb heavy-metal band. But it was also somehow reassuring. Within the macabre fantasy world of Depeche Mode's music, even a hint of lighthearted reality—albeit a reality that itself was twisted beyond recognizable proportions—was welcome.

It Sounds

Nothing Like a

Pygmy

EVEN IN EXTINCTION, Route 66 is one of America's most cherished institutions. Its two-thousand-mile trek across the American heartland bisects both the land and its culture, a cement artery that connected the glittering riches of Los Angeles with the old-world romance of Chicago, immortal long before it was immortalized in three chords and one of the best-known lyrics in American literature. The lights were always bright on Broadway, and you could see all the stars as you walked down Hollywood Boulevard. But there was only one place where you were *guaranteed* to get your kicks.

The archetypal rock 'n' roll road, the archetype of American rock 'n' roll—when Bobby Troup first put pen to paper and traced the highway in song, could he have even dreamed how far his song would travel, how much farther than the very highway itself?

From the Rolling Stones to the Manhattan Transfer, from the U.S.A. of Tom Petty to the England of Billy Bragg—during a John Peel radio session in 1983, the British singer-songwriter recast "Route 66" into exclusively English terms, renaming it for the A13, "Trunk Road to the Sea," and winding it to Southend from Wapping ("There ain't no stopping!"), through Barking and Dagenham, and then down to Grays Thurrock, "rather near Basildon!"

In Basildon the locals bristled warmly, happy to hear their hometown on the radio. And though they would return the actual lyric to its true American heritage, Depeche Mode knew that one day they would repay the compliment in full.

Pop history is littered with "classic" songs, moments that remain preserved in their listeners' memories for all time, so that even when every other name, face, and fancy of the year is forgotten, you can still remember precisely what you were doing the first time you heard . . .

Depeche Mode's rendition of "Route 66" was one of those moments. But it was not merely a memorable moment for its listeners. For Depeche Mode, too, "Route 66" marked a critical juncture in their development, that at which they finally crossed the Rubicon upon whose banks they had halted so many times in the past.

For it was one thing for Martin to wear an acoustic guitar on stage, unplugged and unplayed, for the benefits of the TV cameras; another for the band to pose, as they had done in the past, gazing wistfully up at a row of inviting axes while a photographer fired off his film. But it was something else entirely for Martin to enter a recording studio, set the tapes rolling, then strike that first resounding guitar chord, and to keep striking until the whole performance was captured forever. By the time the take was finished, the entire studio was hushed. They were waiting for the world to end.

<180>

Finally Martin broke the silence. "It's all right. I write songs on this thing all the time!"

Another legend bit the dust.

"We don't think of ourselves as a keyboard band at all," Alan explained patiently, and for the umpteenth time, as Depeche Mode ran the gauntlet of American interviews. "We like to consider sound itself as our only restriction. We work within the practicalities of what we do, and most of the time that tends to involve keyboards. But we will use guitar sounds and all kinds of different sounds, too. Often we'll sample them, and use them with keyboards, rather than play them live, because it's a bit easier for us to work that way."

In the studio, however, anything goes, and Depeche Mode's sixth album was to be their most unrestricted yet. They had learned from past problems; more important, they had learned from the pressures that came so close to aborting *Black Celebration.* Never again would Depeche Mode do something simply because it was the one thing they weren't expected to do; never again would they worry about a record's reception before it was even recorded.

<|8|>

The biggest wrench was making the decision not to work with Daniel Miller for the first time in the band's history. Like the individual group members themselves, Miller understood intuitively what Depeche Mode needed, could lead them blindfolded through the complexities of the studio.

But the routine was becoming stale. After their initial qualms, Depeche Mode had come to accept what a lot of outsiders were saying all along, that *Black Celebration* really was their greatest album yet, the culmination of six years of recording.

Daniel and co-producer Gareth Jones had played a crucial part in that achievement, just as they had on the albums that preceded it. Reconvening the same team for yet another record might result in an even greater album. But it might also run the risk of simply reiterating a formula that had already reached its own nirvana. It was time for a change.

David Bascombe was the band's chosen replacement, an English engineer best known for his work with Peter Gabriel and Tears for Fears. *Music for the Masses* was to be his first major production project, and his brief was simple—to shift the band's focus, to rechannel their basic energies, but to never lose sight of the things they held sacred.

It was a tall order, but one that Bascombe eagerly leaped toward. "He helped us find ourselves in the music more," was Dave's approving summary of Bascombe's eventual impact. He opened up the band's sound, and in so doing, brightened it. Over and over again, when the band members were asked to sum up the album, one word kept springing to mind. *Music for the Masses* was "optimistic."

<182> But it was also incomplete. In the past, Martin had presented his songs to the band in an almost skeletal form, sparse guitar-and-keyboard demos that the band would then slowly flesh out. This time, Martin delivered his demos in what amounted to their finished state, then simply waited while the band, as Fletch put it, "copied what he had done and added Dave's vocals." For the first time, Martin was adamant, the group was going to perform his songs as he originally visualized them.

It was a mistake. According, again, to Fletch, "We feel we do our best when we're all working on the songs together, right from the beginning." *Music for the Masses* left no room for musical maneuvering, few places in which even Alan, the musical dynamo of the group, could insert the independent inventiveness that led songs away on a whole new tangent.

The only area in which Martin allowed his bandmates lassitude was in the search for new samples. In their constant quest for fresh effects, Depeche Mode had long since abandoned any notion of simply repeating samples from one album to another (the acoustic guitar plucked with a German coin found on "People Are People" is a notable exception), but the group wasn't averse to returning to the scenes of their previous "crimes"—if not the actual sounds.

For *Music for the Masses,* junkyards and construction sites continued to prove fruitful hunting grounds. The band also added toy shops to its list of haunts, feeding toy instruments through an array of different amplifiers, with plenty of cheap reverb and distortion, then sampling the ensuing noise.

Martin had also grown very enthusiastic about "your standard kitchen. Plates, glasses, can openers, pots and pans, make good percussion sounds," he enthused. "And if you hit a saucepan [on a record], maybe a housewife doing her cooking will suddenly start humming that melody."

Briefly, the band toyed with the idea of recording an entire album using kitchen implements, a scheme that more than a decade before had occupied Pink Floyd as they struggled to come up with a suitable follow-up to the massively successful *Dark Side of the Moon.*

<183>

"If you tap a wine bottle across the top of the neck, you get a tabla-like sound close-up. Or you can fill it partly with water and do the same thing," explained Pink Floyd guitarist Dave Gilmour at the time. "We used aerosol cans, and, pulling rolls of [sticky tape] out to different lengths, the further away it gets, the note changes."

Pink Floyd aborted the sessions after recording no more than three tracks; "It seemed like a good idea at the time, but it didn't really come together," said vocalist Roger Waters. Now Depeche Mode was taking those same principles and creating entire albums from them. The difference was, whereas Pink Floyd had been attempting to *replicate* the effects of different instruments without actually playing them—one elaborate construction duplicated a bass using rubber bands, matchsticks, and a cigarette lighter!—Depeche Mode was creating whole new sounds.

"We've sampled a pygmy doing his wail, but we've turned that into something that sounds nothing like a pygmy," laughed Alan. "We also do a lot of reversing and looping, so by the time you've used a sound, like a loon on 'Strangelove,' you sometimes can't remember what it was when you started." Another favorite was the dull "WHUMP" obtained by hitting the pipe of a vacuum cleaner.

Not all of Depeche Mode's electronics arsenal was so unconventional. Over the years, Daniel Miller had amassed an immense collection of what were now vintage analog synthesizers, and was more than happy to offer them up to the band. "He's got an EMS, one of the suitcase-type keyboards," Martin raved. "It's not good for melodies, but it's great for sound effects." Other favorites included a Moog Series 3, and an enormous Oberheim. Martin was even able to turn to the band's advantage the analog synthesizer's penchant for constantly going out of tune. "We get some really good sounds, then sample them to overcome that problem."

<184>

Another analog factor the band appreciated was the fact that the vast majority of the machines were built before keyboards had developed the preset-sound ability, forcing the group to work from scratch, as opposed to purchasing some cartridges and flicking through sounds until they found something they liked.

A further sign of the changing times was provided by Depeche Mode's choice of studios—the Guilliame Tell complex in Paris, and the Kinks' Konk setup in north London. Like Daniel and Gareth Jones, Hansa and Berlin had simply grown too familiar.

But there was another reason for the group to remain so close to London: Dave and Joanne were about to become parents, with the baby due around the same time the new album was expected to be completed.

In both instances, the precise timing was far from an exact science, and as the band put the finishing touches to the record, Dave was jumping every time the phone rang. The band's schedule was such that he would have precious little time with the child during the crucial first year, and Dave was adamant that he wouldn't waste a single moment. Baby Jack

Gahan was just three weeks old when he attended his first gig, but flying visits aside, he would be a year old before he saw his father again.

Depeche Mode wound into their latest touring schedule with a pair of European festival shows, alongside Elton John and Rod Stewart. The group's latest single, "Strangelove," had confirmed their high billing at the shows, gatecrashing a U.K. chart that had otherwise surrendered itself to either adult-oriented easy listening or revamped oldies masquerading beneath the sheen of modern technology—or else a combination of the two.

Vince Clarke's Erasure had now overcome their early aversion to chart success, but while "Victim of Love" was eventually to reach the Top Ten, it did so despite the protests of even Vince's own old fans. But the very reality of one of Vince's most hackneyed songs becoming one of his best-selling hits was somehow symptomatic of what was wrong with the British charts; that, and the fact that reheated debris such as Jefferson Starship could remain at number one throughout May 1987, before surrendering their status to Whitney Houston. Depeche Mode's highly placed arrival into this ghastly scenario was more than another familiar face turning up at the pensioners' party; it was a clear sign, historically and culturally, that pop's landscape was again shifting.

<I85>

The question was, In which direction was it moving? And who would be best placed to take advantage of it? The old guard—the Starships, Rods, and Eltons for whom both time and fashion had stood still—and whose recent chart rebirth was surely spelled out by the resurgence in sad balladeering? Or the new—the Depeche Modes of this world—for whom pop music was still a viable art form worth fighting for?

"Strangelove" certainly set some bizarre precedents for a major hit single, not least of all in its subsequent recorded history.

Hitherto Depeche Mode had satisfied themselves with no more than three or four different mixes of an individual song, spread across both the regular and the limited twelve-inch singles. "Strangelove" was to manifest itself in a staggering *fourteen* different mixes, ranging from the original album version through the exotically titled "Blind Edit" and "Highland Mix," and on to the positively ominous sounding "Death Mix." Among the producers responsible for this astonishing array of artistry can be counted Bomb the Bass svengali Tim Simenon, Rico Conning, and mix master Phil Harding.

Since then, most Depeche Mode singles have been similarly handled, although not all of these manifold mixes were intended for public consumption. Rather, special versions would be commissioned by different clubs and radio stations, often to be targeted at very specific areas, geographical and otherwise, and frequently without Depeche Mode's approval.

"Remixes are sometimes so demoralizing," Fletch complained once. "You spend quite a lot of time doing this twelve-inch remix that you're really proud of, [only for the record company to] say, 'It's a great track but we'd like to get some Latin hip-hop jazz guy from Brooklyn to do the remix.' So we just feel a bit demoralized when they tear it apart. But part of the problem is that we mix the music for the bedroom. We've never been able to mix twelve-inchers for [club play]."

Yet despite their reservations, Depeche Mode was again in the position of pioneering. It was their admittedly reluctant willingness to allow their records to suffer outside remixes that paved the way for the upsurge of superstar disc jockeys and producers who would themselves be taking over the British charts before the end of the decade.

By the end of the decade, such a credit really could help sell a record, particularly when the remix was masterminded by the likes of Shep Pettibone, Brian Eno, Chris Tsangarides, or the Razormaid team—each of whom has contributed his own personal vision to Depeche Mode's original handiwork. Suddenly, even the most undanceable records were appearing in a multitude of superstar mixes, with defenders of the new faith arguing, somewhat cynically but certainly with some accu-

<186>

racy, that there was now no reason whatsoever for any record to pass by unloved by any major section of the marketplace. It could simply be remixed and remixed until it met their approval.

Despite such flagrant profiteering; despite, also, Depeche Mode's own unwitting role in setting the scene, Dave continued to insist that paramount among Depeche Mode's aims "is to bring credibility back into pop.

"Whereas rock bands like U2 tend to be accepted at the time," he explained, pop groups—a company into which he continued to slot Depeche Mode—seldom were. It was only later, often after the group itself was dead and buried, that they attained the respect they had always deserved. Taking examples from his own childhood, he continued, "Gary Glitter, T. Rex and the glam bands who were very throwaway in the early seventies are . . . real hip now." (Martin himself would acknowledge Glitter's newfound stature, as well as his own long-standing love of Glitter's music, by recording a solo version of the great man's foudroyant "I Love You Love Me Love.") Dave's concern was that Depeche Mode should not be treated as shabbily.

<187>

But the evolution of pop music has sped up immeasurably since the early 1970s, and just as the glorious riffing of the British glam rockers was eventually transformed, via a series of sometimes inexplicable convolutions, into punk rock, so that of Depeche Mode was itself poised to mutate, furiously and ferociously, regardless of whether or not that mutation was forged in the heat of human ingenuity or mere technological advances.

In their hearts, Depeche Mode still allied themselves with those bands that had never suffered the attentions of the teen press. Asked once to name which other bands he would like to be a member of, Dave unhesitatingly replied, "New Order, the Smiths, maybe the Cure. I think there are similar areas in all three bands to Depeche Mode."

There were similarities—in the electronic delivery of

New Order, the moody atmospherics of the Cure, the lyrical intensity of Smiths front man Morrissey. But musically, Depeche Mode's lineage stretched back to the pioneering German acts whose early-Eighties experiments in sound had proven such an influence upon Martin's songwriting techniques. And from there, it reached forward again, to encompass a whole new generation of industrial bands.

At the very forefront of this new movement, Ministry and Skinny Puppy could both trace their own development back through firm flirtations with a distinctly Depeche Mode–influenced sound; both, too, had supported Depeche Mode on past North American tours: Ministry in 1983, on the heels of their own *With Sympathy* debut album; Skinny Puppy's Celvin Key during his earlier life with the Vancouver-based Images in Vogue.

<188> Both bands had now long since distanced themselves from their early role models, reinventing themselves as skillfully, in fact, as Depeche Mode had. But still their careers brushed the occasional shoulder. It was only after hearing what Adrian Sherwood did with "People Are People" that Ministry's Al Jourgensen contacted the producer to work on his own next album, *Twitch*. And it was only after Depeche Mode coined a pounding, mechanical "Aggro Mix" for their latest single, "Never Let Me Down Again," that Jourgensen took to referring to his own music as "aggro."

Released in August 1987, "Never Let Me Down Again" was, in many ways, the most typical Depeche Mode song on the forthcoming *Music for the Masses* album—one of the very few that retained both the instant melodic flow that had established the band in the first place, and the lyrical simplicity and ambiguity that forged their reputation. Could the song really have documented something so mundane as an airplane ride?

Certainly its "Aggro Mix" was far removed from the air of near-innocence with which Depeche Mode performed the album version, but even in its original state, "the travelogue becomes a metaphor for drugs or gay sex," growled New York's *Village Voice*; "the hard-rock beat is too bombastic, David Gahan sings too suggestively [and] the melody rises and falls with too much symphonic drama." One critic even compared the song to Laibach, the Slovenian art collective, whose Wagnerian sense of musical proportion the song did indeed share some common ground with.

Elsewhere, it was suggested that Martin wrote the song either for or about Marc Almond—the song's coda was practically identical to the chorus of Soft Cell's now five-year-old "Torch." "But that's one of the nicest things about Martin's words," Alan countered. "The fact that they can mean different things to different people, depending on how people decide to interpret them."

This confusion was not to be resolved by the single's accompanying video, either. Anton Corbijn's recruitment as the band's video director and official photographer (roles he retains today) was the third and final change made by Depeche Mode as *Music for the Masses* came together.

<189>

Corbijn was a former photographer with *New Musical Express,* and his stark, monochromatic studies had long since earmarked him as one of the key cameramen of the 1980s, a title he justified when he moved into video work with U2 (a rarely seen version of "Pride") and Echo and the Bunnymen ("Seven Seas").

But his stark black-and-white treatment of "Never Let Me Down Again" did little to aid pat summarizations of the song. Culled from the strong six-song mini-movie *Strange,* it made little enough sense in that context. Removed from *Strange,* where at least a hint of continuity was provided by a series of running visual gags, it stood no chance!

Despite Corbijn's input, "Never Let Me Down Again" did little in either Britain or the U.S., a fate that was reserved, too, for the new year's "Behind the Wheel" single. Indeed, when neither made even the traditionally loyal U.K. Top Twenty, they represented the worst-ever displays by two successive Depeche Mode singles—and that despite "Wheel" being backed with that revolutionary treatment of "Route 66," itself enjoying an even wider market after a Nile Rodgers remix made the *Earth Girls Are Easy* movie soundtrack.

It was, then, something of a relief when the band scored a totally unexpected British hit with "Little 15," a single released in Germany alone, but imported into Britain in such quantities that it actually charted! It proved that Depeche Mode's hard-core following remained desperately loyal—a fact that, as 1987 slipped away, appeared increasingly doubtful.

Music for the Masses itself had struggled to reach the U.K. Top Ten, and while "Little 15" scraped no higher than number sixty, only Cliff Richard in 1961, and the Jam—whose "That's Entertainment" single charted twenty years later—had previously scored so high with a foreign release. Even though, in the eyes of Britain's hypercritical music press, Depeche Mode could do little right, in the marketplace they remained untouchable.

<190>

"I think the problem [in Britain] is very much due to the people who control the BBC," Alan explained in America—where his complaints could not be added to the BBC's little black book. "Because the BBC controls all the major television and radio, the BBC producers decide what people will listen to." Depeche Mode was still granted "a certain amount of hearing" because of their track record, "and because we have this hard-core following that demands it. But the BBC producers play our songs reluctantly—they'd rather not, but they have to."

Depeche Mode's "crime," of course, was the hoary old chestnut of "suitability." In terms of radio broadcasting, music that did not meet the historical criteria of Top Forty material traditionally had its own slot in the evenings, away from peak listening hours, in the capable hands of disc jockeys like John Peel. But this procedure only worked, as Dave Gahan once commented, because most "experimental" bands were by their very nature acts whose music would not come close to Top Forty stature.

Depeche Mode derailed that rule by attaining mass popularity, then retained it through a series of complex musical and emotional shifts. According to Martin, one Radio One deejay, Steve Wright, always introduced Depeche Mode records by saying, "I hate that band! Aren't they the most depressing thing in music?"

"A lot of pop music is about escaping," condemned Alan. "There's all these pop songs [whose] words make no sense whatsoever!" Depeche Mode did not want to restrict their audience to superficiality, he continued. Their songs were intended for those people "who want to find something in the words."

Such people were out in force when Depeche Mode toured Europe throughout the fall of 1987 and the United States in the run up to Christmas. Despite their lowering record sales, the band remained a major concert draw, and in November they even conquered the one territory that had previously remained resistant to their magic—France. At the end of the month, six years of comparative disinterest were finally ended by a triumphant show in Paris.

<191>

The American visit was somewhat less well starred. Despite opening with the first of four sold-out California shows, at the Cow Palace in San Francisco, the next four shows—intended as a warm-up for a longer visit in the spring—only highlighted the quixotic nature of Depeche Mode's Stateside following. Their December 8 performance in Phoenix attracted less than six thousand fans to a venue that could hold twice that many. Fairfax, Virginia, and Montreal were scarcely more welcoming.

The band members themselves remained philosophical about their tempestuous relationship with both America's ticket buyers and critics. "We don't get good live reviews," Fletch admitted to the *Los Angeles Herald Examiner,* "so it's not that we've got this great reputation for being a live band. Our *fans* think so, but the critics don't."

Journalist Todd Everett noted that "Other than in

markets like L.A., where they receive strong radio exposure on stations like KROQ-FM [expatriate British disc jockey Richard Blade was a confirmed Depeche Mode cheerleader], Depeche Mode's reputation rests largely on word of mouth."

But as Martin explained, "I never had any kind of great expectations for us in America. I'd always thought of our music as not suited to the American music scene. When it first started turning around, we were very shocked by the great reception we were getting from some of the audiences here." It was with America ("and other places where we don't sell all that many records!") in mind, he continued, that Depeche Mode titled their latest album *Music for the Masses* in the first place.

"We called it [that] to make people laugh. In Europe, most bands wouldn't use such a title—it's so blatant." Depeche Mode's German record company, in particular, missed the joke altogether, "because over there, we really are music for the masses," laughed Fletch. "They were saying, 'Oh, so what is this, you are making commercial music?' They just don't understand sarcasm."

<192>

In other countries, however, the title did take on more of an ironic angle, allowing Martin the opportunity to reiterate a remark he had made two years previous, in an interview with the New York–based *Island Ear* magazine. He sincerely believed, he told his interrogator, that it was impossible for music to make any kind of profound statement to the masses; if it tried, the masses would either miss it—or be prohibited from hearing it.

Depeche Mode's love-hate relationship with American radio—so fervently behind them while "People Are People" was ascendant; so apathetic ever since—was one example, as was the official response to Depeche Mode's attempts to bring their own support act to America with them, the highly rated Nitzer Ebb.

Natives of Basildon's near neighbor Chelmsford, Nitzer Ebb were refused the necessary work permits—"I guess their reasoning is, 'Why can't you have an American band opening up?' " Martin said with a sigh; and Depeche Mode's December 1987 shows, sure enough, were instead supported by San Francisco's Voice Farm, a keyboard-based band whose choice in costuming was even more revealing than Martin's leather dresses. Myke Reilly and Charly Brown appeared on the band's debut album, *The World We Live In* ("and life in general!" as one observant critic punningly quipped), clad only in their underwear.

Neither were Nitzer Ebb's visa difficulties resolved in time for the second leg of Depeche Mode's American tour in May, although the apparent xenophobia of the immigration department had relaxed a little. Opening the series of concerts that stretched from the end of April until the middle of June was Orchestral Maneuvers in the Dark, a band that might once have headlined over Depeche Mode with ease!

<193>

Back in 1981, Vince laughed understandingly when *Melody Maker* compared Depeche Mode to the (then) far more established OMD, and the mock rivalry between the two bands—given an even sharper edge as the two groups matched one another hit for hit in the U.K. charts—was only exacerbated as Depeche Mode slowly began to come out on top.

But OMD had retained their chart profile, long after many of their other contemporaries had faded. Like Depeche Mode, they were old-timers, the last true survivors of a very endangered species. The other synthesizer bands were now tumbling like ninepins, with even the once-almighty Human League releasing a new album, *Crash,* with the back cover credit "No sequencers used on this record."

To those people who remembered the similar claims that had once so amused Queen, the previous decade of rock music had completed a dreadful cycle. "The early electronic bands were an extension of the punk scene, moving away from bands [and claims] like that," Martin complained. "Now they've gone full circle."

Those bands that were left, then, had to stick together, and by the time the spring tour reached its climax at Pasadena's seventy thousand-capacity Rose Bowl on July 18, 1988, the affair had taken on the appearance of a veritable synth-poppers reunion.

Joining Depeche Mode and OMD on the bill were Thomas Dolby—the nerdlike electronics genius whose career jolted into hyperspace when his "Blinded Me with Science" became a freak godfather of America's dance-music scene in the early 1980s—and Mute stablemates Wire, an equally eccentric English quartet whose entire career was built around a refusal to play even front man Colin Newman's delicious pop songs by the numbers.

Hardly surprisingly, the American press was swift to dub the six-and-a-half-hour festival "Monsters of Techno-Rock." Depeche Mode responded with the banner that was to be draped over the back of the stage: Concert for the Masses.

<194>

Chapter 11

It Came Out of the Backyard

THE 1988 AMERICAN tour was Depeche Mode's first truly nationwide outing, a mammoth undertaking that encompassed twenty shows in fifteen states and two countries (Montreal, Toronto, and Vancouver all slipped into the itinerary), and this time, almost all were completely sold-out.

Music for the Masses had debuted in the *Billboard* charts at number thirty-five. Now, some nine months later, the album was still lurking around the lower reaches of the Top 100, accumulating sales of over half a million. It was an impressive performance, and the success of the tour simply reinforced Depeche Mode's position.

Nineteen eighty-eight had seen a number of established "rock" bands move back onto the live circuit, including several whose record sales outstripped Depeche Mode's by almost embarrassing percentages.

Poison, for instance, had a Top Five album, but, according to Fletch, "We're doing better business than them. The kids are buying [their] records, but not coming to see them live. It baffles us, really."

So did the attitude of many of the supporters Depeche Mode was meeting on the road. The group thought their supporters would be glad to see Depeche Mode finally making inroads into the American consciousness. Instead, Martin murmured incredulously, they discovered that "our fans don't *want* us played on Top Forty radio. In some way, we're their little secret." He had even heard of Top Forty stations being overwhelmed, not by requests to play Depeche Mode, but by requests *not* to play them. "People call in . . . telling them they haven't got the right to play our records because they're a Top Forty station!"

Unhampered by similar dreams of elitism, Sire continued pulling out all the stops in promoting the tour. Sensing victory after so many years of near misses, realizing that Depeche Mode was truly poised on the brink of a major breakthrough, the record company kept both the music press and the conventional entertainment magazines well-fed with news.

One particularly inspired stunt was joining with Long Island's premier "new music" college radio station, WDRE, to sponsor a dance contest at the Malibu discotheque. Eight teenaged winners would then be placed aboard a chartered bus and, for one week, they would follow the trail of the old Route 66 as it wound its way toward Pasadena for the Rose Bowl climax. To add to the occasion, the bus would also host a film crew, Joel DeMott and Jeff Kreines, working under the directorial eye of D. A. Pennebaker.

To those bands that dream of celluloid immortality, Pennebaker is something of a Holy Grail among rock chroniclers. His record of Bob Dylan's 1965 British tour, *Don't Look Back,* and the following year's *Eat the Document,* remain the ultimate examples of the documentary maker's craft, while

1967's eponymous study of the Monterey Pop festival set standards that even today remain in-concert film staples.

Certainly Pennebaker had yet to eclipse this brilliant pop triumvirate; his only other concert movie to offer the dramatic potential of those earlier events—David Bowie's *Ziggy Stardust* farewell show—was released so long after the fact (shot in 1973, it made the cinemas in 1981) that even its historical value was negated by another eight years of Bowie's infuriating stylistic dilettantism. Music is not made in a vacuum; it exists according to the precepts of the time in which it was made. In 1973 Ziggy Stardust was God, and his abdication was headline news. By 1981, the whole thing was simply quaint.

As reports of Pennebaker's involvement with Depeche Mode became popular knowledge, the fears were not that one party or the other had bitten off more than it could chew (the union was unlikely, to say the least!), but that—as *Interview*'s Lauren Swift pointed out—Pennebaker's personal style had become so heavily imitated that it was now all but clichéd. Would the master still be able to rise above the servants?

<197>

"I don't think of [this project] as a documentary. I find the word misleading," Pennebaker explained. "Most people are bored with documentaries. To me, if you are making a documentary, you are telling the viewer everything about the subject that you think they ought to know. With a regular movie, you try and tell them as little as they need to know. I prefer the latter and feel [this] works on that level. I wanted to make a film about real people in real life." It was all a long way from the simple, live video that the band had been planning since the "Live in Hamburg" release.

With a prescience that was, perhaps, lost on many of Depeche Mode's traditional friends and foes, Pennebaker explained why, after filming the likes of Dylan, Hendrix, Joplin, and Bowie, it was now Depeche Mode who appealed to him. "You should compare passion, not technique," he admonished. Depeche Mode "bring a real passion to what they do." Pennebaker agreed with Martin's own, long-standing conviction that "a lot of people think you cannot make soul music with synthesizers. But the soul in music comes from the song. The instrumentation doesn't matter at all."

To Pennebaker, it was of no consequence whatsoever that Depeche Mode neither burned their guitars, like Hendrix at Monterey, nor incinerated their audience, like Dylan on a nightly basis. Nor did it matter that Depeche Mode was "serious" about their music—most musicians are. What was important was the fact that they were serious about what that music could achieve. "We'd never go for shock for shock's sake," Alan once remarked. "But there's a certain edge to what we do that can make people think twice about things." Pennebaker spotted that "certain edge" the very first time he saw Depeche Mode perform, in San Francisco the previous December. The brief he set himself was to capture it on film.

<198> Pennebaker's approach to the movie was disarmingly simplistic. Together with Chris Hegedus and David Dawkins, he would merely point his cameras and roll, with as little directorial interference as possible. Nothing would be scripted, no scenes were engineered, and even more surprisingly, perhaps, Depeche Mode themselves would be granted as little input into the finished film as possible. Pennebaker admitted that he knew next to nothing about the band when he started work on the movie. For him, the challenge was to get to know them through the camera lens. Depeche Mode for their part were fascinated to see what the great director would make of them.

Pennebaker ended up with over a hundred and fifty hours of film—and a budget that barely allowed for two. Not since Bob Dylan's four-hour *Renaldo and Clara,* in 1976, had the scriptless "direct cinema" approach that Pennebaker inevitably pioneered received such a grueling workout; and Pennebaker himself confessed that Depeche Mode themselves grew increasingly restless as the editing process stretched into a long, unceasing future.

"It must get [very] frustrating as we say, 'Well, we haven't got the foggiest notion of what it is about!' "

Pennebaker's team followed Depeche Mode everywhere, even to those cities where their reputation *still* hadn't preceded them. In Atlanta, and again in Nashville, band and audience alike drowned within the vast emptiness of underpopulated arenas. Even moving the portable stage forward, a space-killing device the band had occasionally used in the past, could not dent the gaping chasm at the back of the hall. Spliced in with footage from the fans' own odyssey across America, such scenes offered a poignant contrast to the real star of the tour, the Rose Bowl concert.

The idea for this final show was the band's own, and they stuck with it even against the advice of their accountants. Of all the major venues in the area capable of accommodating a major audience, the Rose Bowl was by far the most expensive. It was also among the least experienced at handling a major music event—the Depeche Mode show would be the first concert staged at the Rose Bowl since Stevie Wonder and Jackson Browne had headlined the Peace Sunday event in 1982.

<199>

But Depeche Mode was adamant. "We wanted to do something special to finish the tour, to give us something to look forward to." They arranged for a live KROQ broadcast of the press conference where the gig was announced from the Rose Bowl itself, and the band's words made it plain that the show was intended as a thank you to Southern California for the support it had given Depeche Mode over the years.

Yet there was a genuine element of risk involved. Depeche Mode had no real idea of just how many tickets the show would sell, and while Dave tried to put a brave face on the band's nervousness, claiming that the possibility of failure "was half the fun! That's what made it exciting, and I think that's what excited Pennebaker as well"—still, it was an inestimable relief when the gamble paid off.

More than a month before the show, Rose Bowl ticket sales had topped 53,000; the final total of 66,233 represented a 95 percent sellout of the enormous stadium, and to top it all, relates KROQ deejay Richard Blade, the band even affected the weather that night.

"They were doing 'Blasphemous Rumours' when suddenly it began to thunder and rain. Do you know how rare that is in the middle of L.A. in July? And then the band followed that up with 'Sacred' and the rain stopped. It was really weird!"

Depeche Mode's set that night was essentially the same one they had been performing all tour, concentrating on *Music for the Masses,* with just a sprinkling of old favorites thrown in for good measure. But there was one surprise: when the band broke their own self-imposed embargo on material from their first two albums and rescued Vince's "Just Can't Get Enough" from the annals of history.

<200>It may have been the song that had started everything for Depeche Mode in the United States—seven years before, when it ripped up the college charts—but it was also wholly at odds with the Depeche Mode most of the audience knew and loved. The roars it received, however, were the closest rock 'n' roll can come to a secret Masonic handshake. "I remember this!" the audience seemed to be crying. "It's amazing that you do, too!"

When it was all over, Martin swore that the Rose Bowl was "definitely *the* highlight of my, and probably the band's, career. It was just a feeling that I'll never forget, and I don't think the people who were there will either. The power between us was just incredible." Pennebaker's cameras had already caught the glances of sheer joy that passed between Dave and Martin onstage; now, with the empty stadium still echoing with the cheers of his fans, Martin sat alone in a corner, silent and close to tears. He was feeling completely lost. All he could think was, How are we ever going to top *that*?

The original title for Pennebaker's Rose Bowl movie was *A Brief Period of Rejoicing,* a somewhat self-conscious reference to Depeche Mode's renowned shroud of gloominess being lifted for as long as they were onstage. Within weeks, however, that title was dropped in favor of the more prosaic *101*—the Rose Bowl had been the 101st concert of the *Music for the Masses* tour.

The title also camouflaged a second agenda. The music and the tour, of course, dominated the on-screen action, but the end result of so much activity, too, received considerable coverage as well—and that end result was numerical. The Rose Bowl concert was phenomenally profitable—gross receipts for the show amounted to a staggering $1,360,193—and toward the end of the movie, a promotor looks gleefully at the attendance figures and announces, "We're gonna be rich!" A title like *101* simply opened the audience's minds to the ensuing bombardment of similarly astronomical figures.

As the parent of Depeche Mode's Sire label, Warner Brothers (who joined radio syndication giants Westwood One and the magazine *Radio and Records* in distributing the film) took considerable exception to Pennebaker's flaunting of Depeche Mode's profit margin. When "Everything Counts" was culled from the inevitable soundtrack album as a single, the European video clip opened with an accountant marveling, "We made loads of money, tons of money!"—an obvious, but nevertheless effective juxtaposition. In America, the scene was promptly excised.

<201>

But the point was still made, in the movie and on the jacket of the accompanying *101* soundtrack album. At the band's insistence, the album appeared in the racks wrapped within Anton Corbijn's photograph of a Rose Bowl merchandising stall, its T-shirts priced at eighteen dollars and twenty-three dollars each, posters and programs at ten dollars, simple pins at six dollars.

Such harsh intrusions, many critics felt, defied Pennebaker's own description of the movie as "a musical fantasy, a . . . fragmented, simultaneous vision of the lives of its participants, layered like the music it's set to, with what was funny and what mattered." And certainly these moments detracted from the almost otherworldly qualities with which

Pennebaker's cameras embraced the true stars of the movie: the fans, whose antics Depeche Mode still found incredible.

But that contrast, the band was adamant, was deliberate. "We didn't want to make a film that just shows the band onstage," Dave insists. "We wanted to show the effect we've had on American culture and on the American fan in particular. The film really shows you what it's like for a band in the Eighties—now." The sheer economics of touring, both expenses and profits, was inescapably a part of that.

There was another juxtaposition to be considered as well, however, one that highlighted the now immeasurable gulf that existed between modern rock 'n' roll and that on which Pennebaker had cut his pop directorial teeth. The Rose Bowl show was staged twenty years to the very day after the Monterey Pop Festival, at which money had been all but irrelevant to the performers, fans, and organizers. Viewers cognizant of that piece of trivia could not help but agree that if the irony of that contrast was not deliberate, then the forces of cosmic coincidence were working overtime that day!

The Route 66-ers, whose journey to the Rose Bowl added a third storyline to the movie, themselves brought another dimension to this private humor. The Monterey audience, like that which gathered at Woodstock two years later, came together in the most natural way possible, growing together over the course of one weekend, united in the joy of the expected music. It became very easy to compare that event with the sense of forced community that permeated the blue bus as it traveled rock's most historic road map—and to do so very unfavorably.

But the teens also formed the adhesive that bound together a series of otherwise disjointed concert segments, and that despite their antics becoming increasingly intrusive as the movie wore on. Aboard their bus, they danced, fixed their hair, played to the cameras which never switched off, and showed just how single-minded their devotion to Depeche Mode was when they were offered the chance to visit Graceland—home to America's greatest living dead pop star.

"What's Graceland?" asked a spikey-haired traveler.

"It's where Elvis lived. Boring!" answered his similarly coiffeured girlfriend. Throughout *101*'s theater run, audiences cheered that dialogue as loudly as any musical highlight—and never before or since has the 1980s' rejection of rock 'n' roll's past been so dramatically captured. As Depeche Mode themselves had warned in the past, the kids knew intuitively that it was Elvis, and "American critics—staff writers at newspapers who've been there about thirty-five years, who wrote about Elvis," who were Depeche Mode's greatest enemies. "Our music is just so alien to them that some people are always going to hate us."

Despite the obvious weight of its joint distributors, *101* was to be treated very much as a low-budget independent movie—which, of course, it was. *101* was brought in for just $600,000—mere peanuts compared to the $5.3 million U2 dropped on their *Rattle and Hum* documentary, produced and released almost simultaneously with Depeche Mode's effort.

<203>

Even the cost of the *101* cinema prints was borne independently, and while that did restrict the number of films that could be made available to the country's theaters, John Beug, vice president of Warner's creative-services-and-marketing department, informed *Variety*, "This is a bit of test marketing." Rock films were traditionally sporadic drawers, unpopular with theater owners because with multiple showings a day, "an exhibitor is spending all this money and the audience is often not there. He runs it on a Tuesday night, and there are maybe four people in the theater."

The solution, Beug determined, was to release *101* for limited runs only, beginning with weekend screenings at four theaters in Los Angeles and Houston. The same principle that had created a cult success of the *Rocky Horror Picture Show,* which had originally debuted as a weekends-only, midnight-only feature, was employed with equal success for Pennebaker's own *Don't Look Back.*

The intention was for *101* to be given a shot at similar status.

The gambit worked. Following its premier at the Berlin International Film Festival, *101* made its American debut on April 28, 1989. After just two weekends, it grossed over $50,000, $13,568 of that during its first weekend in Los Angeles alone. Spread over just eight performances, that sum gave *101* the highest per-screen average in the city that weekend—and accomplished it without any newspaper advertising.

By early May, screenings were set for fourteen more cities throughout North America; by mid-August, *101* was even figuring on *Variety*'s daily box-office report—a stringently tabulated ranking of the top fifty highest-grossing movies. Despite being shown on just two screens nationwide, *101* was the forty-eighth-most-profitable movie of the weekend in terms of overall receipts—tenth according to per-screen averages. Among the considerably better-known movies it outranked were *Turner and Hooch, Batman,* and *Ghostbusters II.*

<204>

Critical reaction to *101* was, unsurprisingly, mixed. Journalist Danny Kelly offered *New Musical Express* readers the chance to exchange Depeche Mode for "two split conkers and a flavored condom." There were no takers, Kelly went on, because "in this country the Modies don't matter a thre'penny toss."

But such indifference was not reserved simply for Depeche Mode. The very concept of rock movies was in the doldrums at the time, the consequence of too many artists making too many films, and few of them being very good. Besides, videos frequently did the same job a lot faster! It is no coincidence that both Michael Jackson's "Thriller" and David Bowie's "Jazzing for Blue Jean"—"long-form" videos that built storylines both within and without the central song—played in cinemas before they became television staples.

For adherents of the movie format, too, there was no doubt that the genre was becoming increasingly stale. The Rolling Stones' *Let's Spend the Night Together,* documenting one night on the band's 1981 *Still Life* tour, and Sting's *Bring on the Night* failed not because the performances were flawed, but because the medium was. The concert movie was at its height, conceptually, at a time when touring superstars visited only the major cities, leaving vast tracts of the country untouched. Led Zeppelin's *The Song Remains The Same,* Eric Clapton's *Rock 'n' Roll Hotel,* and the Band's *Last Waltz* succeeded because they allowed people a glimpse of an event they might never see again—and in the latter case, certainly wouldn't; *The Last Waltz* was the Band's farewell concert.

It was ironic, then, that it was the Rolling Stones who both crippled the movie format *and* became the first victims of their actions. The fifty-city *Still Life* tour grossed an astonishing $50 million in just twelve weeks, simply by setting up in cities where massive arena shows were something that happened to other folks. Other bands had appreciated the importance of rock 'n' roll's backwaters, of course—Kiss and the Police both courted their eventual superstardom by slogging around cities no other band would touch.

<205>

But the Rolling Stones were different. They not only took their music to the masses, they took their corporate sponsors with them. Guaranteed several million dollars of somebody else's money, a band could now *afford* to visit an echoing stadium in the middle of nowhere. It was in hindsight they realized that by releasing a movie of the event, they were simply spoiling an audience who was already sated.

The only genuine exception to this rule was a movie made by the one band that could rightfully claim the crown that the Rolling Stones' increasingly tepid 1980s output had let slip—Ireland's U2. Nineteen eighty-four's *Under a Blood-Red Sky* was originally shot for television by the latest pretender to Britain's ever-contested Authoritative Pop Program throne, "The Tube," and was comprised almost exclusively of concert footage.

It was short (under an hour in length), sharp, and to the point, but more than that, it succeeded partly because of the sheer drama of the concert's setting—the spectacular Red Rocks arena in Colorado—and partly because, like *The Last*

Waltz, it captured the end of an era: U2's transition from traditional stadium rockers to the more esoteric experimentalists of *The Unforgettable Fire* and beyond.

So once again it was ironic that U2's next movie attempt, director Phil Joanou's *Rattle and Hum,* should join the lengthening list of box-office failures—at precisely the same time *101* was painstakingly restoring some dignity to the rock-movie genre. *Rattle and Hum* premiered at the beginning of November 1988, recouped more than two-thirds of its budget in its very first weekend, and by the end of the month had disappeared from almost every cinema in America—the remainder of its costs still barely covered.

101, on the other hand, was released with minimum fuss, minimum promotion, and minimum screenings. And that, insisted Martin, "was a better way to do it. If for some reason it does well, people are pleasantly surprised. If not, then it can just come out on video and nothing's lost.

<206>

"I think the way U2 went about it was a bit of a mistake in some ways. They had this massive promotional budget, went out and there were big adverts everywhere, and then everyone was just let down at the end of that. Everybody expected this massive box-office thing and it didn't happen."

Financing aside, there was nevertheless much in common between the two movies. Both caught their subjects on- and offstage; both allowed them plenty of room in which to decry the stereotypical image of the star as a rock 'n' roll animal. U2 wandered through Graceland and mumbled through interviews; Depeche bought country tapes in Nashville and posed with baby Jack Gahan. For all superficial intents and purposes, the only real difference was that U2 came to life when their guitars were plugged in. Depeche Mode left *their* guitars backstage.

But there were other, considerably deeper conflicts, too. Even at its most inspired, *Rattle and Hum* had a strangely scripted sense to it, as though even its most impromptu moments were selected and edited to order. "Rather than a documentary," complained *Rolling Stone*'s Anthony DeCurtis, "it's merely a documentary of events that often were staged and arranged for the express purpose of being filmed. . . ."

101, however, took its momentum from its sheer chaos, and only once that momentum had reached its maximum speed did the chaos resolve itself. Certainly the bus scenes became wearing, and it was hard to escape the impression (denied by Pennebaker) that the eight travelers were falling into preconceived roles. But still, there remained a natural quality to their behavior that even their constant awareness of the cameras could not disturb—and that was certainly more believable than U2's "Pop Stars on Vacation" antics.

The end result, most apparent in the conflict between crass commercialism (six dollars for a pin!) and outright hero worship, was best summed up by Pennebaker himself, discussing perhaps the single element that has remained constant to Depeche Mode ever since *A Broken Frame:* "The songs have a double edge. Martin will write a song one way, but David will come along and sing it with a different impression." When the two interpretations clashed, that was when Depeche Mode made magic. *101* caught a taste of that magic.

<207>

As *101* wound its inexorable way around the United States—a series of engagements that ended in August, with the movie's release as a home video—each city was treated to its own special "premier." In Sacramento, the local Inn Theater offered prizes to the best Depeche Mode look-alikes; in Hollywood, Depeche Mode themselves won an introduction to Guns n' Roses front man Axl Rose—who promptly declared himself a big fan, and proved it by reciting the plaintive lyrics to "Somebody." He also invited the band to join him at the Cat House heavy-metal nightclub, and among themselves, Depeche Mode was impressed.

But Rose blew it. From the Cat House, the vocalist headed off to a friend's Beverly Hills barbecue, where, the following day's scandal sheets reported, he shot a pig.

In London, a Mute Records spokesman tersely informed the British media that "as strict vegetarians, the band were appalled by [Rose's] behavior and do not wish to associate themselves with anyone who goes round shooting pigs for fun." But still, marveled the press, Axl Rose digs Depeche Mode.

"I think everybody likes to be respected, and we're no different," agreed Alan. "We'd like to think that in the future, people will look back and see us as having made some sort of forward step." That, he presumed, was the original concept for *101*—"the Eighties, and how we fit into the decade. We really wanted to explore why we were so indicative of the Eighties, as opposed to earlier decades."

Pennebaker dismissed Alan's vision, but argued that what *101* captured was of considerably greater importance. "I think [Alan] imagined we were going to interview a lot of people, and out of that, the band would find something that would beguile them. These are four young guys who have this enormous cult audience that somehow came out of the backyard. Here's a band that doesn't get played a lot on the radio, they go into town for a concert and there isn't a lot of advertising, most people don't know who they are, but suddenly the place is full to capacity.

"And the people aren't just there 'cause it's a place to get away with smoking pot. They've really thought a lot about the music; they know the words and are right into it. For the band, this must be a kind of wonder. They're not all that old, they haven't thought this through philosophically. Alan is probably the most intellectual of the four, and he was hoping that we'd find some kind of answer. I always told him, 'Alan, there is no easy answer.'"

Or maybe there was. Throughout the summer of 1989, readers of the personal ads in various British magazines were arrested by the offer of their "own Personal Jesus." For further details, they should just call a certain telephone number. And if it wasn't the Messiah himself who answered the call with a song, the promises he made were convincing all the same:

"Pick up the receiver, I'll make you a believer. . . ."

<208>

Chapter 12

We Remember

Being Punk

THE FIRST BRICKS flew a little after ten P.M. For the past hour, the police had been trying to maintain some order to a line that had been growing for forty-eight hours now, and stretched for close to fifteen blocks. But even with riot-ready reinforcements arriving throughout the evening, a crowd of almost ten thousand people was simply too overwhelming.

Streets away, passersby marveled incredulously at the scene, and their murmuring could be heard throughout Los Angeles. Some people suggested that the President was visiting. Others thought maybe Michael Jackson was in town. Only those who listened to KROQ knew what was really happening. . . . It was March 20, 1990, and Depeche Mode was in town, signing copies of their new album at a La Cienega Boulevard record store.

The first complaints were filed earlier in the afternoon, as local residents panicked at the buildup of teenagers around the mid-Wilshire branch of the Where-house. Graffiti was springing up on walls as boredom was relieved with a quick scrawl. The noise from the portable stereos and boom boxes went on without remission. Traffic was backing up as the line spilled across neighboring roads. People were tired of telling kids to get out of the trees.

Depeche Mode reached the Wherehouse exactly on schedule, a little before nine P.M. Even as they were shepherded through the store's back door, they were amazed at the number of people who had turned out to see them—the event had only been arranged a week before, and the general conviction was that attendance would be light. Just thirty security guards had been hired for the event, which would be over by midnight—so far as the organizers were concerned, it was just another record signing in a store that had staged so many.

<210>

But there was something different about this one, something Los Angeles should have learned two years earlier, when sixty-five thousand of these same teenagers crammed the Rose Bowl to welcome a band that, in the only slightly exaggerated words of the local *Herald Tribune,* wouldn't have filled a bowling alley anywhere else.

There was a sense of expectation in the air, a sense not of simple longing, but of emotional, sexual, cultural, explosive longing. Later, L.A. police captain Keith Bushey admitted that something had to give. "You can't put that many people in that small an area without something [happening]."

And when it did happen, he didn't blame the crowd. They were, he assured the media, "really good, solid young people. There was no evil intention on anybody's part." He sounded almost helpless as he added, "There was just so many of them."

From the moment Depeche Mode was spotted arriving, the crowd began to surge toward the door, pushing and screaming into the store. Police and security guards alike were overwhelmed; at the back of the shop, the four musicians simply looked bewildered—they, too, had believed this would be just another record signing. Now, as the Wherehouse's giant plate-glass windows buckled ominously close to the breaking point under the pressure of so many bodies pushing against it, it was obvious that it wasn't.

"It actually got quite scary!" Dave still sounded shaken, even after the band members returned to the safety of their hotel. "There was no way we could have known there was going to be so many people!"

Alongside the band members, KROQ deejay Richard Blade tried to maintain calm, keep the line moving, make sure that the band members each signed every record jacket, item of clothing, scrap of paper or piece of flesh that was presented to them. But it was always a hopeless task. By ten, the crush inside the shop was intolerable—and outside, the police had had enough. It was time to close the operation down. The band would have to leave.

‹211›

Depeche Mode didn't need to be asked twice. "You could just feel the atmosphere in the place building up," Dave said, shuddering. "We just all looked at each other and said, 'We gotta get out of here!' " They slipped out of the same back door they had entered through, and the announcement was bullhorned into the crowd: The event was canceled. Everybody should just get themselves home.

"No one wanted to believe they had left, even though we had seen them leave," one fan anguished to the *L.A. Times.* "We had been waiting here all day, and we wanted to see them so badly."

Her disappointment was manifest. Elsewhere, however, it was rapidly channeled into anger. Battling against a hail of flying bricks, a hundred and fifty police officers in full riot gear moved to disperse the crowd. Next door, at the Daily Grill restaurant, manager John Cook could only watch helplessly as two neon signs were destroyed by the mob, and plaster was chipped and kicked off the walls.

The evening cost the city twenty-five thousand dollars in riot control alone, and it was miraculous that there weren't any more injuries—just seven people were hurt, including a seventeen-year-old girl who was trampled when her knee gave out and she fell to the ground.

It was, all things considered, a suitably apocalyptic welcome for a band whose latest American album was called *Violator*.

Depeche Mode was still in the studio when "Personal Jesus" was released in August 1989. They had thirteen songs programmed into the computers—as usual, everything was written and demo-ed long before any studio time was booked, and at that early stage, thoughts turned not only toward a full-length album, but also to an EP of material that Fletch described as "pretty interesting and quite apart from the normal stuff we do."

<212> That project was eventually scrapped; in its place came two new releases by individual members of the band: Alan's Recoil project, and Martin's *Counterfeit* EP, both of which were released during the fall of 1989.

Of the two, *Counterfeit* came in for the greatest attention, if only because Martin was the most unpredictable member of the group. For several years, there had been talk of Martin joining forces with Genesis P. Orridge, the uncompromising mastermind behind industrial pioneers Throbbing Gristle and their spiritual successors, Psychic TV.

Despite his often brutal musical reputation, P. Orridge had become almost the spiritual father to many of the early-1980s electronic bands—at the very height of Soft Cell's fame, he linked up with Marc Almond for the "Discipline" single, while he continues to work with Almond's erstwhile partner Dave Ball to this day.

P. Orridge and Martin were long-standing friends; both had spoken longingly of their urge to work together. "We share a similar love of decadence and naughtiness," P. Orridge says in explanation. Unfortunately, *Counterfeit* was not to be the long-awaited consummation of their proposed "marriage."

Rather than siphon away some of his own unreleased compositions on what he admitted was simply a time-killing exercise, Martin instead opted to record an eclectic clutch of cover versions: the Comsat Angels' "Gone," Tuxedomoon's "In a Matter of Speaking," Durutti Column's "Smile in a Crowd," the traditional gospel song "Motherless Child," Sparks' "Never Turn Your Back on Mother Earth," and Joe Crow's "Compulsion." (He also recorded but, sadly, left unreleased, a version of Gregory Phillips's "Down in the Boon-docks"—coincidentally, one of the first-ever releases on the original British independent label, Immediate.)

Of all the criticisms aimed at *Counterfeit,* therefore, the most common was that creatively it was a dud. Not only did Martin not write anything new for the record, his arrangements scarcely deviated from the originals (hence the project's title, of course!). Rather, like the all-covers albums unleashed in swift mid-Seventies succession by David Bowie (*Pin Ups*), Bryan 213 Ferry (*These Foolish Things*), and John Lennon (*Rock and Roll*), *Counterfeit* spoke merely of what the performer listened to, not what he had to say himself.

"I think that the covers make perfect sense," Martin defended himself. "When you're in [that] situation, a Phil Collins/Genesis situation, you only write a certain number of songs. And obviously I'd want to use the best ones for my solo record and the band would want to use the best ones for the band, and there can be conflicts. I didn't want to wind up neglecting the band."

In any event, the opportunity for Martin to air some of the closet gems from his personal record collection was itself of value. The British bands Comsat Angels and Durutti Column were both critical favorites during the early–mid-1980s, but had never made much of a mark on the public taste; Tuxedomoon and Joe Crow were even more cult-oriented, while Sparks, the Anglo-American band that erupted in Britain in 1974, had never come close to repeating its U.K. success in America. "Never Turn Your Back," the band's third U.K. hit that year, was an achingly beautiful song that still deserved, even *demanded,* to be heard in 1989.

If Martin used his solo project to simply kill time, Alan used his to kill frustration. He had tasted the solo waters before, in 1986, when he first got his hands on a sampler. "I was experimenting, chopping up pieces of Depeche Mode songs and [making them] into a weird piece."

That was *1+2,* a barely noticed twelve-inch single, and both it and his latest Recoil project, the five-track *Hydrology,* grew directly out of Alan's own perception of his role within Depeche Mode.

Widely regarded, even by his bandmates, as the most accomplished musician in the group, Alan had also grown pleasantly accustomed to seeing himself described in print as the band's *other* songwriter, and that despite the fact that his credited contributions to Depeche Mode's output still numbered in single figures—half a dozen B-sides and just three album tracks, spread between *Construction Time Again* and *Some Great Reward.*

<214>

It was, he said with a smile, a rather pathetic tally, but in all honesty, none of those tracks particularly pleased him. "I never felt [those songs] came from me," he confessed in a moment of surprising candor. "They came from something *in* me that said I should be writing songs. Consequently, when I listen to my songs being done by Depeche Mode, I don't like them."

Hydrology, if not aptly described as Alan's revenge, was nevertheless a reminder that his own energies were not laying dormant until the band called him in to program the computers one more time—and also his acknowledgment that there were deficiencies within the Depeche Mode setup.

"The main thing that unifies *Hydrology* is that kind of hypnotic effect it gives you," he commented. "I like that feeling. There are elements of it within Mode music, but because the band is so based around three- or four-minute songs, it's very difficult to have that idea of drawing people gradually into the music as it goes on. It would be nice to become a bit more flexible within the group."

Happily, Alan admitted that "I didn't know how anything would end up until I was finished." Ideas would be followed to their ultimate musical conclusion, then scrapped or retained as Alan saw fit. Starting from a single sequence, "a bass line or some kind of mid-range part," he would "let it play around, let myself be hypnotized, and then see where that led me."

This sense of discovery even permeated through to Recoil's promotional photographs—which pictured Alan lying facedown in a bathful of water.

Of course, the proximity of *Counterfeit*'s release to Recoil's caused some good-natured rivalry to erupt between the two burgeoning soloists. "[*Counterfeit*] was quite good, but I thought it was a little bit incomplete—a little bit like well-recorded demos," Alan pondered; and compared to his own *Hydrology,* that was a fair criticism. But, as more than one reviewer pointed out, at least you could sing along to *Counterfeit*!

<215>

Neither *Counterfeit* nor *Hydrology* made any inroads into the mass consciousness (*Counterfeit*'s sales barely topped ten thousand), but among Depeche Mode's own rabid following—despite the burgeoning club impact of "Personal Jesus"—the coincidence of their release did not go unnoticed. "You make one solo album," Martin said with a sigh, "and some people swear you're about to leave the band, or there are creative differences. None of that is true."

His words were no different from those uttered by a thousand other people as they quit a thousand other bands, but when Martin spoke, it was final. There can be no greater indication of the trust that their fans vest in Depeche Mode than the fact that nobody ever mentioned a possible breakup again.

Like *Music for the Masses,* the new Depeche Mode album was pieced together in new surroundings, with a new producer, Mark "Flood" Ellis, and a legendary mixer, Francois

Kervorkian, the New York–based producer who has created danceable club hits for the most unlikely of artists, U2 and the Smiths included!

The sessions themselves shifted between Milan's Logic Studios, Axis in New York, London's Church and Master Rock studios, and the Danish Puk complex, where *Music for the Masses* was mixed.

Flood, a former London disc jockey, had been working within the Mute setup since the early 1980s, engineering for Yazoo among others, and establishing himself as Daniel Miller's heir apparent simply through his familiarity with the label's requirements. When Depeche Mode first started talking with him about their plans for the album, already titled *Violator,* Flood understood intuitively what they demanded.

<216>

The key to the album, as Fletch explained, was to create "an atmosphere. I felt that we'd previously perfected a formula, [so this time] we jammed. Instead of just perfecting songs, we worked on an overall sound, [which] suits us because we're still not strictly technical. We still like to remember being fifteen and inspired by punk. We could never be Emerson, Lake and Palmer."

The band's Milan studio dates were not even preserved on the album. Depeche Mode spent their entire time in that city partying, cutting loose with friends and fans, and not getting a stroke of recording done. "But we had a good time," laughs Fletch, "and it cemented the spirit of the whole album." In Denmark, on the contrary, "the studio was in the middle of nowhere, and we got eight tracks recorded."

As usual, the album boasted its fair share of private jokes. Again according to Fletch, the title itself was chosen because the band wanted a name that sounded like it belonged on either a heavy-metal disc . . . or a hardcore porn book. *Violator* fit both bills.

One track, "World in My Eyes," borrowed its title from fellow Mute artist Loop's album *World in Your Eyes.* Elsewhere, responding to the escalating percentage of reviewers

who labeled Depeche Mode the "new Pink Floyd," one track—
the moody "Clean" finale—lifted its opening bass line almost
directly from the Floyd's own "One of These Days." Typically,
the joke backfired—Depeche Mode was promptly accused, in
New Musical Express, of covering a Tangerine Dream song!
They hadn't, of course, but sharp-eared clubgoers might have
noticed the Kraftwerk samples littered through Razormaid's
remix of "World in My Eyes"!

The burgeoning success of "Personal Jesus" only
urged Depeche Mode on—its success, and the ensuing controversy.

It was some weeks into the "Personal Jesus" telephone campaign before the British press got wind of what was
happening. A handful of callers had complained, claiming that
their prayers for redemption were met by a simple pop song.
Newspaper ad managers dialed the number, either smiled or
scowled, and a few of them canceled the advertisement. Martin <217>
noted their approbation calmly. "I can see their point," he
deadpanned. "Imagine someone about to top themselves and
they see [that ad] in the paper; my last savior, my last chance
. . . and it's Depeche Mode!"

Other editors, however, left the ad alone. If the song
made even one or two lonely souls think twice before diving
headlong into the embrace of one of the real religious cults that
had turned the Personals columns into a happy hunting ground,
then maybe their prayers were being answered after all.

Afterward, Depeche Mode themselves were ada-
mant that despite the most obvious conclusions that could be
drawn, "Personal Jesus" was not an assault on religion, even if
there was something mildly disturbing about a seductively
choppy blues tune that recommended its listeners pick up the
telephone and win instant conversion.

According to Martin himself, the song was actually
based upon Priscilla Presley's portrait of her late ex-husband in
the book *Elvis and Me.* "It's about how Elvis was her man and
her mentor and how often that happens in love relationships,

how everybody's heart is like a god in some way. It's . . . about being a Jesus for somebody else, someone to give you hope and care."

The song was both a logical and a dangerous choice for a single release—dangerous because, like "Blasphemous Rumours" before it, it set the group up against the countless organizations and individuals (and not only the fundamentalist Christian sects) for whom the very use of Jesus's name, outside of strictly proscribed contexts, amounted to sacrilege; logical because, flying in the face of much of Depeche Mode's recent singles catalog, it at last afforded the band the opportunity to shatter the last boundary that restricted them—in Martin's opinion, at least.

"We've really been concerned over the years that with some people—especially in the States—we're just labeled a dance band, and to some people, that's just throwaway. When we release a record, we seem to be heavily promoted on the dance front, [which] puts a lot of pressure on us, because really we like to release any single we like—whether it's dance or not. Whenever we release a record, the reaction in the States is, 'Great song, great song, but the B-side is better for us because the B-side is more throwaway.' " The ghost of "But Not To-night" still rankled. "We don't really understand the American market. . . ."

<218>

But the American market certainly appeared to understand Depeche Mode. Although it was to take six months to register on the *Billboard* Top Forty (it eventually peaked at number thirty-one), "Personal Jesus" entered immediately into heavy airplay on MTV, its stunning video directed again by Anton Corbijn, and excerpted from another mini-movie, *Strange Too.* The Southwestern flavor of the "Personal Jesus" set, the band hanging out in a sleazy desert bordello, simply added to the multitude of inferences that could be drawn from the song—maybe sex was the salvation that Depeche Mode so salaciously offered?

Suitably impressed by the single's success (by the

time its chart run was over, "Personal Jesus" ranked among the best-selling singles in their American record company's history), reviews of *Violator* were almost unanimously positive.

Spin magazine, conscious of the sheer emotional impact Depeche Mode was capable of having on their audience, described the album as "this generation's 'You've Got a Friend,' [catching], maybe even creating, the national mood. Dread, doubt, uncertainty. Fear of self and surroundings. It was everywhere you turned; even Mariah Carey suffered from alienation." Other publications offered similarly thoughtful prognoses.

Back in Britain, of course, Depeche Mode's history still offered a convenient peg from which to hang the occasional disparaging comment. Having described the album as "a veritable dungeon of songs for you to jangle your manacles at," *Record Mirror*'s Tim Nicholson then accused Depeche Mode of simply "playing pretend"—a confession that he was still unable <219> to take the band seriously after all these years.

Sounds' Damon Wise went even further. "If [William] Burroughs wrote for Gahan, Depeche Mode would be terrifying. But he doesn't. Martin Gore writes for Gahan and Depeche Mode are hilarious. The charm of [their] doggedly glib platitudes is wearing thin."

But Wise tempered his own apparent dislike with the admission that Depeche Mode was now "insufferably credible . . . although it took their absence to occasion the media thaw." The only question that remained to be answered, he believed, was, Would anyone dare tell them that to their face?

This newfound credibility, if that is the correct word for it, in many ways came down to Depeche Mode taking control of their own immediate destinies for the first time in their career. In the three years that had passed since *Music for the Masses,* the changes in the musical landscape that Depeche Mode's own past machinations had both predicted and presaged were finally being wrought—musically and culturally. Now they were reaping the benefits.

When Depeche Mode first emerged, the synthesizer itself was a novel instrument, and the bands that rode into view on that novelty were swiftly seized upon not only as musical visionaries, but also as prime tasties for the ever-voracious teen meat machine, handsome pinups who looked as fresh as they sounded. The pioneers of the genre, the Kraftwerks, Enos, and Pink Floyds, of course, didn't get a look in. To put it bluntly, they were *old.*

Now it was sampling technology that was the new kid on the mass-marketing block, and the new darlings of the pop poster press were those bands who emerged, equally new, equally kidlike. Now it was Jesus Jones, Ned's Atomic Dustbin, EMF, the Beloved (whose Jon Marsh executed a fabulous "Mayhem Mode" remix of "World in My Eyes"), even Carter the Unstoppable Sex Machine, the south London duo whose irrepressible riotousness was by their own admission that of long experience, not youthful exhuberance, who would be waging the wars Depeche Mode had fought a full decade before; waging them and, so long as they were equipped to maintain their original zealousness for the long haul, perhaps win them as well, just as Depeche Mode had won theirs.

Old habits died hard—Depeche Mode was still approached by the teen magazines for photos, posters, and impressions of their lips, and occasionally the band members would kowtow to those demands, and with nerdish abandon rush once more into the embrace of a market they had long since outgrown—and grown to detest as well.

"Perhaps if we'd called ourselves a rock band from day one," Martin mused, "we would have had a lot more credibility from day one." Instead, the group went out on the pop limb and earned their credibility the hard way—by gaining so much success that people simply couldn't ignore them any longer.

The band's homeland image, as *Alternative Press*'s Rachel Felder put it, of "leather coated pinups, somewhere between George Michael, the Clash, and a Robert Mapplethorpe

<220>

portrait," had indeed "clouded the somber messages of songs like 'Blasphemous Rumours' and 'Strangelove.' " But according to Alan, "We didn't care much . . . at the time." It was only as time passed that "we've come to realize that sort of thing hasn't done us much good. It's a learning process—as you go on, you realize the important things and the less important things."

"There was this band that everybody loved to hate," Dave reasoned to *Rolling Stone,* "and yet they were incredibly successful. *'Why?'* "—he began mimicking so many of the journalists the band had encountered in the past. " '*Why* do you think you're so successful? *Why* do you think you're on this planet?' It got to the point in interviews where we'd just say 'Fuck you' and walk out." The response to *Violator* was the sound of the world running out after them.

Fresh fuel was added to the band's hurtling momentum by the growing acknowledgments of Depeche Mode leaking from the house-music community—perhaps the most blatant beneficiary of the advent of sampling. Depeche Mode themselves acknowledged this influence when Alan grafted a housey beat onto Martin's original, organ-powered, vision of "Enjoy the Silence," but still, Depeche Mode and, in their wake, their fans and detractors alike were first stunned, then in many instances gratified to discover that an entire generation of Detroit house deejays and producers had grown up imbibing their music.

<221>

"We were never conscious of our influence on Eighties dance music," Dave confessed. "That's the charm of . . . all the compliments that were paid to us by the people in Detroit. We've just gone about things in our own way, unaware of how much influence we're having on other groups."

"I think it was in our approach, rather than the sound itself," Martin continued. "We've always tried to be on the so-called forefront of technology, and I suppose the way we work has been quite influential."

It was amid this atmosphere of unexpected jubilation that Dave wandered into some unaccustomed controversy when he was approached by singer Jimmy Somerville to add his chest to the growing number of artists willing to sport gay pride Act-Up T-shirts. Dave declined, "vociferously," according to the British magazine *No. 1,* a refusal that surprised many people.

It had been, after all, less than three years since "Never Let Me Down Again" was gratefully championed by many within the homosexual community—as indeed many of Depeche Mode's biggest club hits had been. In America especially, the gay club circuit has long been regarded as the dominant factor in many bands' subsequent breakthroughs, or lack thereof, and Depeche Mode was no exception. It would have been very easy for Dave's refusal—which he never did attempt to justify—to be taken as a deliberate snub toward one of Depeche Mode's most important audiences.

<222> Fortunately for him, then, the incident barely provoked a ripple of interest in either the mainstream music press or its gay counterpart. But Dave did not appear willing to let the incident drop. In the same week he rejected Somerville's request, he was involved in a minor fracas at a nightclub when he threw a sofa from a fifteenth-floor window when the club deejay insisted on spinning . . . a Jimmy Somerville record!

That, however, was nothing compared to the events of just two weeks later, when Depeche Mode celebrated the American release of *Violator* with their ill-fated record signing at the La Cienega Wherehouse.

Depeche Mode themselves put a brave face on the incident. "As bad and as dangerous as the situation was," Alan candidly commented, "it was good PR. We were in the news all across the country." Sitting back at their hotel, with every news station reporting how "English pop group Depeche Mode brought traffic to a standstill," they found it difficult to hide their jubilation—even more difficult than it was to pretend that Depeche Mode was not at last living out their ultimate pop fantasies. Recognition, respect, and riots? Who could ask for anything more?

But the band was not to escape the fallout from so shocking an event. According to *Rolling Stone,* one Los Angeles venue had "expressed reservations about booking the band on its upcoming U.S. tour."

That tour was to be part of Depeche Mode's longest ever, a worldwide outing that would keep the group on the road well into 1991, and involved thirty-one stops in the United States and Canada alone, before heading off to the band's first-ever full tours of Australia and Japan. Europe and Britain would round off a frenetic year.

The portents were already good—Martin's two-year-old dream of taking Nitzer Ebb to America was finally fulfilled, and a full month before the tour kicked off, *Violator* peaked at number seven on the *Billboard* charts.

As fast as ticket offices opened, the demand swamped them. In New York, Depeche Mode sold forty-two thousand tickets for their Giants Stadium show within a day. <223> Dallas's twenty thousand-seat Starplex Ampitheater was sold out within a week; so was the World Music Theater in Tinley Park, Chicago. In Los Angeles, where the now traditional tour closer was to take place, forty-eight thousand tickets for the August 4 show at Dodger Stadium were sold within an hour of going on sale, two months before the gig. Within seventy-two hours, a second night was added—and that sold out even faster.

Even in Florida, a state whose radio had notoriously avoided Depeche Mode records in the past, and which the band had never previously visited, there was a volley of four sold-out gigs. Indeed, the tour would actually be opening in the Sunshine State, at the Pensacola Civic Center, where Depeche Mode's pretour rehearsals were taking place. Pensacola itself is known locally as the "Redneck Riviera," and Depeche Mode themselves delighted in putting its reputation to the test. "I've been called a faggot about twenty times today," Alan complained to *Rolling Stone*'s visiting Jeff Giles. "It's the haircut," Dave replied.

Not everything went according to plan, of course.

Depeche Mode's scheduled show at the Ottawa Civic Center was canceled on the very day of the show, after the band's road crew—resplendent in T-shirts that bellowed "Depeche Fuckin' Mode"—accidentally dislodged a quantity of asbestos from a ceiling beam.

Depeche Mode refused to go ahead with the concert unless the promoters, Bass Clef Entertainments, could prove the venue was still safe. The best efforts of an emergency cleanup team were no consolation and, as the local *Sun* newspaper punned, six thousand fans were left with "nothing to do but 'enjoy the silence.' "

"Those guys completely overreacted," Bass Clef's Dennis Ruffo complained. He insisted that the band was shown two recent independent engineering studies that proved the venue's asbestos levels were safe—the bulk of the material, in the building's ceiling tiles, had been removed some seven months earlier. "[But] we couldn't convince them. They were adamant that they would not perform the show."

Elsewhere, however, problems tended to be reserved for those occasions when the band came face-to-face with their critics, that breed of provincial newspaper reporter whom Fletch himself had long since branded for being as old and hidebound as rock 'n' roll itself.

Among their number, there was the need not only to report on Depeche Mode's show, but also to reply to the band's musical blasphemies. To them, it was inexplicable that any band could have survived so long, and risen so high, purely on the strength of synthesizers, sacrilege, and sex.

"Live, Depeche Mode is about the silliest thing in pop music since *Spinal Tap*," complained the *Orlando Sentinel*'s Parry Gettelman. " 'But gee, Dick, it's got a great beat, you can dance to it, I give it an 11.' " The reporter then explained the joke—instantly proving Fletch's point. "Of course, if you actually saw Depeche Mode, you're probably too young to remember 'American Bandstand.' " The direct lineage between

<224>

his humor, and that still-memorable line in *101*—"What's Graceland?"—could not have been drawn any tighter.

Such grumblings, however, could not even dent the juggernaut that now enveloped Depeche Mode. In March 1990 the follow-up to "Personal Jesus"—the majestic "Enjoy the Silence"—burst into the U.K. charts at number seventeen. Weeks later, it was number six—their biggest single since "People Are People."

When *Violator* was released that same month, it shipped gold, outsold both Madonna and Prince, and came to rest at number two on the charts. By the time the album had completed its transatlantic chart runs, and the world tour was finally winding down, *Violator* had spawned two more hit singles: "Policy of Truth" (sensationally remixed by KLF) and "World in My Eyes." "In 1990," Andrew Harrison wrote in *Select,* "three Depeche Modes would not be enough to sate the demand."

<225>

Depeche Mode themselves could not have agreed more. "We can't keep up like this," Martin lamented. "We need a few years' break from all this. We've been doing it for ten years without any huge breaks. There's something insane about this business—about the cycle of making albums and going on tour to promote them. All of us in the band could use a long stretch of sanity."

And some more than others.

It would be harsh to say that Dave was cracking under the pressure, but all three of his bandmates, and the band's entourage as well, had noticed that he was changing. Irritable, even irascible, he had apparently stopped enjoying himself, on- and offstage. He snapped when he was questioned, barked demands where once he would have offered suggestions.

There wasn't even any respite when he finally came off the road, mentally shattered, physically exhausted, and hovering on the brink of his thirtieth birthday, toward which he had never shown less than unequivocal hatred. "You go past thirty, that big three-oh, and you've got to start kicking arse."

Otherwise . . . otherwise you might as well pull the blanket over your knees and start sipping that bedtime cocoa right now.

But there was no peace, even at home. Trips back to Basildon to visit his mother were like attempting an army assault course, as well-meaning neighbors came to pay their respects, and the old crowd of knockers came to hurl imprecations. In the end, Dave was having to ask his mother to visit *him,* "and bring the old house with you."

Once he had craved attention. Now he loathed it. There were, after all, only so many mornings that one could wake up to find another group of fans sitting on the lawn, singing Depeche Mode songs! Dave had already moved house twice, simply to escape the attentions of his own fan club.

"Because it's not the normal fans you tend to meet," Alan reminded him. "You only tend to meet the obsessive ones. So you get this sort of warped vision of what your fans are like."

<226>

Warped . . . like the kid who hired a private detective, a real live Philip Marlowe, to follow Dave home from the recording studio and report back on the singer's address. Then he turned up at Dave's front door, in the same clothes he'd seen Dave wearing, expecting to be rewarded for his diligence.

Dave went ballistic. "I lost my rag and really shouted at him. I told him, basically, to fuck off." The boy retreated, close to tears.

A few days later, Dave sat down and wrote the fan a letter: " 'I apologize but you must respect my privacy . . .' He [wrote] back saying, 'I'm sorry I bothered you and I won't ever do it again. . . . [P.S.] Would it be possible for me to come round next weekend?'

"I just thought, Well, that's it. It's time to move."

Only this time, he wasn't going around the block, or down the road. This time he was going halfway around the world. And he was going alone.

Chapter 13

Time to Start

Kicking Arse

DEPECHE MODE PARTED company at the end of the *Violator* tour, not knowing whether they would ever work together again.

They were sick of touring, they were sick of one another, and if—as so often in the past when frayed feelings reached flash point and boiled over into battle—the pressure points seemed minor to outsiders, within the group's closest circles, they represented more than the end of a tour. They marked the end of an era.

Ten years is a long time in the life of a rock 'n' roll band. The Beatles barely scraped a decade together, and the Rolling Stones only survived by taking longer and longer breaks from each other. When they started out, rock 'n' roll was still a hobby, something to fill in time before the real world came knocking. It was only later, in the mid–late

1970s, that people perceived it as a career in itself, and began changing bands like others change jobs.

Was that, Depeche Mode asked themselves, what their band had become? A job? As the tour wound down, exhausted and exhausting, it certainly felt like one.

Everybody had their own plans, their own vision of their immediate future. Fletch and Martin were looking forward simply to spending time with their own families—or families to be: Both were getting married the moment the madness was over. Alan was planning a new Recoil album, an outlet for the musical demons who preyed so heavily on his mind while he toured with Depeche Mode. And Dave . . . Dave was considering uprooting his entire world.

Dave's marriage had suffered rough patches before, but none like this. Just as he had feared, he'd almost completely missed his son's first year; now he'd just missed his fourth. Even if mother and child did make it out to some of Depeche Mode's foreign dates, Dave mourned, "It was [still] a very difficult time . . . because of [my] not being able to be around much. It all created a lot of friction at home, and [we] did come very close to splitting up." That particular breach was eventually healed in the excitement of Dave's immediate homecoming. But others were not to be mended so easily.

As the tour wound down, Dave found his own thoughts turning more and more toward his age, toward the big three-oh, which was suddenly bearing down upon him. His bandmates had already passed that milestone, and none of them looked any worse for the wear. But somehow, that wasn't enough for Dave. Thirty wasn't a birthday, it was a deadline, and it was getting closer all the time. "As hippie as it sounds," he explained, "I had to find out what Dave Gahan wanted to do. You go past thirty and you've got to start kicking arse."

He packed a suitcase and flew to Los Angeles.

"Over the years I think I was a pretty shitty person," Dave confessed to the British *Vox* magazine. "I didn't like what I was creating . . . in my own life."

<228>

He and Joanne had been together since their teens, "and we used to be really good friends. That had deteriorated, mostly on my part." There was nothing specific; maybe he got drunk more than before, maybe he was faster to lose his temper. But gradually, "you tug away until you lead separate lives. I decided the only way I was going to get a focus on my life was to crush everything down. I had to regain perspective on what I really wanted to do."

And that, he was adamant, was to put his heart and soul into making music. With Joanne, his career had always come between them. "I'd like a life outside rock," Dave would moan, "but . . ." And his voice would trail guiltily away. Now he had nothing to feel guilty about. Now he could admit, "I'm in it right up to my fucking neck, and I'm going to remain in it."

Dividing his time between London, where his old life was ending, and Los Angeles, where his new one was beginning, "living out of a suitcase," as he put it, Dave set about completely reinventing himself. <229>

The ill-fitting beginnings of a goatee beard sprouted on his chin. His flesh was constantly raw from the fallout of his visits to what *Alternative Press* called "some truly brutal tattoo parlors." His once-broad Essex accent now grated against the slang Los Angeles colloquialisms that incongruously peppered his speech. And he got into what even he admitted was "some silly stuff. I got involved with people and things that were over my head, and for a little while there I was lost."

He was found again by Teresa Conway, Depeche Mode's press officer throughout their 1988 American tour, now working for the Triad booking agency. Through her, he would see the world—or, at least, the world according to L.A.

Reliving his teens, when life was a riot of live shows, Dave reveled not in the freedom of going out unrecognized, but in going out and being whoever—or whatever—he wanted. And when Teresa took him along to the final show of Lollapalooza 1991, the explosive climax to the last-ever Jane's Addiction's tour, he realized precisely who—and what—that was.

"I was like, 'I fucking do that! I can do that!' " Dave still roars with excitement as he talks of his musical rebirth, the abrupt, shattering realization that whatever he may have represented in the past, whatever he could be in the future, right now he was a rock 'n' roll singer. All he needed now was to put a rock 'n' roll band behind him.

At the back of his mind, Dave was already half-convinced that maybe Depeche Mode had made the right decision when they parted company at the conclusion of the *Violator* tour with barely a backward glance. He was still proud of all the band had accomplished, but it all seemed so long ago right now, a different life, a different Dave Gahan. All around him, America was bursting at the seams with excitement—the metallic harshness of the new industrial bands, the punk-fused metal of grunge, the burning desire of techno and rave. For the first time in years, he felt excitement when he bought new records.

<230>

The new buzzword was "alternative rock," and Dave grasped the concept by the horns. He wondered how the rest of Depeche Mode would react to it—"I'm not saying I listen to better music than anyone else," he said with a sigh, "but I like seeing a lot of new bands." The first time he'd mentioned Rage Against the Machine to Alan, Alan's response had been, "Who?" "Get a clue, man!" And if Martin even suggested that Depeche Mode reconvene to make another dance album—"I probably wouldn't . . . bother making another record with Depeche Mode.

"Unless we pushed it a lot further," Dave said, "there was no point going on." And unless he could have more input into the band, could shatter the rigid hegemony that eleven years of recording had established, he wouldn't.

Martin, Alan, and Fletch had only a dim understanding of all that Dave was going through, felt only a dim concern as well. Martin was still writing songs, was still thinking in terms of another Depeche Mode album, but he wasn't in too much of a hurry.

His first child had just been born, and he didn't intend making the same mistakes Dave had, missing the first year of his daughter's life while he slaved over a hot synthesizer. Besides, having a daughter "was just more enjoyable than going back into the studio." Instead, he spent his spare time playing computer games and watching Disney movies. "Actually, I'm quite worried about the influences of Disney songs [on my writing]," he joked. "Because that's all I listen to now."

Fletch, too, was contemplating parenthood, and while he waited, he threw his energies into establishing a restaurant partnership in north London's St. John's Wood. He might not, he admitted, be the first pop star to open a restaurant, but he was the only one who actively enjoyed doing the accounts. As it was with Martin, the idea of returning to the band was tempting . . . but first things first.

Alan alone retained his musical vision, the consummate musician spending his time the only way he knew how. <231> Almost as soon as Depeche Mode came off the road in 1991, Alan was back in the studio under his Recoil disguise, beginning work on what would become the *Bloodline* album.

As usual, he worked in seclusion; even as a member of Depeche Mode, he had often found himself alone in the studio, working out the arrangements the others would drop by to listen to the following morning. He called it the "screwdriver work," sifting through endless tapes and restructuring them to meet the moods of each song.

But his style had changed in the years since Recoil had last stirred. *Bloodlines* was intended to be an instrumental album, but track after track suddenly appeared incomplete, calling out for lyrics, and with them, vocalists—Curve's Toni Halliday, techno-raver Moby, and Nitzer Ebb's Doug McCarthy repaying Alan for co-producing (with Flood) his own band's next Mute album, *Ebbhead*.

It was McCarthy, too, who took control of what became *Bloodline*'s most astonishing track, a spine-chilling rendition of the Sensational Alex Harvey Band's classic "Faith

Healer." But Alan would have little time to enjoy the enthusiasm with which both "Faith Healer" and *Bloodline* were to be greeted. After no more than a year in seclusion, Depeche Mode was stirring again.

When, just after Christmas 1991, Martin called Dave in Los Angeles to announce that he had another album's worth of songs demo-ed up, Dave's first thought was to tell him to find another singer. Instead, he told him to send the tapes over. After all that he and Martin had been through together, the least he could do was listen to the new songs first. Who knows? There may even be something salvageable there!

He was still thinking in those terms when Martin's package arrived, and he placed the first tape in the player. Idly, he flicked the play button and picked up the pile of lyrics that accompanied the songs. The first track was called "Condemnation."

<232>

Dave still sounds excited, discussing his first impressions today. "Condemnation" was like nothing Martin had ever written in the past: soaring, majestic, beautiful. "It was a total relief! I couldn't believe it!" Long before the new record was complete, Dave was describing "Condemnation" as the best he'd ever sung. "I wish I could have written it."

The song ended, and Dave turned to the next page of lyrics—then dropped them in shock. Even in rough demo form, the next song was electrifying, a tightly coiled blues groove that built and burned. It was called "I Feel You," and that was the moment, Dave informed an astonished *Rolling Stone* reporter, that he grabbed a broomstick, rushed to the mirror, and started playing air guitar. The only reason he'd considered leaving Depeche Mode, he knew, was because he couldn't ever see them matching his dreams. Not only did these songs match them, they equaled them. "I was ready to do something with a purpose, and suddenly things started to fall into place."

Alan was already in Madrid, renting a private villa for the rest of Depeche Mode to share, and organizing a temporary studio there. Dave and Teresa, already pregnant with the couple's first daughter, flew out there in March, but even as the couple greeted Alan, Martin, and Fletch, the magic that they'd felt in the tape was dissipating. The looks of shock and disgust that the rest of the band bandied about saw to that. By the time Dave had finished explaining the direction in which he saw the new album progressing, he was ready to simply fly back to Los Angeles.

"It was really traumatic," Dave described later. "There were lots of little struggles going on. Depeche Mode is a very English setup, and I came back [from L.A.] with a lot of aggressive influences, like, 'I wanna do this, I wanna do that.' "

Understating what other observers have described as a thoroughly miserable couple of weeks, Dave concludes, "It took a bit of time for us all to feel comfortable together."

All their old fears and doubts had doubled back to haunt Depeche Mode. No longer a band, they were four adults coming together in the hopes of rekindling a forgotten child- <233> hood camaraderie that none of them required any longer. Suddenly, each had his own life and loves; each had his own faults as well, and as dismal days in the studio turned into hectic nights on the town, those faults were magnified, blown into cinemascopic proportions.

It was as though somebody had decided to spring-clean Depeche Mode's closets, but instead of skeletons, they hauled out old grudges. And Dave was at the center of most of them.

It wasn't because his approach to music had altered, either. His sudden enthusiasm for new bands, the way he boiled over with new ideas, that was fine. That was what Depeche Mode was all about. But his entire personality had changed as well. Privately and publicly, Alan disparaged his bandmate's choice of life-style.

"I think Dave's very, very easily influenced, and I don't think that living in Los Angeles has had a good effect on him," Alan said.

Over a year later, *New Musical Express*'s Gavin

Martin agreed with him. Dave, he wrote, "has all the trappings, and a few of the problems, of a Rock God.

"He doesn't look or sound like a well man. His skin is sickly gray, his eyes sunk into bluish sockets. The insides of his long skinny arms are all bruised and scratched." The journalist hinted deeper about Depeche Mode's "dirty little secret," but though he was adamant that "everybody" in the band's entourage knew about Dave's " 'problems,' no one mentions them."

Instead, curious journalists were informed that the scratches were "inflicted by rabid fans who tore their idol apart . . . in Germany"; but still the rumors built, until Dave finally, and vehemently, spoke out. He knew what people were saying, and it wasn't true—he had never had a drug problem.

Nothing that came out of the Madrid sessions was usable, with the exception, perhaps, of the tension that strained Depeche Mode's bonds toward a fresh breaking point. Martin and Fletch showed their traditional lack of interest in the studio process, even exceeded it, while Dave's input was restricted to an endless stream of complaints. The sounds weren't hard enough, or live enough. At times it was as if the singer had spent the last year rereading every criticism that had ever been directed at Depeche Mode, and had now decided to agree with them.

Even the arrival of Daniel Miller in town, so often the oil that calmed Depeche Mode's stormy waters, did not resolve the conflicts. Neither did the increasingly tempting nightlife of Madrid. Finally, Flood—drafted in to produce the new album, but feeling increasingly useless as the arguments dragged unresolvedly on—announced that enough was enough. It was time for this most unpartylike party to move, to the Château du Pape in Hamburg.

Since he had last worked with Depeche Mode, on *Violator,* Flood had been in the studio with U2, bringing home their seventh album, the experiment-in-waiting that was *Achtung Baby.*

<234>

Recalled now to help Alan grapple with the reborn Depeche Mode, Flood intuitively grasped the concepts Dave was trying to put across. Like U2, Dave felt his music was getting too polished, too slick, too predictable. He wanted to shake some preconceptions; he wanted to shake up his bandmates.

"The differences between working with . . . Depeche Mode and . . . U2 are actually far less than you might think," Flood explained to *Alternative Press*. "It's really only the instrumentation that makes you perceive them as being different. Their modus operandi to get to the end thing might be different, but that's about the extent of [it]."

And even that gap was lessening. It was Flood's idea to recruit Brian Eno, who had been working with U2 since 1984's *Unforgettable Fire* album, to mastermind the inevitable program of remixes. And when Dave first suggested using live drums on the new album, and "bullied" Alan into playing them, Flood was as enthusiastic as Fletch was incredulous.

<235>

"Fletcher said, 'Dave's gone crazy, he wants drums,'" Dave said with a smirk. "'Next thing, he'll want backing singers.' And I did." Under Flood's guidance, the gospel trio of Hilda Campbell, Bazil Meade, and Samantha Smith was brought in for "Get Right with Me."

Neither was that the end of Dave's demands. A string section, led by Will Malone, was recruited for the aching "One Caress"; Uileann piper Steafan Hannigan was featured on "Judas." And as each outsider filed through the studio, the clouds that had hung over Depeche Mode for so long lifted a little farther—from Dave, who was getting his own way, and from his bandmates, who abruptly realized that Dave's own way wasn't so bad after all.

Slowly, the band members slipped into their accustomed roles. The consuming passion now was to make a record "with a bit more edge to it," as Flood put it, and deep into the night, he and the band discussed "marrying live performed things with what I suppose is the core of the band—synthesizers, computers, stuff like that." The end result, he reckoned, was 85 percent in favor of "real instruments, though it's still been treated, or sampled from original live performances."

According to Alan, Flood's contribution was "the rare ability to step back and have a producer's perspective and also the technical know-how to be completely hands-on with all the equipment."

As much as Daniel Miller—who still stopped by the studio to offer advice, and who actively pushed the band to "try and break down ideas that were done before, and move forward," Dave continued—Flood was now "a crucial member of our team." The results of this unity, roaring out of the studio speakers as the band listened to yet another playback, never ceased to amaze them.

Only as the sessions drew to a close, and Alan and Flood wrestled with the handful of loose ends that plagued each song, did that unity begin to splinter once again. Bored with the studio, eager to spend time with their families before their inevitable return to the rock 'n' roll circus, and restlessly awaiting the reaction to the album, they found the same old pressures beginning to rebuild. A remix of "In Your Room," performed by Nirvana producer Butch Vig, was vetoed despite Dave's enthusiasm for the results. Thwarted, Dave retaliated in kind.

"There was a bit of apathy from certain people," Alan detailed. "We couldn't agree about direction on a couple of songs, various things." He laughed. "We seem to have slipped into a cycle where we have to have a clear-the-air argument every few months."

One subject that the band did agree upon—or three-quarters of the band at any rate—was Dave and Teresa's forthcoming marriage, timed for just weeks before the group went back on the road. Neither Alan, Martin, nor Fletch was present at the ceremony, an apparent snub the music press was swift to make an issue of. It says much for Depeche Mode's ability to keep their dirty laundry to themselves that not one of the band rose to the bait. For them, the only thing worth talking about was the new album, dubbed—with a certain irony—*Songs of*

<236>

Faith and Devotion, and proudly previewed by Alan as "very much a record for the Nineties."

The only question left to be answered now was, Did the Nineties need such a record from Depeche Mode?

They were, after all, elder statesmen now, as old as the Rolling Stones were when punk first sank its teeth into their aging carcass, as antique as Elvis was when psychedelia swept him swirling into irrelevance.

Now it was the bands who had grown up listening to Depeche Mode's earliest hits, with the same exuberance as Depeche Mode themselves had listened to the pop of their youth, who commanded the attentions of the media—and who gleefully turned the musical equations Depeche Mode had once questioned back on their own heads.

Suede, widely and rightfully regarded as Britain's brightest new band in years, harked back to the Bolans, Glitters, and Bowies of old—contorted androgyny colliding with joyous angst-pop. The distorted punk-metal pioneered by Seattle bands Mudhoney and Nirvana had already spawned two of the best-selling albums of the not-so-new decade, and looked set to spawn a few more.

<237>

A bewildering kaleidoscope of new dance fusions had turned the entire concept of disco upside down, even as the rebirth of sharp guitar-driven pop threw the synthesizer back into the shadows. For any band attempting to stake a place within such confused, chaotic parameters, 1993 was not a good time to be starting. For Depeche Mode, it amounted to madness.

"I Feel You," the song that had so radically altered even Dave's perceptions of what Depeche Mode represented, was chosen as the single that would preview *Songs of Faith and Devotion,* in February 1993. It was an intriguing choice, one that—like so many of the band's decisions—was fraught with danger.

Opening with what *Alternative Press* described as "a high-octane sample from Lou Reed's *Metal Machine*

Music," "I Feel You" had little in common with either Depeche Mode's past output or, as it transpired, the remainder of *Songs of Faith and Devotion.*

"Screeching unwillingly into patent robot throb," the song had a primal savagery that was wholly at odds with the introspective hopefulness that permeated the album, a vivid contrast that was only emphasized by Anton Corbijn's accompanying video.

Returning to the southwestern bordello theme of the "Personal Jesus" video, "I Feel You" was dominated by Dave's slow seduction by a writhing blonde—a seduction that concluded with Dave launching into a vaudevillian semi-striptease designed solely to give the maximum impact to the public unveiling of his new tattoos. The scene should have bristled with sexual drama. But somehow, the general consensus insisted, Dave just looked silly. As silly, he responded, as a man who has just landed on top of the world.

<238>

Songs of Faith and Devotion was released in early March 1993, crashing onto both the American and British charts at number one. It was the first truly "alternative" album ever to achieve so distinguished a double.

It remained at the top for just one week, then slipped so swiftly that by November, *Rolling Stone* had already spotted the seven-month-old album clogging the bargain bins. But such statistics did not seem important—were, in fact, no more than Depeche Mode expected, because that is the way the charts operate today. Nineteen ninety-three albums by Aerosmith and Kiss, Nirvana and Porno for Pyros, Duran Duran and Smashing Pumpkins also peaked in their first weeks on the chart, then dropped—one more indication that, in the mid-1990s, the most successful bands are no longer those that "cross over" among the multitude of specialist charts that clog the pages of the trade magazines, but those that *pass* over, whose appeal is so great—as *Rolling Stone* put it—that they have arrived at "that rarefied career plateau where chart positions never cloud the skies."

Unquestionably, Depeche Mode had attained that

status. By the end of the summer of 1993, they had topped festival bills all over Europe; by December, they'd headlined two of the biggest gigs London had seen all year—their own Christmas extravaganza at Wembley Arena, and six months earlier, a massive open-air show at the Crystal Palace Bowl.

They were also celebrating another hit album, a track-by-track recreation of *Songs of Faith and Devotion,* recorded live around Europe and North America, and farther in both intent and execution than any Depeche Mode album before it.

Gone were the synth-driven textures of *101,* or the album's worth of live cuts that had made it onto the B-sides of various singles. Even during those tracks recorded without the benefit of Martin's guitar and Alan's pounding drums, there was a driving bombast to the performances, over which Dave's voice soared, harsher and more confident than ever, while Hilda Campbell and Samantha Smith—both retained from the studio album—were now featured on almost every cut, and not just one.

<239>

Gone, too, however, was the delicacy of previous performances. "Irrtitatingly," complained *Vox* magazine's Martin Townsend, "some of the [lyrics] are lost in [Dave's] quest to involve the audience in a singalong." Coupled with his constant cries of "Yeah!" and the battery of stadium-sized roars that accompanied his every pelvic jerk (caught in vivid color by the accompanying *Devotion* concert video), listening to *Songs of Faith and Devotion—Live* could indeed seem a frequently grueling experience—and for what purpose?

It was a calculating release, expecting fans to shell out for markedly inferior renditions of a set of songs they had purchased once that year already. But it was a calculated move, as well; Depeche Mode rising above the last surviving accusations of computer-controlled pop gibberish in the most defiant manner imaginable—with live guitar and drums—and doing it with such assurance that few people even questioned the nature of their victory: Pure? Or Pyrrhic?

For thirteen years, Depeche Mode had championed their synth-driven lineup, had castigated those bands that broke down and dismissed electronics while the technology was stil young. For Depeche Mode to now break down themselves and make the same transition with such undisguised pleasure went beyond mere hypocrisy. It was positively heretical.

Or was it? At the same time as they played one game, that of synthesized independence till death do us part, Depeche Mode had always been watching another—the notion of electronics as a simple means to an end. For them, sound has always been the principle concern, whether it is the distorted wailing of a sampled pygmy or the fuzz-drenched roar of electric guitars. Both have played their part in Depeche Mode's sound, and for all the music that has been generated through their computers, there has been as much again that was captured live—a claim that few "traditional" rock 'n' roll bands, sequestered in their own multi-track ivory towers, can make.

<240>

But it is not the recording process itself that matters, nor is it the nit-picking debate that continues to rage between proponents of this sound and that and the other. Just as a book cannot be judged by the make of the pen it was written with or art by the canvas it was painted on, so music is not to be judged by its instrumentation. It is the effect of the instrumentation, and the uses to which it is put, that matters most.

Depeche Mode, over the years, has been bagged with movements as diverse as synth-pop, industrial, and techno—has made their presence felt in house, rave, and disco. But the fact that one band can embrace so many disparate genres, without once disrupting their own musical equilibrium, makes a mockery of such pigeonholing.

Rock 'n' roll is a stream of constant development and decay, and the longer a band survives, the faster the rate of attrition. Only through its lyrics, and the themes expressed within them, can the genres so beloved of the rock cognoscenti be truly determined, for it is through lyrics that an artist finds true common cause with, or draws the most lasting inspiration from, his contemporaries.

That is how Elvis Costello could be called a punk in 1977, or Mott the Hoople a glam band five years before; it resolves, too, the apparently unbridgeable gulf between the fresh-faced synthesized pop group Depeche Mode used to be, and the multifaceted, multilayered, multicathartic icon they have become.

Musically, the transition remains all but unimaginable. Lyrically, the intent has been there all along. The band Diesel Christ proved that when they released their own tribute to Depeche Mode in 1993, performing *Songs of Faith and Devotion* in its entirety, but rearranging each song in pure *Speak and Spell* style. The emotional punch remained the same.

Other bands refuse to take people for granted, or politics or policies. Depeche Mode refuses to take life itself for granted. It is that realism, a notion that goes beyond anything so <261> transient as mere music, or even art, that is conveyed through Depeche Mode's music, that reaches out to touch the souls of the band's vast audience, and that remains there ever after.

It doesn't concern that audience in the slightest whether or not Depeche Mode are considered "happening" or "hip"; whether they play Oberheim Xpanders, or Gibson Les Pauls. They don't care whether Martin's lyrics are ever placed on the same slab as a Dylan, Young, or Morrissey, for discussion and dissection; they aren't even particularly bothered if they ever hear the band on the radio.

And if they don't care, Depeche Mode doesn't either.

"What is credibility anyway?" Dave once asked. "Credibility is usually lost when any band enters the Top Fifty, so for us, that went out of the window . . . years ago."

The only credibility Depeche Mode demands is that which you have to retain in yourself. "You've got to know that what you're doing is valid. Not whether it makes people think, or whether it changes things—this business is about entertainment, and it's about whether [or not] you're just traveling along.

"I don't think we are. I think we're a very unconventional band."

And Martin whirled around, his face burning with delight. "See, I told you! Depeche Mode are so fucking weird."

<242>

\<Discographies\>

Despite the best efforts of everybody involved in this book's production, the following discographies are not complete. Very early on in their career, Depeche Mode realized the advantages of multi-format releases, both in the singles and albums markets; consequently, many of their records have appeared in a variety of guises, often (as is the case with the On-U Sound, Razormaid, and Disconet remixes) in extremely limited editions. The introduction of compact discs in the mid-1980s, and the subsequent rush to translate entire catalogs to the new format, also opened the way for a great deal of confusion.

The wholesale reissue of Depeche Mode's singles catalog to CD in 1991 saw many of their earlier CD singles deleted and reissued with minor track variations; several of these releases may have inadvertently been omitted. Similarly, certain variations between vinyl and CD versions of Depeche Mode albums may have been overlooked; it should also be noted that a number of European and Asian imports, which do offer extra bonus tracks (the German *Speak and Spell* appends five, drawn from Depeche Mode's first three singles), have not been listed here.

Also absent, in the section detailing solo projects, is a breakdown of Vince Clarke's post–Depeche Mode career with Yazoo/Yaz, The Assembly, Paul Quinn, and Erasure.

<244>

<Depeche Mode U.S. Discography>

7"/CASSETTE SINGLES

Sire 50029	Just Can't Get Enough / Tora! Tora! Tora! [11/81]
Sire	Meaning of Love / See You [5/82]
Sire	Everything Counts / Work Hard [7/83]
Sire 29221	People Are People / In Your Memory [3/84]
Sire 28918	Master and Servant / Remotivate Me [8/84]
Sire	But Not Tonight / Stripped [2/86]
Sire 28697	A Question of Lust / Christmas Island [4/86]
Sire 28366	Strangelove / Fpmip [5/87]
Sire 28189	Never Let Me Down Again / Pleasure Little Treasure [9/87]
Sire	Behind the Wheel / Route 66 [12/87]
Sire 27777	Strangelove (remix) / Nothing [8/88]

Sire 22993	Everything Counts (live) / Nothing (live) [2/89]
Sire	Personal Jesus / Dangerous [9/89]
Sire	Enjoy the Silence / Memphisto [2/90]
Sire 19842	Policy of Truth / Kaleid [9/90]
Sire	World in My Eyes / Happiest Girl [2/91]
Sire 18600	I Feel You / One Caress [2/93]
Sire 18506	Walking in My Shoes / My Joy [5/93]
Sire	Condemnation / Rush [9/93]

12" SINGLES

Sire	Just Can't Get Enough (schizomix) / Any Second Now (altered mix) [11/81]
Sire 29957	Meaning of Love / See You / See You (extended) / Now This Is Fun [5/82]
Sire	Everything Counts (in larger amounts) / Work Hard (East End mix) [7/83]
Sire 20214	People Are People (different) / Are People People? (On-U Sound) / In Your Memory (slick) [3/84]
Sire 20383	Master and Servant (black & blue) / Remotivate Me (release mix) / Are People People? (On-U Sound mix) [8/84]
Sire 20402	It's Called a Heart (emotion) / It's Called a Heart (emotion dub) / It's Called a Heart / Flexible (deportation) [9/85]
Sire 20578	But Not Tonight (extended) / Breathing In Fumes / Stripped (Highland) / Black Day [2/86]
Sire 20530	A Question of Lust / Black Celebration (live) [4/86]
Sire 20783	Never Let Me Down Again (split) / Never Let Me Down Again (aggro) / Pleasure Little Treasure (Glitter) / Pleasure Little Treasure (join) / Never Let Me Down Again (Tsangarides) [9/87]

Sire 20858	Behind the Wheel–Route 66 (megamix) / Behind the Wheel–Route 66 (megadub) / Behind the Wheel (extended) / Behind the Wheel (Beatmasters) [12/87]
Sire 21022	Strangelove (Highland) / Strangelove (edit) / Nothing (two mixes) [8/88]
Sire 21328	Personal Jesus (Holier Than Thou) / Personal Jesus / Personal Jesus (pump) / Dangerous / Dangerous (Hazchemix) [9/89]
Sire	Enjoy the Silence (2 mixes) / Memphisto / Sibeling [2/90]
Sire 21534	Policy of Truth (single) / Policy of Truth (Capitol) / Policy of Truth (Beatbox) / Kaleid (remix) / Policy of Truth (transcentral) [9/90]
Sire	World in My Eyes (2 mixes) / Happiest Girl (Jack) / Sea of Sin [2/91]
Sire	I Feel You (5 mixes) / Dangerous [2/93]
Sire	Walking in My Shoes (Grungy Gonads) / Walking in My Shoes (7″) / My Joy (7″) / My Joy (Slow Slide) [5/93]
Sire 41058	Condemnation (live) / Enjoy the Silence (live) / Halo (live) / Death's Door (jazz) / Rush (spiritual guidance) / Rush (nitrate) / Rush (wild planet) / Condemnation (Paris) [9/93]

<247>

U.S. 12″ PROMO SINGLES

(Note: All Depeche Mode singles have been made available as promotional issues, usually featuring the A-side cut only, in long/short or mono/stereo form only. Following is a select listing only of promos containing exclusive couplings or mixes.)

Sire 1025	Big Muff / Photographic / Nodisco / Boys Say Go [3/82]

Sire promo	Master and Servant (Servant and Master remix) [8/84]
Sire promo	It's Called a Heart (dub) / It's Called a Heart (emotion) [9/85]
Sire PRO 2504	A Question of Lust / A Question of Lust (extended) [4/86]
Sire PRO 2780	Strangelove (pain) / Strangelove (7″) / Agent Orange [5/87]
Sire PRO 2847	Never Let Me Down Again (LP version) [9/87]
Sire PRO 2952	Behind the Wheel (extended) / Behind the Wheel (remix) / Behind the Wheel (dub) / Behind the Wheel (beatmasters) [12/87]
Sire promo	Behind the Wheel (power mix) [12/87]
Sire promo	Behind the Wheel (Pettibone) / Behind the Wheel (LP) / Route 66 (single) [12/87]
Sire promo	Behind the Wheel (megamix) / Behind the Wheel (megadub) [12/87]
Sire promo	Everything Counts (original/live medley) [2/89]
Sire promo	Everything Counts (long/short) [2/89]

U.S. CD SINGLES

Sire 21328	Personal Jesus (Holier Than Thou) / Personal Jesus / Personal Jesus (Pump) / Dangerous / Dangerous (Hazchemix) [9/89]
Sire 20490	Enjoy the Silence (Hands and Feet) / Enjoy the Silence (Bass Line) / Enjoy the Silence (Rickie Tik Tik) / Enjoy the Silence (Ecstatic Dub) / Enjoy the Silence (Harmonium) [2/90]
Sire 21490	Enjoy the Silence / Mephisto / Sibeling [4/90]
Sire 21534	Policy of Truth (7″) / Policy of Truth (Capitol) / Policy of Truth (Beatbox) / Kaleid

<248>

(remix) / Policy of Truth (transcentral) [9/90]

Sire 21735   World in My Eyes (Mode mix) / World in My Eyes (7″ mix) / World in My Eyes (Oil) / Sea of Sin (Tonal) / Sea of Sin (Sensoria) / Happiest Girl (Orbital) / Happiest Girl (Jack) [2/91]

Sire 40289   Dreaming of Me / Ice Machine [1991]

Sire 40290   New Life / Shout / New Life (7″ version) [1991]

Sire 40291   Just Can't Get Enough / Any Second Now / Just Can't Get Enough (schizomix) / Any Second Now (altered) [1991]

Sire 40292   See You (ext.) / Now This is Fun / Now This is Fun (ext.) [1991]

Sire 40293   Meaning of Love / Oberkorn / Meaning of Love (fairly odd) / Oberkorn (development) [1991]

‹249›

Sire 40294   Leave in Silence / Excerpt from My Secret Garden / Leave in Silence (longer) / Further Excerpts from My Secret Garden / Leave in Silence (quieter) [1991]

Sire 40295   Get the Balance Right / The Great Outdoors / Get the Balance Right (combination mix) / Tora! Tora! Tora! (live) [1991]

Sire 40296   Everything Counts / Work Hard / Everything Counts (in larger amounts) / Work Hard (East End mix) [1991]

Sire 40297   Love in Itself 2 / Fools / Love in Itself 3 / Fools (Bigger) / Love in Itself 4 [1991]

Sire 40298   People Are People / In Your Memory / People Are People (different) / In Your Memory (slick) [1991]

Sire 40299   Master and Servant (slavery whip mix) / Remotivate Me (release mix) / Master and Servant (voxless) [1991]

Sire 40300	Blasphemous Rumours / Told You So (live) / Somebody (remix) / Everything Counts (live) [1991]
Sire 40314	Shake the Disease / Flexible / Shake the Disease (remix extended) / Flexible (remix extended) / Shake the Disease (edit the shake) / Something to Do (metal mix) [1991]
Sire 40315	It's Called a Heart / Fly on the Windscreen / It's Called a Heart (extended) / Fly on the Windscreen (extended) / Fly on the Windscreen (death) [1991]
Sire 40316	Stripped / But Not Tonight (Highland) / Stripped (Highland) / But Not Tonight (extended remix) / Breathing in Fumes / Fly on the Windscreen (quiet) / Black Day [1991]
Sire 40317	A Question of Lust / Christmas Island / Christmas Island (extended) / People Are People (live) / It Doesn't Matter Two (instrumental) / A Question of Lust (minimal) [1991]
Sire 40318	A Question of Time (Newtown) / Question of Time (live) / Black Celebration (Black Tulip) / More Than a Party (live) [1991]
Sire 40319	Little 15 / St. Jarna / Sonata No. 14 in C# M [1991]
Sire 40328	Strangelove (edit) / Strangelove (remix) / Strangelove (blind edit) / Strangelove (Highland) [1991]
Sire 40329	Never Let Me Down Again (CHR single edit) / Never Let Me Down Again (aggro) / Never Let Me Down Again (split) / Never Let Me Down Again (Tsangarides) [1991]
Sire 40330	Behind the Wheel / Route 66 / Behind the

<250>

	Wheel (Pettibone) / Behind the Wheel (LP) [1991]
Sire 40331	Everything Counts (Simenon-Saunders remix) / Nothing (Strauss remix) / Strangelove (Simenon-Saunders remix) [2/89]
Sire 18889	Personal Jesus / Policy of Truth [1991]
Sire 18890	Enjoy the Silence / World in My Eyes / Everything Counts (live) [1991]
Sire 40767	I Feel You (single) / One Caress (LP) / I Feel You (throb) / I Feel You (Babylon) [2/93]
Sire 40784	I Feel You (Life's Too Short) / I Feel You (swamp) / I Feel You (Afghan Surgery) / I Feel You (Helmet at the Helm) [2/93]
Sire 40852	Walking in My Shoes (plus seven) [5/93]
Sire	Condemnation (Paris) / Enjoy the Silence (live) / Halo (live) / Death's Door (jazz) / Rush (spiritual guidance) / Rush (nitrate) / Rush (wild planet) / Condemnation (live) [9/93]

U.S. CD PROMO SINGLES

(Note: All Depeche Mode singles 1987–present have been made available as promotional issues, usually featuring the A-side cut only. Following is a select listing only of promos containing exclusive couplings or mixes.)

Sire PRO 2953	Behind the Wheel / Route 66 [12/87]
Sire PRO 3696	Personal Jesus (Telephone Stomp) / Personal Jesus (Pump) / Personal Jesus (Acoustic) / Dangerous (Hazchemix) / Dangerous (Sensual) [9/89]
Sire PRO 3976	Enjoy the Silence (Hands and Feet) / Enjoy the Silence (Bass Line) [2/90]
Sire/Wherehouse	Something to Do (Metal Mix) / interview

[issued via KROQ to fans attending the ill-fated Wherehouse signing, 3/90]

12″/CD RAZORMAID REMIXES have been produced for a number of Depeche Mode tracks, including the following: Sea of Sin / Behind the Wheel / Master and Servant / Set Me Free / It's Called a Heart / World in My Eyes / Enjoy the Silence / Strangelove / New Dress / Happiest Girl.

Depeche Mode feature on the following Razormaid collections: *Class X* (CX-1, CX-4, CX-6); *Chapter* (3); *Anniversary* (5, R-1, SP-CD 07, RM-DOUBLE-CD-05, RM-CD-09).

12″/CD DISCONET REMIXES have been produced for a number of Depeche Mode tracks, including the following: Strangelove / People Are People / Master and Servant / Behind the Wheel / Route 66 / Just Can't Get Enough / Set Me Free.

These tracks are additionally featured in the *Disconet* medley.

CD SINGLES COLLECTIONS

Sire 9362 40284   *The Singles 1–6* [six discs, 1991]
Dreaming of Me / Ice Machine / New Life / Shout / New Life (7″ version) / Just Can't Get Enough / Any Second Now / Just Can't Get Enough (schizomix) / Any Second Now (altered) / See You (extended) / Now This Is Fun / Now This Is Fun (extended) / Meaning of Love / Oberkorn / Meaning of Love (fairly odd) / Oberkorn (development) / Leave in Silence / Excerpt from My Secret Garden / Leave in Silence (longer) / Further Excerpts from My Secret Garden / Leave in Silence (quieter)

Sire 9362 40285   *The Singles 7–12* [six discs, 1991]
Get the Balance Right / The Great Outdoors / Get the Balance Right (combination

<252>

mix) / Tora! Tora! Tora! (live) / Everything Counts / Work Hard / Everything Counts (in larger amounts) / Work Hard (East End mix) / Love in Itself 2 / Fools / Love in Itself 3 / Fools (Bigger) / Love in Itself 4 / People Are People / In Your Memory / People Are People (different) / In Your Memory (slick) / Master and Servant (slavery whip mix) / Remotivate Me (release mix) / Master and Servant (voxless) / Blasphemous Rumours / Told You So (live) / Somebody (remix) / Everything Counts (live)

Sire 9362 40285   *The Singles 13–18* [six discs, 1991]

Shake the Disease / Flexible / Shake the Disease (remix extended) / Flexible (remix extended) / Shake the Disease (edit the shake) / Something to Do (metal mix) / It's Called a Heart / Fly on the Windscreen / It's Called a Heart (extended) / Fly on the Windscreen (extended) / Fly on the Windscreen (death) / Stripped / But Not Tonight (Highland) / Stripped (Highland) / But Not Tonight (extended remix) / Breathing in Fumes / Fly on the Windscreen (quiet) / Black Day / A Question of Lust / Christmas Island / Christmas Island (extended) / People Are People (live) / It Doesn't Matter Two (instrumental) / A Question of Lust (minimal) / A Question of Time (newtown) / Question of Time (remix) / Black Celebration (black tulip) / Black Celebration (live) / Stripped (live) / A Question of Time (extended remix) / Something to Do (live) / More Than a Party (live) / Little 15 / St. Jarna / Sonata No. 14 in C# M

ALBUMS

Sire 3642	*Speak and Spell* [3/82] New Life / Puppets / Dreaming of Me / Boys Say Go! / Nodisco / What's Your Name? / Photographic / Tora! Tora! Tora! / Big Muff / Any Second Now / Just Can't Get Enough
Sire 23751	*A Broken Frame* [9/82] Leave in Silence / My Secret Garden / Monument / Nothing to Fear / See You / Satellite / Meaning of Love / Further Excerpts / A Photograph of You / Shouldn't Have Done That / The Sun and the Rainfall
Sire 23900	*Construction Time Again* [8/83] Love in Itself / More Than a Party / Pipeline / Everything Counts / Two-Minute Warning / Shame / The Landscape Is Changing / Told You So / And Then . . .
Sire 25124	*People Are People* [6/84] People Are People / Now This Is Fun / Love in Itself / Work Hard / Told You So / Get the Balance Right / Leave in Silence / Pipeline / Everything Counts
Sire 25194	*Some Great Reward* [9/84] Something to Do / Lie to Me / People Are People / It Doesn't Matter / Stories of Old / Somebody / Master and Servant / If You Want / Blasphemous Rumours
Sire 25346	*Catching Up With Depeche Mode* [9/85] Master and Servant / It's Called a Heart / Just Can't Get Enough / See You / Flexible / Shake the Disease / New Life / Fly on

the Windscreen / Blasphemous Rumours /
Somebody / Love in Itself / Dreaming of
Me / The Meaning of Love

Sire 25429   *Black Celebration* [9/86]
Black Celebration / Fly on the Windscreen
(final) / A Question of Lust / Sometimes /
It Doesn't Matter Two / A Question of
Time / Stripped / Here Is the House /
World Full of Nothing / Dressed in Black /
New Dress / But Not Tonight

Sire 25614   *Music for the Masses* [9/87]
Never Let Me Down Again / The Things
You Said / Strangelove / Sacred / Little 15 /
Behind the Wheel / I Want You Now / To
Have and to Hold / Nothing / Pimpf /
Agent Orange

<255>

Sire 25614 [CD]   *Music for the Masses* [9/87]
Never Let Me Down Again / The Things
You Said / Strangelove / Sacred / Little 15 /
Behind the Wheel / I Want You
Now / To Have and to Hold / Nothing /
Pimpf / Agent Orange / Never Let Me
Down Again (Aggro) / To Have and to
Hold (Spanish Taster) / Pleasure Little
Treasure

Sire 25853   *101* [2/89]
Pimpf / Behind the Wheel / Strangelove /
Sacred / Something to Do / Blasphemous
Rumours / Stripped / Somebody / Things
You Said / Black Celebration / Shake the
Disease / Nothing / Pleasure Little Trea-
sure / People Are People / A Question of
Time / Never Let Me Down Again / A
Question of Lust / Master and Servant /

	Just Can't Get Enough / Everything Counts
Sire 26081	*Violator* [3/90]
	World in My Eyes / Sweetest Perfection / Personal Jesus / Halo / Waiting for the Night / Enjoy the Silence / Policy of Truth / Blue Dress / Ocean
Sire PROCD 5192	*Selections 1–12* [1991]
	(featuring cuts from CD singles collection)
Sire PROCD 5242	*Selections 13–18* [1991]
	(featuring further cuts from CD singles collection)
Sire 45243	*Songs of Faith and Devotion* [3/93]
	I Feel You / Walking in My Shoes / Condemnation / Mercy in You / Judas / In Your Room / Get Right With Me / Rush / One Caress / Higher Love
Sire 45505	*Songs of Faith and Devotion—Live* [12/93]
	I Feel You / Walking in My Shoes / Condemnation / Mercy in You / Judas / In Your Room / Get Right with Me / Rush / One Caress / Higher Love

<256>

SIGNIFICANT SAMPLER ALBUM APPEARANCES

Celluloid 6595	*Some Bizzare Album* [1981]
	(includes "Photographic" [demo])
Sire 25665	*Just Say Yes* [1987]
	(includes "Never Let Me Down Again" [remix])
Sire 25745	*Just Say Yo* [1988]
	(includes "Behind The Wheel / Route 66 [megamix])
Warners 25526	*Modern Girls* soundtrack [1986]

	(includes "But Not Tonight" [Robert Margouleff remix])
Sire 25947	*Just Say Mao* [1989]
	(includes "Everything Counts" [Bomb Behind the Yalu Mix])
Sire 26240	*Just Say Da* [1990]
	(includes "Personal Jesus" [Kazan Cathedral mix])
Sire 25835	*Earth Girls Are Easy* soundtrack [1992]
	(includes "Route 66" [Nile Rodgers remix])
Sire 26707	*Until the End of the World* soundtrack [1992]
	(includes "Death's Door" [1992])

VIDEOS

<257>

Sire 3-38107	*The World We Live In and Live in Hamburg* [1986]
Sire 3-38124	*Some Great Videos* [1986]
Sire 3-38147	*Strange* [1988]
Sire 3-38155	*101* [1989]
Sire 3-38181	*Strange Too* [1990]
Sire	*Devotion* [1993]

SOLO APPEARANCES

Martin Gore

COUNTERFEIT EP

Sire 25980	*Counterfeit* EP [1989]
	Gone / In a Matter of Speaking / Smile in a Crowd / Compulsion / Never Turn Your Back on Mother Earth / Motherless Child

Alan Wilder

SINGLE WITH RECOIL

Sire 40345 CD   Faith Healer [1991]

ALBUM WITH RECOIL

Sire 26950   *Bloodline* [1989]

SINGLE WITH NITZER EBB (PRODUCED WITH FLOOD)

Geffen PRO 4350 I Give to You (Wilder mix) plus three

ALBUM WITH NITZER EBB (PRODUCED WITH FLOOD)

Geffen 24456   *Ebbhead* [1992]
Reasons / Lakeside Drive / I Give to You / Sugar Sweet / DJVD / Time / Ascend / Godhead / Trigger Happy / Family Man

<258>

<Depeche Mode U.K. Discography>

7″ SINGLES

Mute 013	Dreaming of Me / Ice Machine [2/81]
Mute 014	New Life / Shout [6/81]
Mute 016	Just Can't Get Enough / Any Second Now [9/81]
Mute 018	See You / Now This Is Fun [1/82]
Mute 022	Meaning of Love / Oberkorn [4/82]
Mute BONG 1	Leave in Silence / Excerpt from My Secret Garden [8/82]
Mute BONG 2	Get the Balance Right / The Great Outdoors [1/83]
Mute BONG 3	Everything Counts / Work Hard [7/83]
Mute BONG 4	Love in Itself 2 / Fools [9/83]
Mute BONG 5	People Are People / In Your Memory [3/84]
Mute BONG 6	Master and Servant / Remotivate Me [8/84]
Mute BONG 7	Blasphemous Rumours / Somebody [10/84]
Mute BONG 8	Shake the Disease / Flexible [4/85]

Mute BONG 9	It's Called a Heart / Fly on the Windscreen [9/85]
Mute BONG 10	Stripped / But Not Tonight [2/86]
Mute BONG 11	A Question of Lust / Christmas Island [4/86]
Mute BONG 12	A Question of Time / Black Celebration (live) [8/86]
Mute BONG 13	Strangelove / Pimpf [5/87]
Mute BONG 14	Never Let Me Down Again / Pleasure Little Treasure [8/87—limited edition in red vinyl]
Mute BONG 15	Behind the Wheel (remix) / Route 66 [12/87]
Mute BONG 16	Everything Counts (live) / Nothing (live) [2/89]
Mute BONG 17	Personal Jesus / Dangerous [9/89]
Mute BONG 18	Enjoy the Silence / Memphisto [2/90]
Mute BONG 19	Policy of Truth / Kaleid [9/90]
Mute BONG 20	World in My Eyes / Happiest Girl [2/91]
Mute BONG 21	I Feel You / One Caress [2/93]
Mute BONG 22	Walk in My Shoes / My Joy [5/93]
Mute BONG 23	Condemnation / Rush [9/93]
Mute BONG 24	In Your Room (live) [1/94]

<260>

7" EP

Mute BONG 7E	Blasphemous Rumours / Told You So (live) / Somebody (remix) / Everything Counts (live) [10/84]

7" GATEFOLD-SLEEVE SINGLES

Mute GBONG 17	Personal Jesus (acoustic) / Dangerous (Hazchemix)

7" PROMO SINGLES

Mute BONG 16r	Everything Counts (radio edit) [1989]

DISCOGRAPHIES

7" MAGAZINE FREEBIES

Lyntone LYN 10209	Sometimes I Wish I Was Dead / FAD GAD-GET track (red vinyl flexi, free w/ *Flexipop* No. 11) [9/81]
Record Mirror 1	New Dress (remix) plus other artists [2/86]

SIGNIFICANT IMPORT 7" SINGLES

RCA SPB 7475	Photographic (demo) [Spain—1981]
Mute LITTLE 15	Little 15 / St. Jarna [Germany—5/88]

10" SINGLE

Mute 10BONG 16	Everything Counts (absolute) / Everything Counts (1983 12") / Nothing (U.S. 7") [1989]

12" SINGLES

<261>

Mute 12014	New Life (remix) / Shout (Riomix) [2/81]
Mute 12016	Just Can't Get Enough (schizomix) / Any Second Now (altered mix) [6/81]
Mute 12018	See You (extended) / Now This Is Fun (extended) [9/82]
Mute 12022	Meaning of Love (Fairly Odd) / Oberkorn (Development) [4/82]
Mute 12BONG 1	Leave in Silence (longer) / Further Excerpts from My Secret Garden / Leave in Silence (quieter) [8/82
Mute 12BONG 2	Get the Balance Right (combination mix) / The Great Outdoors [1/83]
Mute 12BONG 3	Everything Counts (in larger amounts) / Work Hard (East End mix) [7/83]
Mute 12BONG 4	Love in Itself 3 / Fools (Bigger) / Love in Itself 4 [9/83]
Mute 12BONG 5	People Are People (different) / In Your Memory (slick) [3/84]

Mute 12BONG 6 Master and Servant (slavery whip mix) / Remotivate Me (release mix) / Master and Servant (voxless) [8/84]

Mute 12BONG 7 Blasphemous Rumours / Somebody (live) / Two-Minute Warning (live) / Ice Machine (live) / Everything Counts (live) [10/84]

Mute 12BONG 8 Shake the Disease (remix) / Flexible (remix) [4/85]

Mute 12BONG 9 It's Called a Heart (remix) / Fly on the Windscreen (remix) [9/85]

Mute 12BONG 10 Stripped (extended) / But Not Tonight (extended) / Breathing in the Fumes / Fly on the Windscreen (quiet) / Black Day [2/86]

Mute 12BONG 11 Question of Lust (extended) / Christmas Island (extended) / People Are People (live) / It Doesn't Matter Two / Question of Lust (minimal) [4/86]

<262>

Mute 12BONG 12 Question of Time (extended remix) / Black Celebration (live) / Something to Do (live) / Stripped (live) [8/86]

Mute 12BONG 13 Strangelove (maximix) / Fpmip / Strangelove (midimix) [5/87]

Mute 12BONG 14 Never Let Me Down Again (split) / Pleasure Little Treasure (glitter) / Never Let Me Down Again (aggro) [8/87]

Mute 12BONG 15 Behind the Wheel (Pettibone) / Route 66 (Beatmasters) [12/87]

Mute 12BONG 16 Everything Counts (live) / Nothing (live) / Scared (live) / Question of Lust (live) [2/89]

Mute 12BONG 17 Personal Jesus (Holier Than Thou) / Personal Jesus (7″) / Personal Jesus (Pump) / Dangerous (Hazchemix) / Dangerous (7″) [9/89]

Mute 12BONG 18 Enjoy the Silence (2 mixes) / Memphisto / Sibeling [2/90]

DISCOGRAPHIES

Mute 12BONG 19   Policy of Truth (2 mixes) / Kaleid (remix)
                 [9/90]
Mute 12BONG 20   World in My Eyes / Happiest Girl (Jack) /
                 Sea of Sin [2/91]
Mute 12BONG 21   I Feel You (2 mixes) / Dangerous [2/93]
Mute 12BONG 22   Walking in My Shoes (Grungy Gonads) /
                 Walking in My Shoes (7″) / My Joy (7″) /
                 My Joy (Slow Slide) [5/93]
Mute 12BONG 23   Condemnation   (Paris) / Condemnation
                 (Death's Door Jazz) / Rush (Spiritual Guid-
                 ance) / Rush (alternate) [9/93]

LIMITED 12″ SINGLES

Mute LBONG 2   Get the Balance Right / My Secret Garden
                 (live) / See   You   (live) / Satellite   (live)
                 [1/83]
Mute LBONG 3   Everything Counts / New Life (live) / Boys
                 Say Go (live) / Nothing to Fear (live) /
                 Meaning of Love (live) [7/83]
Mute LBONG 4   Love in Itself / Just Can't Get Enough
                 (live) / Shout (live) / Photograph of You
                 (live) / Photograph (live) [9/83]
Mute LBONG 5   People Are People (remix) / In Your Mem-
                 ory / People Are People [3/84]
Mute LBONG 6   Master and Servant (sci-fi dancehall clas-
                 sic) / Are People People? / Master and Ser-
                 vant [8/84]
Mute LBONG 8   Shake the Disease (edit the shake) / Master
                 and Servant (live) / Flexible (pre-deporta-
                 tion mix) / Something to Do (metal mix)
                 [4/85]
Mute LBONG 9   It's Called a Heart (extended) / Fly on the
                 Windscreen (extended) / It's Called a Heart
                 (slow) / Fly on the Windscreen (death)
                 [9/85]

<263>

Mute LBONG 12	Question of Time (newtown) / Question of Time (live) / Black Celebration (black tulip) / More Than a Party (live) [8/86]
Mute LBONG 13	Strangelove (blind) / Pimpf / Strangelove (pain) / Agent Orange [5/87]
Mute LBONG 14	Never Let Me Down Again (Tsangarides) / Pleasure Little Treasure (Join) / To Have and To Hold (Spanish Taster) [8/87]
Mute LBONG 15	Behind the Wheel (beatmasters) / Route 66 (casualty) [12/87]
Mute LBONG 16	Everything Counts (Simenon-Saunders remix) / Nothing (Strauss remix) / Strangelove (Simenon-Saunders remix) [2/89]
Mute LBONG 18	Enjoy the Silence (Quad: Final Mix) [2/90]
Mute LBONG 20	World in My Eyes (mode to joy) / Happiest Girl (pulsating orbital vocal) / World in My Eyes (dub in my eyes) [2/91]
Mute LBONG 23	Condemnation (live) / Personal Jesus (live) / Enjoy the Silence (live) / Halo (live) [9/93]

<264>

SIGNIFICANT IMPORT 12" SINGLE

Mute 12LITTLE 15	Little 15 / St. Jarna / Sonata No. 14 in C# M [5/88]

12" DANCE MIX SINGLES

Mute DANCE-BONG 13	Strangelove (Fresh Ground mix) [5/87]

12" PROMO SINGLES

Mute RR12 BONG 10	Stripped (Highland) [2/86]
Mute SHOP-BONG 13	Strangelove (single) / Pimpf / Strangelove (maximix) [5/87]
Mute PP12-BONG 16	Strangelove (hijack) / Nothing [5/87]

DISCOGRAPHIES

HMV 1	Strangelove (maximix) / Never Let Me Down Again (Split Mix) [5/87—free with limited edition of *Music for the Masses*]
Mute MOD 101	Violator Megamix [2/90]
Mute PBONG 18	Enjoy the Silence (Bass) / Enjoy the Silence (Ricki Tik Tik) / Enjoy the Silence [2/90]
Mute PBONG 21	I Feel You / I Feel You (Throb) / I Feel You (Babylon) / One Caress [2/93]
Mute PBONG 22	Walking in My Shoes / Walking in My Shoes (Grungy Gonads) / My Joy / My Joy (Slow Slide) [5/93]
Mute PBONG 23	Condemnation (Paris) / Death's Door (jazz) / Rush (spiritual guidance) [9/93]

12″ DOUBLEPACK SINGLES

Mute D12BONG 9	It's Called a Heart (extended) / Fly on the Windscreen (extended) / It's Called a Heart (slow) / Fly on the Windscreen (death) [9/85]

<265>

12″ ON-U SOUND REMIXES were produced of the following:

Just Can't Get Enough [Mute 016]
Photographic [LP cut]
Death Wish [unreleased track]
Are People People? [Mute BONG 5]
Master and Servant [Mute BONG 6]
Strangelove (Photogenic) / Strangelove (Death Mix) [Mute BONG 13]

CASSETTE SINGLES

Mute CBONG 11	Question of Love (Flood) / If You Want (live) / Shame (live) / Blasphemous Rumours (live) [4/86]
Mute CBONG 14	Never Let Me Down Again (split) / Never

| | Let Me Down Again (aggro) / Pleasure Little Treasure (glitter) [9/87] |
| Mute CBONG 15 | Behind the Wheel (Pettibone) / Route 66 (Beatmaster) / Behind the Wheel (LP) [12/87] |

CD SINGLES

CDBONG 13	Strangelove (maximix) / Strangelove (midimix) / Strangelove (LP mix) / Agent Orange / Pimpf / Fpmip / Strangelove (blind mix) / Strangelove (pain mix) [5/87]
CDBONG 14	Never Let Me Down Again (split) / Pleasure Little Treasure (remix) / To Have and To Hold (Spanish Taster) [8/87]
CDBONG 15	Behind the Wheel (remix) / Route 66 / Behind the Wheel (Pettibone) / Behind the Wheel (LP) [12/87]
CDBONG 16	Everything Counts (live) / Nothing (live) / Sacred (live) / Question of Lust (live) [2/89]
CDBONG 17	Personal Jesus (2 mixes) / Dangerous [9/89]
CDBONG 18	Enjoy the Silence (2 mixes) / Memphisto/ Sibeling [2/90]
CDBONG 19	Policy of Truth (2 mixes) / Kaleid (remix) [9/90]
CDBONG 20	World in My Eyes / Happiest Girl (Jack) / Sea of Sin [2/91]
CDMUTE 013	Dreaming of Me / Ice Machine [1991]
CDMUTE 014	New Life / New Life (remix) / Shout (Riomix) [1991]
CDMUTE 016	Just Can't Get Enough / Any Second Now / Just Can't Get Enough (schizomix) / Any Second Now (altered) [1991]
CDMUTE 018	See You (extended) / Now This Is Fun / Now This Is Fun (extended) [1991]

<266>

DISCOGRAPHIES

CDMUTE 022	Meaning of Love / Oberkorn / Meaning of Love (fairly odd) / Oberkorn (development) [1991]
CDBONG 1	Leave in Silence / Excerpt from My Secret Garden / Leave in Silence (longer) / Further Excerpts from My Secret Garden / Leave in Silence (quieter) [1991]
CDBONG 2	Get the Balance Right / The Great Outdoors / Get the Balance Right (combination mix) / Tora! Tora! Tora! (live) [1991]
CDBONG 3	Everything Counts / Work Hard / Everything Counts (in larger amounts) / Work Hard (East End mix) [1991]
CDBONG 4	Love in Itself 2 / Fools / Love in Itself 3 / Fools (Bigger) / Love in Itself 4 [1991]
CDBONG 5	People Are People / In Your Memory / People Are People (different) / In Your Memory (slick) [1991]
CDBONG 6	Master and Servant (slavery whip mix) / Remotivate Me (release mix) / Master and Servant (voxless) [1991]
CDBONG 7	Blasphemous Rumours / Told You So (live) / Somebody (remix) / Everything Counts (live) [1991]
CDBONG 8	Shake the Disease / Flexible / Shake the Disease (remix extended) / Flexible (remix extended) / Shake the Disease (edit shake) / Something to Do (metal) [1991]
CDBONG 9	It's Called a Heart / Fly on the Windscreen / It's Called a Heart (extended) / Fly on the Windscreen (extended) / Fly on the Windscreen (death) [1991]
CDBONG 10	Stripped / But Not Tonight (Highland) / Stripped (Highland) / But Not Tonight (extended remix) / Breathing in the Fumes /

<267>

	Fly on the Windscreen (quiet) / Black Day [1991]
CDBONG 11	A Question of Lust / Christmas Island / Christmas Island (extended) / People Are People (live) / It Doesn't Matter Two (instrumental) / A Question of Lust (minimal) [1991]
CDBONG 12	A Question of Time (extended remix) / Black Celebration (live) / Something to Do (live) / Stripped (live) [1991]
CDBONG 21	I Feel You (7″) / I Feel You (Babylon) / I Feel You (Throb) / One Caress [2/93]
CDBONG 22	Walking in My Shoes (Grungy Gonads) / Walking in My Shoes (7″) / My Joy (7″) / My Joy (Slow Slide) [5/93]
CDBONG 23	Condemnation (Paris) / Death's Door (Jazz) / Rush (Spiritual Guidance) / Rush (alternate) [9/93]
CDBONG 24	In My Room / Fly on the Windscreen / World in My Eyes / Condemnation (live)

<268>

SIGNIFICANT IMPORT CD SINGLE

| Mute LITTLE15 | Little 15 / St. Jarna / Sonata No. 14 in C#M |

LIMITED CD SINGLES

Mute LCD-BONG 16	Everything Counts (Simenon-Saunders remix) / Nothing (Strauss remix) / Strangelove (Simenon-Saunders remix) [2/89]
Mute XLCD-BONG 18	Enjoy the Silence (Quad: Final Mix) [2/90]
Mute LCD-BONG 19	Policy of Truth (transcentral) / Policy of Truth (Pavlov's dub) / Kaleid (remix) [9/90]
Mute LCD-BONG 20	World in My Eyes (mode to joy) / Happiest Girl (pulsating orbital vocal) / World in My Eyes (dub in my eyes) [2/91]

Mute LCD-BONG 21	I Feel You (Life's Too Short) / I Feel You (Swamp) / I Feel You (Afghan Surgery) / I Feel You (Helmet at the Helm) [2/93]
Mute LCD-BONG 22	Walking in My Shoes (7″) / Walking in My Shoes (Random Carpet) / Walking in My Shoes (Ambient Whale) / Walking in My Shoes (Anandamidic) [5/93]
Mute LCD-BONG 23	Condemnation (live) / Personal Jesus (live) / Enjoy the Silence (live) / Halo (live)

CD SINGLES COLLECTIONS

Mute DBMX 1 *The Singles 1–6* [six discs, 1991]
Dreaming of Me / Ice Machine / New Life / Shout / New Life (7″ version) / Just Can't Get Enough / Any Second Now / Just Can't Get Enough (schizomix) / Any Second Now (altered) / See You (extended) / Now This Is Fun / Now This Is Fun (extended) / Meaning of Love / Oberkorn / Meaning of Love (fairly odd) / Oberkorn (development) / Leave in Silence / Excerpt from My Secret Garden / Leave in Silence (longer) / Further Excerpts from My Secret Garden / Leave in Silence (quieter)

<269>

Mute DBMX 2 *The Singles 7–12* [six discs, 1991]
Get the Balance Right / The Great Outdoors / Get the Balance Right (combination mix) / Tora! Tora! Tora! (live) / Everything Counts / Work Hard / Everything Counts (in larger amounts) / Work Hard (East End mix) / Love in Itself 2 / Fools / Love in Itself 3 / Fools (Bigger) / Love in Itself 4 / People Are People / In Your Memory / People Are People (different) / In Your Memory (slick) / Master and Servant (slavery

whip mix) / Remotivate Me (release mix) / Master and Servant (voxless) / Blasphemous Rumours / Told You So (live) / Somebody (remix) / Everything Counts (live)

Mute DBMX 3   *The Singles 13–18* [six discs, 1991]
Shake the Disease / Flexible / Shake the Disease (remix extended) / Flexible (remix extended) / Shake the Disease (edit the shake) / Something to Do (metal mix) / It's Called a Heart / Fly on the Windscreen / It's Called a Heart (extended) / Fly on the Windscreen (extended) / Fly on the Windscreen (death) / Stripped / But Not Tonight (Highland) / Stripped (Highland) / But Not Tonight (extended remix) / Breathing in the Fumes / Fly on the Windscreen (quiet) / Black Day / A Question of Lust / Christmas Island / Christmas Island (extended) / People Are People (live) / It Doesn't Matter Two (instrumental) / A Question of Lust (minimal) / A Question of Time (newtown) / A Question of Time (remix) / Black Celebration (black tulip) / Black Celebration (live) / Stripped (live) / A Question of Time (extended remix) / Something to Do (live) / More Than a Party (live) / Little 15 / St. Jarna / Sonata No. 14 in C#M

<270>

ALBUMS

Mute STUMM 5   *Speak and Spell* [9/81]
New Life / Just Can't Get Enough / I Sometimes Wish I Was Dead / Puppets / Boys Say Go / Nodisco / What's Your Name /

Photographic / Tora! Tora! Tora! / Big Muff / Any Second Now

Mute STUMM 9 *A Broken Frame* [9/82]
Leave in Silence / My Secret Garden / Monument / Nothing to Fear / See You / Satellite / Meaning of Love / Further Excerpts / A Photograph of You / Shouldn't Have Done That / The Sun and the Rainfall

Mute STUMM 13 *Construction Time Again* [8/83]
Love in Itself / More Than a Party / Pipeline / Everything Counts / Two-Minute Warning / Shame / The Landscape Is Changing / Told You So / And Then . . .

Mute STUMM 19 *Some Great Reward* [8/84]
Something to Do / Lie to Me / People Are People / It Doesn't Matter / Stories of Old / Somebody / Master and Servant / If You Want / Blasphemous Rumours

<291>

Mute MUTEL 1 *The Singles 1981–85* [9/85]
People Are People / Master and Servant / It's Called a Heart / Just Can't Get Enough / See You / Shake the Disease / Everything Counts / New Life / Blasphemous Rumours / Somebody / Leave in Silence / Get the Balance Right / Love in Itself / Dreaming of Me / The Meaning of Love

Mute STUMM 26 *Black Celebration* [9/86]
Black Celebration / Fly on the Windscreen (final) / A Question of Lust / Sometimes / It Doesn't Matter Two / A Question of Time / Stripped / Here Is the House / World Full of Nothing / Dressed in Black / New Dress / But Not Tonight

Mute STUMM 47 *Music for the Masses* [9/87]
Never Let Me Down Again / The Things

You Said / Strangelove / Sacred / Little 15 / Behind the Wheel / I Want You Now / To Have and to Hold / Nothing / Pimpf

Mute STUMM 47   *Music for the Masses* (w/ free 12″—HMV 1) [9/87]

Never Let Me Down Again / The Things You Said / Strangelove / Sacred / Little 15 / Behind the Wheel / I Want You Now / To Have and to Hold / Nothing / Pimpf / Strangelove (maximix) / Never Let Me Down Again (split)

Mute CDSTUMM 47   *Music for the Masses* [9/87]

Never Let Me Down Again / The Things You Said / Strangelove / Sacred / Little 15 / Behind the Wheel / I Want You Now / To Have and to Hold / Nothing / Pimpf / Agent Orange / Never Let Me Down Again (Aggro) / To Have and to Hold (Spanish Taster) / Pleasure Little Treasure

CSTUMM 5   *Music for the Masses/Black Celebration* [9/87]

Black Celebration / Fly on the Windscreen (final) / A Question of Lust / Sometimes / It Doesn't Matter Two / A Question of Time / Stripped / Here Is the House / World Full of Nothing / Dressed in Black / New Dress / But Not Tonight / Never Let Me Down Again / The Things You Said / Strangelove / Sacred / Little 15 / Behind the Wheel / I Want You Now / To Have and to Hold / Nothing / Pimpf (cassette)

Mute MOD 101   *Megamix—live 1988* [2/89]

Mute STUMM 101   *101* [2/89]

Pimpf / Behind the Wheel / Strangelove / Sacred / Something to Do / Blasphemous Rumours / Stripped / Somebody / Things

	You Said / Black Celebration / Shake the Disease / Nothing / Pleasure Little Treasure / People Are People / A Question of Time / Never Let Me Down Again / A Question of Lust / Master and Servant / Just Can't Get Enough / Everything Counts
Mute STUMM 64	*Violator* [3/90]
	World in My Eyes / Sweetest Perfection / Personal Jesus / Halo / Waiting for the Night / Enjoy the Silence / Policy of Truth / Blue Dress / Ocean
Mute Verbong 1	*Songs of Faith and Devotion—the Interview* [3/93]
Mute STUMM	*Songs of Faith and Devotion* [3/93] I Feel You / Walking in My Shoes / Condemnation / Mercy in You / Judas / In Your Room / Get Right With Me / Rush / One Caress / Higher Love
Mute STUMM	*Songs of Faith and Devotion—Live* [12/93] I Feel You / Walking in My Shoes / Condemnation / Mercy in You / Judas / In Your Room / Get Right With Me / Rush / One Caress / Higher Love

SIGNIFICANT SAMPLER ALBUM APPEARANCES

| Some Bizzare 1 | *Some Bizzare Album* [1981] (includes "Photographic") |
| Band of Joy 25 | *One and Only: 25 Years of Radio One* [1992] (includes "Boys Says Go" [Richard Skinner radio]) |

VIDEOS

| Mute | *The World We Live In and Live in Hamburg* [1986] |
| Mute | *Some Great Videos* [1986] |

Mute   *Strange* [1988]
Mute   *101* [1989]
Mute   *Strange Too* [1990]
Mute   *Devotion* [1993]

SOLO APPEARANCES

Martin Gore

COUNTERFEIT EP

Mute STUMM 67   *Counterfeit* EP [1989]
Gone / In a Matter of Speaking / Smile in a Crowd / Compulsion / Never Turn Your Back on Mother Earth / Motherless Child

Alan Wilder

<274> ## SINGLE WITH DAPHNE AND THE TENDERSPOTS

Disco Hell [1979]

SINGLE WITH RECOIL

Mute 110   Faith Healer [1991]
12MUTE 110   Faith Healer (Trance) / Faith Healer (Conspiracy) / Faith Healer (Theory) / Faith Healer (Disbeliever) / Faith Healer (Deformity) / Faith Healer (Barracuda)

ALBUMS

Mute STUMM 31   *1 + 2* [1986]
Mute STUMM 51   *Hydrology* [1989]

ALBUM WITH NITZER EBB (PRODUCED WITH FLOOD)

Mute STUMM   *Ebbhead* [1992]
Reasons / Lakeside Drive / I Give to You / Sugar   Sweet / DJVD / Time / Ascend / Godhead / Trigger Happy / Family Man